IN PURSUIT OF
THE TRUTH

DCI CLIVE DRISCOLL

IN PURSUIT OF THE TRUTH

My Life Cracking the Met's Most Notorious Cases

EBURY
PRESS

1 3 5 7 9 10 8 6 4 2

Ebury Press, an imprint of Ebury Publishing
20 Vauxhall Bridge Road
London SW1V 2SA

Ebury Press is part of the Penguin Random House group of companies whose addresses can be found at global.penguinrandomhouse.com

Penguin
Random House
UK

First published by Ebury Press in 2015

www.penguin.co.uk

A CIP catalogue record for this book is available from the British Library

ISBN 9781785030086

Printed and bound in Great Britain by Clays Ltd, St Ives PLC

MIX
Paper from
responsible sources
FSC® C018179

Penguin Random House is committed to a sustainable future for our business, our readers and our planet. This book is made from Forest Stewardship Council® certified paper.

For my mum, Christine Helen Rose Driscoll
and my brother, Barry Leslie Driscoll.
Without them, I would not be where I am today.

To Alfred and Doreen Laurence,
I will never be able to repay you.

Contents

Foreword

In Pursuit of the Truth gives its reader a snapshot of what it was like in the 80s and 90s for a police officer working in South London at the time, and Clive Driscoll's no-holds-barred description of those who he had been in contact with.

I found it amazing that some officers would put so many obstacles in the way of someone who wanted to catch criminals, but this book outlines the fairness in the job that Clive was trying to do for individuals. This always came across to me too.

Clive's book gives the reader in-depth knowledge into how he worked; his methodology of getting to the truth. For victims, they need an officer with integrity, someone who cares about them and what they are going through, and this is what you get with Clive.

Reading this book throws light on some of the problems that happened in my own case; that botched job has been well documented over the years. But it is not just my case that suffered from a lack of commitment from officers. How many families have suffered over the years from police incompetence and, in some cases, lack of commitment to the job? The public want to have the trust and confidence in the police force because, as we know, we need them to protect and uphold the law. There needs to be a continued root and branch into the history of police misdemeanour in order to turn the police force around, and to get public support and encourage young people to join the police.

Doreen Lawrence, Baroness Lawrence of Clarendon, OBE
June 2015

In April 1993, my son Stephen Lawrence was stabbed and brutally murdered when he was on his way home in Eltham, London. This murder was to change my family's lives forever.

In the beginning, we spent a few years being frustrated and pushed around. A number of assumptions were made by police officers about my son and my family. Some told lies, possibly to cover for others who might have been complicit in protecting those who were suspected of my son's murder. Others were seen as corrupt, and allegedly in the pockets of known criminals and drug dealers. To this day, some of those suspicions have not gone away.

We were accused of using the murder of Stephen to promote a secondary agenda to seek publicity for ourselves and to create a state of distrust and a loss of confidence in the Metropolitan Police. There was so much concern about our quest for justice that the Home Office used a secret force, the Special Demonstration Squad (SDS) to infiltrate the legitimate campaigns my family and other families had organised, in order to gather intelligence and possibly even distract and smear some campaigns to stop us from getting justice. This process was not limited to just the Met but across some police forces across the UK as well.

My family was, however, not deterred by the lack of support from the police service and their attempts to discourage us. We started to make inroads into what was a strongly resistant environment and we were against huge powerful authorities who were not willing to be defeated by a small unrelenting black family.

We worked hard with the support of lots of people, including very dedicated police officers who recognised the need to investigate what had then become seen as a racist murder and to tackle the endemic issues which existed in society as well as within the Met.

One such fine police officer was Detective Chief Inspector Clive Driscoll. He took over what became the Stephen Lawrence

Investigation and was very determined to tell my family the truth. He gave us a commitment that he would do everything in his power to secure a conviction for the murderers of my son.

It became patently clear right from the start that Clive had a great deal of integrity, a drive to put criminals behind bars and was determined to interrogate all the available evidence again and again. As a result, he identified new crucial evidence – including photographs of the then suspects disposing of evidence and blood specks on a jacket – which was eventually used to jail two men.

Clive Driscoll helped my family and I to regain some of the lost confidence in the Met, due to the way he treated us. He understood the need for us to have a proper investigation for the murder of our son. He did not hide behind the need to save the blushes of the Met and other police forces by managing the truth. He even sometimes put his own position at risk because he felt he needed to go to where the evidence and the investigation led him.

My family and I feel wholly vindicated by our commitment to secure justice for Stephen. This was made possible by lots of people but Clive Driscoll contributed hugely, making it possible for us to have a successful trial and secure a conviction.

In the end we achieved some justice, but it is only some justice.

It is a great privilege to write a foreword for this book, which I hope captures the great effort made by people like Clive who dedicate their lives to fighting crime and securing justice for people who are entitled to it, sometimes in the face of great resistance.

Thank you, Clive for your contribution to policing in the UK.

Neville Lawrence, OBE
June 2015

What Is Wrong With Me?

'What, what, nigger!'

It was 10.30 p.m., Thursday 22 April 1993, when one of the five white youths charging across Well Hall Road in Eltham, south London, yelled those words at the two young black men walking on the other side of the street. Three people at the bus stop saw them. One of the two young men saw them. But the other, the one wrapped up for winter even though it was a mild April night, didn't budge. Didn't flinch. Didn't alter his path.

Stephen Lawrence wasn't the type of lad to run away if he'd done nothing wrong. If he had been, like his good friend, Duwayne, he would probably be alive today. Completely unprovoked, one, possibly two, of the white men stabbed Stephen, both times from behind. A more cowardly act cannot be imagined.

The first incision, delivered at frightening pace with a downward 'bowling' arm action, plunged into the boy's left shoulder, ripping through his clavicle and severing a main artery.

The second jab went in, vertically, under the left arm. The blade was wide, five inches long and razor sharp, slicing everything in its path. When the knife was withdrawn, Stephen's blood was already gushing out.

The assailants were like a pack of hunting dogs but Stephen was strong and fast. He tore away from them and chased after Duwayne to safety. It was the most natural thing in the world. But it was also the worst thing he could have done: the quicker he ran, the harder his heart pumped.

And the more blood he lost.

He collapsed 120 yards later, his arms useless at his side. As he looked up at Duwayne, he asked, 'What is wrong with me?'

Those were young Stephen's last words.

Stephen Lawrence was pronounced dead at Brook Hospital in Shooter's Hill an hour later. In truth, his life was over from the moment the first knife had entered his body. Either blow would have killed a man. Both merely guaranteed his fate.

The attackers, according to the witnesses and the dozens of anonymous tip-offs that came in during the next few days, were the area's notorious Acourt Gang: five lads who took pleasure in intimidating locals, more often than not anyone of a different race or colour to them. Their track record of violence and terror in and around Eltham spoke volumes.

The newspapers didn't give the crime much priority. What was the value of another black kid? He was probably in a gang or dealing drugs. That was the story doing the rounds. But the story was wrong. Stephen was an 18-year-old architecture student. He loved football, not drugs. He had friends, not gang runners. He was a lovely, normal lad from a lovely, normal family who happened to be black.

The media might not have been interested but I heard enough from my desk in Brixton to know it was solvable. A stream of information had been coming in since Stephen's death, and the potential for forensic evidence had to be good. From a distance it seemed like a straight-forward outcome, and I almost envied the murder team that would be on it.

How wrong can you be?

2

CHAPTER ONE

There's Always
a Next Time

'Good evening, all.'

From the moment the crackling black-and-white image of Jack Warner delivered those words on a Saturday night, until he wrapped up 30 minutes later with his regular sign-off of 'Goodnight, all', you could hear a pin drop in our house. Everything stopped for TV's first police drama, *Dixon of Dock Green*.

If there's been a greater influence on me outside my own family, then I can't place it. Sergeant George Dixon, the kindly old gent with the downward-pointing triple arrows on his epaulettes, fascinated me. He was so twinkly eyed and friendly, but he struck fear into the hearts of the low-level criminals in the Dock Green area: bike thieves, blackmailers, bank robbers – you name it – every wannabe Big Time Charlie in Dixon's vicinity knew they'd met their match with the Sarge. A mob doing over a bakery before the early crusts had risen? There was George to save the village's buns. On the hunt for a missing child – no one was better at getting information from witnesses because who didn't want to speak to Dixon of Dock Green?

He didn't carry a gun, he didn't drive a fast car – in fact, he wheeled around on a pushbike most of the time, his cape flapping in the breeze. But what George Dixon did have was a sense of community, of putting people first, of knowing what was right and wrong. Some of the other people he brushed up against – officers and criminals alike – were a bit flash, a bit full of themselves or smug. George was never like that. He was fair. He was kind. He had a way with him that put you at ease, even from the other side of the TV set.

And, in 1979, I wished I'd never set eyes on him.

I wasn't exactly thinking of old George when I got on the tube at Morden more than 40 years ago. Nor was he specifically in my thoughts when I emerged, a little lost, an hour later at Colindale. But since Dixon was the inspiration for me applying to join the 'Force', the reason I was lugging a suitcase along Aerodrome Road towards the Metropolitan Police Training College, and the reason I was about to start 17 gruelling weeks away from home, at least part of the sense of dread in the pit of my stomach could be pinned on him. Which was only fair, he'd have to see that.

The Peel Centre they call it now, named after the Met's founding father, Lord Robert Peel, although most coppers just refer to it as 'Hendon'. Whatever its name, I knew I was close when I saw the three dark tower blocks looming towards me, about as welcoming as something from a Hammer Horror film. All they needed was a lightning storm around the top and the sound of wolves howling. To this day, I still break out in a cold sweat whenever I have to go there. Back then, I almost turned on my heels. I certainly stopped and asked myself the same question I'd been anguishing over throughout the long trip north: *Should I be doing this?*

In the entrance hall of the middle tower block, sitting behind a table that looked like it had been put there as a temporary desk many years earlier, a roly-poly geezer in the blue police sweater was thumbing through a paperback.

I hadn't been expecting anyone to rush over with open arms but I did think the bloke might actually acknowledge my presence. He did when I coughed.

Without looking up, he said, 'Name?'

'Driscoll, Clive.'

He grunted and, with one last glance at his thriller, picked up a scuffed clipboard and started rifling through the dozen or so pages fastened to it.

'Driscoll, was it?'

'That's right.'

Another grunt, then he reached into a box and gave me a key.

'Fourth floor,' he said. 'Breakfast is at seven, be down at nine for enrolment.'

I stood there. Was that it? 'Anything else?' I asked.

'Yeah, don't be late.'

Then his nose went back in the tatty Len Deighton and, as far as he was concerned, I ceased to exist.

Things weren't much friendlier up on the fourth floor. If it's possible for a room to have a personality, then mine had modelled itself on the grumpy bastard downstairs. Bed, desk, wardrobe and sink; so stark it was almost monosyllabic. If it could have ignored me, it would have. As for the colour, it was as though autumn had come early. Everything was a muddy blend of orangey-brown, including the walls, which, judging by the noise coming through them, couldn't have been much thicker than the lick of slurry-coloured paint covering them. I couldn't tell if it was my next-door neighbour or an inmate five doors down, but someone was having a right old party.

I sat on the edge of the narrow bed, head in my hands, trying to drown out Studio 54 next door. What was wrong with me? Wasn't this what I'd always dreamed of doing? You can't be a copper without training. Even George Dixon – my fictional hero – would have had to go through something like this.

But did he have as much to lose as me?

Suddenly the revellers got a bit louder and I was aware of a commotion in the corridor. Does anyone do 'happy' like a bunch of 18-year-olds? There was no trouble, no swearing or fighting; just the sheer unbridled joy of a bunch of lads away from their homes, off the leash probably for the first time in their lives, letting it all hang out.

A thump on the door got me up.

'Mate, come and have a drink!' someone shouted from outside.

Here we go.

I opened the door and, if I'm honest, the party died right then. One second I was looking at a dozen or so pimply teenage faces, laughing and joking without a care in the world; the next I was seeing what confusion looked like in human form.

To their credit, the lads' smiles stayed, but they were frozen. One of them might even have sworn.

'We wondered if you was coming out for a bevy?' one of them, a Liverpudlian kid, managed to get out. 'You know, all the new recruits together, and that?'

Bless you for going through with it.

'No, you're all right, lads. I'm going to find a phone, call home, then turn in for the night.'

'OK, nice one.'

He tried not to sound relieved but the smile gave him away.

I couldn't blame him or any of them. After all, what group of kids wants to go out on the lash with somebody's dad?

Dixon of Dock Green wasn't the only inspiration for me joining the Met. I'm actually quite sad to admit that in 1979 there was another much more basic force behind my decision to apply to Hendon.

Money.

In 1979 I was nearly 30 years old. (No wonder my teenage neighbours looked like they'd seen a ghost when they caught sight of my vizog. To them I could have been 50.)

Age brings responsibilities and, as a husband and father I had them in droves. I needed to put food on the table, clothes on the backs of four people. A policeman's salary at the time was actually a very tidy pay packet, even before the new prime minister, Margaret Thatcher, started bumping it up over the next few months. We were barely out of the old Labour government's 'Winter of Discontent', the Irish National Liberation Army had claimed Airey Neave's life in the House of Commons car park, the Irish Republican Army were weeks from assassinating Lord Mountbatten and the country was suffering the worst strikes since the 1920s. To the politicians and the public the police had never been more vital.

But to my family, I was vital, too.

The look on my son Robert's face when I'd packed my suitcase had stayed with me all day. Little Bonita, still in nappies, had had no idea what was going on. But Robert, at four years old, had twigged that something was up and I'd had to say I was going away. I wasn't sure if he'd understood but he'd soon realise when I wasn't there the next day, or the day after or the day after that. The thought of him being sad was more than I could bear; the thought of him getting used to me not being there was even worse.

No kid should feel abandoned by his dad. And I should know…

I was born on 24 February 1951 in the women's hospital on Nightingale Lane, south Clapham, to Christine and Dennis Driscoll.

Mum's dad, Bob Vacher, had been a civil servant in the Foreign Office, but with five kids money had been tight: when Bob had a pork chop for his tea, Mum and her two brothers and two sisters would just get his gravy and be happy with it, because there was nothing else.

I'd say they were proper Clapham working class but then Dennis Driscoll, my father, entered the picture and showed them what *real* working class was. Dennis came from a long line of steelworkers and what they used to call 'pipe fitters' – plumbers we'd say today – from a village in Monmouthshire on the South Wales borders. The menfolk would work hard and drink hard and the women would do the rest – although everyone had their breaking point. When Grandad Driscoll used to stagger home from the pub blinding drunk, he'd open the front door, chuck his hat in and wait. If the hat stayed in, he could enter. If it came flying back out, that was the cue to find somewhere else to sleep that night. Grandad married twice and his second wife was cruel to my father, to say the least.

Grandad Driscoll had settled in Monmouthshire for the work. Originally, he was from Tipperary – which, as the song says, is a very long way – or so he told me. Other members of the family said it was Cork. Like a lot of the Irish, he'd dropped the 'O' from O'Driscoll on the way over to help blend in, but since you couldn't walk past his house without copping a 'Top o' the morning' or 'Bejeesus!' or two, I'm not sure it was the best piece of undercover work I've ever seen.

Still, like father like son, and when work led my dad east in the late thirties, he ended up in London, where he met my mum. I think they were getting along quite nicely, nothing too serious, but when World War II started and Dennis' name came up on the draft list, it forced their hand into marriage. They both thought he'd never come back. A wedding seemed the perfect send-off.

But come back he did – although only in body. Everyone agreed Dad was a changed man. Who wouldn't be after five years at war? My parents tried to make a go of it and my brother, Barry, was born in 1946 as proof of that. Dad's work took him here and there over the next few years, but they were together long enough for me to appear five years later. Was I an accident? You could say that. Mum was devastated to discover herself pregnant; Dad wasn't too happy about it either and skedaddled back to Wales for good. The first time I saw him I was five years old.

You can't miss what you've never had, so Dad not being there didn't affect me, not like it did Barry. A five-year-old losing their father is devastating: till the day he died in 2000, I don't think Barry ever quite got over it. Mum was the same. She never stopped loving Dad to the end and wouldn't think of remarrying, even when he found someone else who adored him and had another child, Paul, our half-brother. Even as a single parent, Mum spoilt me rotten. She confessed later it was out of guilt of having not wanted me.

I didn't mind. I liked being spoilt.

So, yes, it was all a bit messy and, without Nan and Grandad Vacher – and, of course, George Dixon – in our corner, I don't know what we'd have done.

I'd have to say the Sarge and my grandad were probably equally responsible for instilling in me a moral code and a sense of fairness which has stayed with me to this day. But there was only one of them who could put food in our stomachs, so Grandad just shades it. A remarkable fella. Shot in the arm during the Battle of the Somme – which was incredible when you consider how many men weren't that lucky – he was the one I turned to for advice or support. Mum used to work 12 hours a day at the St John's Hospital just to make ends meet, which meant looking after us was impossible. There wasn't the benefits system back then so without her parents, my brother and I would have been taken into care. Thousands of post-war babies went through the same thing when their dads didn't return.

Throughout my early years we all shared a house in Galveston Road, Putney. We had the ground floor and Nan and Grandad had upstairs, although us boys flitted between the two. My strongest memory of living there is seeing Uncle Bob, Mum's brother play the piano at parties. I asked him to teach me once but he said he was too busy, so the old man who lived next door stepped in. Even though the piano was horrendously out of tune, he showed me three chords – G, D and C – and said, 'You can play any song in the world with those.' It's a lesson that's served me well my entire life, and tinkling the ivories has always been a good stress reliever in difficult times.

After Galveston Road we all moved one street along to Mexfield Road, us taking number 82 while my grandparents had 72.

I don't remember ever rowing with my brother, probably because of the age difference. Most of my memories of him are pretty happy. One in particular is a bit of both. I remember Barry taking me to the flicks when I was about six or seven. He was at senior school by then and we ran into a few older lads who obviously knew him. Nothing was said but I felt my brother tense up till they passed by. Then, during the film, he went to the toilet. I waited and waited and he didn't come back, which I thought was odd because movies were a real treat for us – you didn't miss a second if you could help it. So off I went, concerned and cross in equal measure, to the gents to find him – and there he was being beaten up by the older lads. I was tiny and as much use against them as a chocolate teapot, but that didn't stop me charging at them, screaming to leave my brother alone. I caused such a row that the usherette came marching in and told everyone off.

Afterwards Barry wouldn't talk about it. He just said, 'You shouldn't have done that. You could have been hurt.'

'I never thought about it,' I replied.

'Well, you should next time.'

'There won't be a next time,' I said, ever the optimist.

'There's always a next time with people like them.'

It turned out this gang always took the mickey out of Barry because he wore short trousers. The thing was, he knew Mum couldn't afford to buy him anything else while they still fitted so he'd kept quiet and put up with the grief.

From that day I had a hatred for bullies that has never left me. In fact, you could argue that I only joined the police as a way of getting back at them.

I don't think I ever told Barry that.

Because of her job, I didn't get as much time with Mum as I'd have liked but I do remember her walking me to McAuley Primary School for my first day. I thought it was great, especially as it was just me and her.

But then she left me there, and I thought, *This isn't what I signed up for.*

So I went home.

I just walked out of the class, out of the school and retraced our footsteps home, across main roads and everything. I was five! How I wasn't skittled is an absolute mystery. But when Mum got back, there I was sitting on the doorstep.

I have to say school wasn't a particularly happy part of my life, especially when I moved up to Wandsworth Secondary Modern. Being dyslexic probably had a lot to do with the problem, although that wasn't diagnosed until years after I left. Back then there was another word for it.

Idiot.

Thicko, dunce, lazy sod – you name it, I was called it. And that was just by the teachers. I lost count of the number of times I got hauled up in front of the class, told to bend over and did my best not to cry as half a dozen whacks with a cane rained down on my backside. And why? Because my written work looked like a drunken spider dragging lead over the page.

There are different types of dyslexia, I've since learned. I have a type that gives me word blindness. I can see a word written down a hundred times and not recognise it as the same one. Whereas most people could look it up once in a dictionary and remember it, I have to look it up every time. The shape of the word just won't sink in. What's more, dictionaries explain a word by using other words – and I usually need to look half of those up, too.

Anyway, none of this was explored at Wandsworth and so, five years after I'd arrived, it surprised no one when I left full-time education with precisely zero qualifications. When you're not expected to achieve anything, that's pretty much what you'll do, isn't it?

But all that didn't matter because I knew what I wanted to do with my life and it didn't require 'O' levels. For as long as I could remember, there was only one thing I wanted to be above all else ...

A footballer.

I'm sorry, Jack Warner. My passion in life, from the moment my grandad threw me a ball, was football. Maybe it was in the blood because my dad's cousin was the mum of England World Cup winner, Martin Peters. I only learned this years later when I went to a family function and there he was. Even closer to the family tree is my uncle Jackie – Dad's brother – who played professionally for West Bromwich Albion and Shrewsbury Town. He was half decent, so they tell me and, if I'm honest, I wasn't that bad at it, either. It helped that I played in goal; no kid wants to play between the sticks so, right there, you've got more chance of getting in the team. I was a bit of a Dracula – afraid of crosses – but as a shot-stopper I was not only pretty handy but fearless with it. The bigger and uglier the number 9 flying at me, the more determined I was to get in his way, especially if he'd flattened a couple of our lads on the way through.

'Anything for the team', that was my credo. I'm not saying it was sensible. I probably saved as many shots with my head as my hands, but they all count. As Mr Williams, the school team coach, used to say, 'Lucky you've got nothing up there to get hurt, Driscoll.'

Football had been all I could think about for as long as I could remember and it was the only thing I ever fell out with Grandad over – for the simple reason that he was a massive Chelsea fan and I supported the other south west London lot, Fulham.

It's his own fault – as I told him many times – for never taking me to a game. That honour went to a neighbour called Alan Bladen, the dad of one of my friends. He knew I didn't have a dad of my own so one day he asked, 'Do you fancy going to see a football match?'

'Yes please!'

The match happened to be at Craven Cottage, between Fulham and Spurs. I remember it to this day. We stood – not sat – in the Stevenage Road stand, now the Johnny Haynes, and with the wind whipping up the Thames and down our spines, I stood there transfixed as Johnny Haynes himself, out on the left wing, squared the ball to Pat O'Connell and he whacked it home. That was it. The place erupted and I was hooked. From that moment on I've supported Fulham ... and it's been a bloody nightmare. For years we finished third or fourth – from bottom. Then we dropped out of the top division and were gone for ever.

While I was little, the Bladens took me when they could, but as I got older I'd go on my own. My mate Stevie Frankham supported Chelsea so one week we'd see his mob at home and the next week we'd see a proper team. Occasionally they played each other, which was job's a good'un. Both our teams for the price of one.

There was always such a great atmosphere at each ground. As kids we'd get passed down to the front where you could almost touch Haynes, Maurice Cook, Jimmy Langley, George Cohen, Alan Mullery, Stan Brown, Dave Metchick, Bobby Keetch, the legend Tosh Chamberlain and the rest as they ran by. They were all heroes, even John Key – possibly the worst player ever known to man, bless him – but, as a keeper myself, Tony Macedo was my all-time hero.

This was the era when men wore ties to games, and when their team scored an important goal they'd all toss their hats up in the air, just like you see on the old Pathé News reels. Even though we were packed in, there were no police officers and never any trouble. That all changed in the sixties, although to this day I have no idea why. Almost overnight we went from grounds where rival fans stood shoulder to shoulder to always being on the brink of tribal warfare. The first evidence I saw of changing times was before a summer game against West Ham. There was a cricket game going on in Bishops Park and suddenly hundreds of Hammers louts stormed the pitch, destroying the game and beating up cricketers and Fulham fans. I'd never seen anything like it: vicious, nasty, cowardly, meaningless violence from nowhere. There are people today who are still injured from that afternoon.

Football violence would later feature in my career, but aged 13 and turning out for the school team, it could not have been further from my mind. After we went on a tour of the northwest, I caught the eye of a couple of scouts: a bloke from Millwall asked Mr Williams if he could speak to me, so he put him in touch with Grandad.

I was buzzing when I went down for my trial and, if I'm honest, I thought, *This is it – goodbye school, goodbye teachers. I'm going to be a footballer.*

But Millwall never got back in touch.

To be fair, Mum tried to sympathise but she didn't get it. Not like a dad would have. Football was a hobby not a career in her eyes.

It was the same story when my beloved Fulham, then the devils Chelsea, invited me down and both ignored me afterwards, like the worst one-night-stand. But it was when Watford actually signed me up on trainee papers that Mum, in her ignorance, played a blinder.

By then I'd left school and got a job at McKinley & Sons hardware firm, which seemed such a boring way for anyone to spend their life. I was commuting twice a week to Watford, Tuesdays and Thursdays, for football training, then back again on Saturday for matches if I was lucky. What with work as well, I was knackered and one Saturday morning I slept through two alarm clocks before rising at half-past ten – the time I should have been getting changed at Vicarage Road.

'Mum! Why didn't you wake me? I've got a match today!'

'You needed your rest, love. You're a growing lad.'

'But I'm playing in goal today!'

And that's when she came out with the immortal words: 'Well, I'm sure they'll find someone else to do it.'

Sure enough, they did.

My name was mud for a while. It didn't help that the local paper ran a match report entitled: 'The Case Of The Missing Keeper'. But I managed to turn it around and had some cracking games for the reserves. I even got chosen to play in the first team for a testimonial at Spurs. We lost but I had a blinder of a game, so much so the reserve goalie asked me afterwards to show him how I made one particular save. The real feather in my cap came in the dressing room, from the gaffer, Ken Furphy himself.

'Nice job, son,' he said. 'I'll be speaking to you soon.'

'What about?' I asked.

'What do you think? A contract.'

That was the dream: to get professional papers from a professional club. Then I could leave my stinking job at McKinleys.

But Ken Furphy never did speak to me because that night, on the way home, I felt so rotten I fell asleep on the train and missed my stop. The next morning my throat was the width of a tyre and I had a fever that could roast a chicken. The doctor diagnosed glandular fever and, because it's so contagious, confined me to the house for weeks, even after I felt OK. In the end, it was two months before I was back on my feet and ready to play again, and by then it was the start of the new season and not only had Ken Furphy moved on to manage Sheffield United, but Watford had signed a keeper from Borehamwood. From rising star on the brink of signing I was suddenly persona non grata.

After that, the manager Len Henry took me to Wimbledon, then in the Southern League, but try as I might I never recaptured the fitness or energy of before. After a run with Tooting and Mitcham Wanderers, I finally admitted I didn't have what it took any more – either on the field or putting up with the bullying from so-called 'senior players' in the dressing room – and so I hung up my boots for good.

I needed a back-up trade and, since a long service medal at McKinley's was never going to happen, I fell back on my childhood dream of law enforcement.

Ironically, however, it wasn't the positive role model of George Dixon that encouraged me, rather a couple of distasteful episodes when I was 15.

The first came after a game of football. The lads and I were coming back from a kickabout in Wandsworth Park when we saw a girl with a quality shiner on her eye. Turned out her dad had beat her up so she was staying out for the night in the park, with a friend, to teach him a lesson.

I didn't know this girl, she wasn't my girlfriend and nor did I think she ever might be, but something in me said, 'Hang on, you can't let two girls stay out on their own.' So me and another one of the crowd said we'd hang around as well.

Not being the brightest, we didn't tell any adults. But when, at about two in the morning, the big Shell garage opposite the park was broken into, I wished we had. Suddenly the park was swarming with Old Bill and one with a dog saw us four, in a park in the middle of the night, and put two and two together.

The first thing the copper did was smack me round the head. Then he asked if we'd robbed the place.

That wasn't the way to do things, I was pretty sure of that. Worse occurred when we were all spirited off to Wandsworth nick. I was OK with Grandad being rung, but when the desk sarge started to phone the girl's house I said, 'You can't do that. Her old man is the reason she's got a black eye in the first place.' Were they interested in the truth? Put it this way: the call was made and, sure enough, this huge man gave her a wallop the second he saw her. It made the ticking off I got from Grandad seem a bit mild.

I said, 'You're meant to protect victims, not help them get hurt,' but it fell on deaf ears. Just as well, Grandad reckoned, or I could have got worse than a ticking off.

A few months later I saw another unflattering glimpse of the boys in blue. That was when Grandad died and my world fell apart. It was 1967 and I was 16 years old. We were all cut up, but it got worse when Mum handed over her stamps book to the 'Man from the Pru' to cash in an insurance policy and he pocketed it and claimed she'd never paid. I'd lost count of how many years she'd contributed weekly to that book, and there she was, ripped off at a time when she was already grieving.

The police were rubbish. The coppers they sent weren't interested, simple as that: not in Mum, not in the crime and definitely not in the truth. If this was real policing then I was not impressed. Years later, I would teach young police officers: 'Look after your witnesses and your investigation will look after itself.' It's the very least we can do for any victim of crime.

Despite these early, unpromising brushes with the law, there I was a year or so later, filling in forms to join the Metropolitan

Police Force. When the reply came back I was disappointed to be told I was too young. But it said, 'Do apply again at a later date.'

The police was only ever meant to be a back-up so I wasn't too heartbroken at the time. When my career as a sportsman fell apart however, I needed something to do so became a painter and decorator. Until I learned I was allergic to paint. Then I worked abroad with friends for a while before the lure of blue flashing lights hooked me again and I became an ambulance man. Aged 24, I was certainly old enough to reapply for the Met but I decided to get a bit more experience before I went for it. Ambulances seemed the next best thing.

I did the statutory six weeks' training at Waterloo, which was essentially a pumped-up first aid course: intubation, infusion, cardiac massage – we ticked off all the big life savers. About halfway through the training, I started to go out on call with a real ambulance man.

My very first call was to the Union Jack Club. If you visit that address today you'll find a fairly salubrious place, but back then it was a doss house, so going to treat a vagrant who'd collapsed was no surprise.

Except, when we got there, he wasn't just collapsed. He was dead.

Honestly, I could have had a year's training and still not have been prepared for that. I wasn't scared or sick. My overwhelming thought was: *You don't look any different.*

Apart from the fast driving course where we got to use the old blues-and-twos – the flashing blue lights and the two-tone 'nee-naa, nee-naa' sirens – it was a bit downhill after that. No more corpses, no real entertainment: once I'd qualified, I had to do the obligatory year driving old folks around, like a glorified bus driver. Only at the end of that did I get accepted onto the accident and emergency team.

Talk about a shift in gear...

I was posted to Battersea, which was a very busy station. From 7 a.m. to 3 p.m. there were two ambulances on shift so that was all right, but from 11 p.m. to 7 a.m. you had only one. 'Battersea 1' was my call sign for the dispatcher and some shifts I was hearing it non-stop. Nights were quite perky, Battersea Rise being just down the road from some inner London addresses, and there were some nasty assaults, especially towards the weekend. On the plus side, there was no time to think about what you were doing: get in, do your stuff, get them to a hospital.

Of course, like any profession, the old hands tried to make it difficult for the newbie. Even in my mid-twenties, I was treated like I was fresh out of school.

'You're not an ambulance man till you've ticked off the Big Five,' I was told on my first day.

'And they are?'

The bloke grinned. 'Number one: you have to have someone under a train.'

Ouch.

'Two: you have to have a hanging. Three: a shooting. Four: you have to deliver a baby. In your vehicle. And five: you need a celebrity, preferably an overdose. Until you've done those, you're not one of us.'

I have to say I was a little intimidated but, Battersea being Battersea, I'd only been there a month before I'd ticked the lot off.

The baby was first. I must declare a bit of a balls-up at this point because if it weren't for pilot error I would never have claimed this one. We were bombing off to Charing Cross Hospital, patient on board, but my driver for the night, a great lad called Smithy, missed the Fulham Palace Road turning around the Hammersmith one-way system and, before you knew it, the woman I was trying to keep calm started going down the final straight.

'Smithy, pull over! I can see the crown!'

'Christ, Clive! I've heard about your goalkeeping!'

By the time the wheels stopped turning it was all over and I was the most relieved man on earth to be holding a tiny newborn. I don't think I'd ever been more scared. You literally have someone's life in your hands. Two people's, actually. But it's probably the easiest job I had on the ambulance service because the mum does all the work, doesn't she? All I had to do was just wrap up the baby and keep the little fella safe till the experts got involved at the hospital.

I don't know if it was because it was my first delivery but I made a point of calling into Charing Cross when my shift ended. There, looking quite radiant, was the mum and in her arms the tiny bundle of life I'd seen enter the world. I admit I felt a tear or two coming, especially as she would not stop thanking and thanking me for saving her son.

'Clive,' she said finally, 'do you know what I am going to call him?'

I could see where this was going.

'Tell me,' I said.

'I'm going to call him... Kalimullah.'

Kalimullah! You'd think she'd have thrown a 'Clive' in there, wouldn't you?

There was humour everywhere in the ambulance service – without it, you wouldn't get through the day.

I got to know one guy, a cracking ambulance man and a fairly normal, balanced bloke outside the job. Then one day it all got on top of him and he took a concoction of drugs that would have killed an army and went and lay down by his dad's grave. You can't underestimate the trauma we were put through, and humour – however dark – was a necessary stress outlet.

A case in point: Smithy and I were on shift one Saturday night and the first five shouts we got were deaths.

'Battersea 1, you've got a drugs overdose, someone sitting in a doorway.'

'On our way.'

That was the first. The second was someone under a train – and let me tell you, *they* look very different when they're dead. The third was more normal, someone just passing away naturally in their sleep, before, finally, we had to scrape up a motorcyclist who'd gone into, and under, a bus.

By now the radio operator was looking for the gag. The next shout that came in began with: 'Calling Euthanasia 1! Euthanasia 1, pick up.'

After the fifth, we were all feeling pretty low and even the radio jokes stopped. It took the sixth job, delivering a baby on the Heygate Estate in Elephant and Castle, to make us feel a bit better. Suddenly we were only losing 5–1 instead of 5–0.

There were good nights too – many times when our actions saved someone's life. And we did get to work with, if I can put it like that, a number of celebrities. I was sad to pick up one of my favourite film actresses for a drugs overdose but not as sad as my driver, who nearly killed us several times because his eyes were fixed on the rearview mirror all the way to the hospital.

The papers never got hold of that story, but nobody could miss the events of 16 September 1977: that was the night we were called out to Barnes Common to discover Marc Bolan's multi-coloured Mini halfway up a sycamore tree. The car, with Marc's girlfriend Gloria Jones behind the wheel, had gone out of control on the humpback bridge. Bolan wouldn't have known anything about it, poor lad, but Gloria was still breathing when we got there – albeit where she landed on the bonnet – so we got her to hospital and she made it.

It wasn't a job for everyone, that was obvious.

By this time I had been in the ambulance service for two years and I was training a newbie, a young woman straight out of Waterloo. Unluckily for her, our first job together was a body under a train.

It was the crack of dawn and the first train into Clapham Junction had spaghettied someone. By the time we got there, the police had shut down power to the line so we could walk the 50 or so yards to the body.

I could sense my young partner tensing as we got close. It wasn't a pretty sight from a distance. When we were about six foot from the body, however, even I nearly had a coronary: I was looking at the victim's open eyes when suddenly they blinked. Then she looked at me and spat: 'You took your fucking time!' Those were her exact words.

That was enough for my sidekick. She screamed, dropped her kit bag and ran across half a dozen live train lines, clambered up the wall on platform 1 and was never seen by us again.

But this victim ... I don't know how she was still alive. Her injuries were astounding, to the extent where we had to put her together like a jigsaw puzzle. Somehow me and a copper got her into the ambulance and all the way to St James's Hospital. But the second they tried to get her into a bed her arm fell off.

'Fucking idiots!' Again, the exact words.

It was like a scene from *Monty Python and the Holy Grail*. If she'd said, ''Tis but a scratch' I would not have been surprised.

Normally you keep patients awake as long as possible to monitor brain function. On this occasion, the docs put her out immediately just to shut her up.

Despite the patient's language, I thought I'd done an OK job so me and the copper who'd helped me out decided to get a cup of tea. In truth, we were both a bit proud of ourselves for being the utmost professionals throughout what was probably the worst day of our lives.

But then a waitress walked by with a plate of tinned tomatoes and that was it. We both just bleughed. All over the nice shiny floor of St James's Hospital.

I suppose it was only a matter of time – you couldn't see what we'd seen without feeling something. We'd managed to hold it together to do our jobs, but the tomatoes were the final straw.

A week later, I was at Battersea and a young bloke walked in.
'Clive Driscoll?' he said.

'That's me.'

'I understand you were very kind to my mother when she had her accident.' Then he threw a fiver down on the desk and walked out. Such a lovely gesture and one that meant a lot.

I'd only intended to do two years on the ambulances then join the Met, but I had such a cracking time that four years in I still didn't want to leave. If I'd been a single man I probably wouldn't have. But by then, having married my girlfriend Tina and having two young children, a better-paid job with shorter hours took priority. Our £11,000 mortgage wouldn't pay itself.

Which is how, in May 1979, I found myself lying face down on a narrow bed at Hendon thinking I'd made a terrible mistake.

CHAPTER TWO

What Are They Doing To You, Officer?

Christ!

You think you've seen everything a lift can throw at you but the sight of the doors sliding open on a Monday morning to reveal at least a dozen coppers in full patrol regalia had me doing a double-take. Until I remembered where I was.

Hendon took in about 40 recruits every week back then. According to my paperwork, you were handed your uniform in the third week and so, in theory, they could have been only a fortnight more experienced than me. But they had the attitude of the hackneyed constables I'd met in Wandsworth Park that night – not one of them budged an inch to let me in so I had to walk down the four flights of stairs to breakfast.

Apparently, Day One at police college wasn't going to be any more warm and fuzzy than the previous night.

The weird thing, I realised, was that I wasn't exactly going out of my way to inspire anything different. If that lift door had opened while I had been on the ambulances, I'd have had something to say. I'm not claiming it would have been the funniest joke in the world but I would have said something. That's the kind of bloke I am: there with the joke, the sharp retort. Keep people smiling, keep them on side. And I'm certainly not shy – far from it. But that morning I didn't say anything.

Not that I didn't think of something – all sorts of things shoot through your mind when you see a dozen coppers squeezed in like sardines – but I just chose to keep it zipped. I'd decided not to be that kind of person any more. That wasn't how policemen behaved in my mind. Not in Dock Green …

The breakfast hall was buzzing. Forty new faces a week is a massive turnover, but it was necessary to keep up with all the retiring old boys: all the coppers who'd come back from the war and signed up in the 1940s were nearing the end, resulting in an almighty recruitment drive.

Looking around the room, I realised London was about to get a police force of spotty teenagers.

I could only see two people who looked like they might be within a few years of my age: one of them was a bloke I recognised from Millwall. Footballers in those days needed another career when they hung up their boots and he'd been fast-tracked into Hendon – but not for his PC Plod skills. The Met had a football team that needed a left-footed player and, guess what? This bloke had a bobby dazzler of one. The other guy, actually a few years my senior, had left the Parachute Regiment for something better paid, which was why he was there.

Of the rest of the intake, the overwhelming majority were 18-year-olds, straight out of school and game for anything. I recognised a few of my neighbours from the all-night party on our wing and they couldn't have looked more chuffed if they'd been on an all-expenses-paid holiday to Ibiza. It was all a laugh for them.

Faced with feeling like a grandad or sitting on my own, I found an empty table in the corner. I was surprised when a young kid in uniform asked to join me.

'Just starting?' he asked.

'First day.'

'I'm in my eighth week,' he said. 'The only advice I can give is don't give up.'

Easier said than done, I thought. But I'd promised myself I'd give it a good go so, after breakfast, I trudged to the designated classroom and sat down with 39 teenagers who behaved like school children until the instructor walked through the door – then they were quiet, trying to suppress their giggling. It was classic childish behaviour. The sort of thing I'd grown out of at 15.

Our training would start in the afternoon, the instructor explained. Until then there was the business of taking our fingerprints, signing the giant black book of candidates and pledging our allegiance.

Off we went to the main hall where a chief superintendent introduced himself and made us run through a few practice goes of swearing the oath to uphold the role of constable, then another one to support the government, and finally a promise of loyalty to the Queen. There was a gap in each one where you said your own name. When we reached that part, it sounded as bad as 10 blokes saying different things would.

The only oath that meant anything to me was the one to Her Majesty. Pledging to look after her and her country without favour or ill will seemed to cover it all to me. If it had thrown in a dig at 'bullies', it would have been perfect.

The chief superintendent looked us all up and down and I was proud to note that I was the only recruit wearing a suit. (The majority of newbies looked like they were queuing for a night at the local disco.) That hadn't been unintentional. Grandad had always looked spot-on – Nan could do her make-up in the reflection from his shoes. 'You have to look smart for business,' he'd said.

Even if I hadn't listened to Grandad, I found myself asking: *What would George Dixon wear?*

What's that phrase? Dress for the job you want, not the one you have. At least I'd seen a policeman or two in action; life experiences didn't exactly rate highly for most of my class's intake.

At least some of the 18-year-olds had probably had a job or two. Another group's experience of the big bad world was the square root of nothing. These were the cadets, those boys and girls who'd decided as kids to join the Job. It's a bit like the Boy Scouts but without the dib, dib, dibbing – all cadets do is train and practise for the day they can be Old Bill for real. Which is fine in principle, but is that the best training for a copper in charge of community work? Not if you ask me.

Luckily, nobody did.

When it came to actual lessons, any thought that my being closer to the group leaders' ages would count in my favour was quickly shot down. It wasn't just the living accommodation that was geared towards the teens; the standard method of teaching was through patronising, ridicule, coercion and outright insults. You could say this is exactly what a mob of scruffy school-leavers needed and, to be fair, they did appear to thrive on the shouting and intimidation. Maybe at 18 I'd have been fine with it as well; but at 28, having seen the things I'd seen and lived the life I had, it didn't work for me.

As my first so-called tutor shouted the odds, I thought, *Hang on, mate. How many lives did you save last week? How many dead bodies did you pick out from under public transport?*

The dyslexia didn't help. There was a lot of written work, tons of overnight reading that they expected you to blast through and, of course, it took me five times longer than anyone else ('therein' and 'therefore' aren't exactly written for the common man, are they?). The wording of laws is very precise: if you don't get every semi-colon or bracket in place it won't stand up in court. For example: 'The judge, says the ass, is a fool' might sound the same as 'The judge says the ass is a fool', but the meaning on paper is a bit different.

Take the theft law: 'A person is guilty of theft if he dishonestly appropriates property belonging to another with the intention of permanently depriving the other of it.' Pick your way through that lot when the words are jumping around like spacehoppers as you try to read them! When my neighbours invited me out again, I had to decline. I knew it would take me till midnight to absorb what most of them could memorise in an hour. Fair play to them for asking, though.

It was a hard first week, I have to admit, and there were many occasions when I questioned why I was putting myself through it. Apparently that wasn't unusual.

On my first Friday, one of the secretaries handed me a brown envelope containing my first week's wages.

'I was expecting to be paid monthly.'

'Not everyone lasts a whole month.' She smiled. 'It's easier this way.'

Hearing that other people found it a struggle sent me off with a bit of a spring in my step, I must admit. But I hadn't got far when I opened the envelope and realised I had to go back to the office.

'There's been some mistake with my money,' I said.

'No mistake.' She was sterner now. 'You're only a trainee. That's all you're entitled to.'

'I meant you've given me too much!'

I knew the police were paid more than the London Ambulance Service but this blew me away. To earn the same amount on the ambulances I would have had to work – as a senior A&E paramedic, not a trainee – about three and a half weeks, including overtime! The difference was quite stunning.

And if the wage was a lot for me, it was like winning the football pools for the youngsters. Envelopes in hand, they all hit the town to celebrate – and yes, they still asked me along. But I had some youngsters of my own I needed to see.

There are some evil minds at work in the police service. There have to be: it could be no coincidence that on Monday morning – *every* Monday morning – there was a test based on the previous week's work. Fail that and you got one chance to re-sit; fail it again, and it was thank you and goodnight, Hendon.

I didn't mind the exam but I despised the timing. I went home that first weekend, had a cracking Saturday with the kids but, come Sunday, when I should have been all family man and loving husband and making the most of our time together, I had to get the books out. I found it quite spiteful, if I'm honest. The powers that be must have known this was our only free time.

Still, nothing was as hard as saying goodbye again to the kids. That was downright torture. Again, Bonnie was too young to take offence, but Robert remembered going through it the week before, followed by not seeing me for what must have seemed like an eternity in his little world. He was distraught and Tina had to peel his arms off me so I could get out of the house. Then, just as I got into the street, there he was running after me down the drive, screaming, 'Daddy, don't go!' Tina had a right struggle to get him back in. When I looked back, I can only imagine it must have been raining because there was a lot of water in my eyes.

I pull Robert's leg a bit about that now but he has the last laugh because, as a Royal Marine, he has spent the last decade disappearing off to fight wars in Afghanistan or wherever for six months at a time. I'm proud as Punch but every time he leaves, part of me wants to cling to him to stop him from going.

My second Sunday night was, if anything, even more miserable than the first. I spent it lying on my bed trying to force the words of a book into my brain, all the while a cascading symphony of drunken teenagers returning to their rooms played like a soundtrack around me.

When it came to Monday morning and sitting down for the test, I felt like death. The fear got worse when I noticed there were only about 30 of us in the room. Had I got the time wrong? Should I have been somewhere else? Then it dawned: I wasn't the only one who'd struggled to come back the night before. I just happened to be one of the 30 who had.

As a bit of a reward after our test, we were told to line up outside the room next to the gymnasium. On the hour, the door was flung open. Yet another weary-looking copper was standing there – in front of racks of blue uniforms. When my turn came, I stepped into the room and was met with a barrage of questions:

'What waist are you?'

'Inside leg?'

'Hat size?'

'Collar?'

Barely a minute later I was being ushered back outside, a large pile of blue and white in my arms: two pairs of trousers, one winter, one summer; one hat; an overcoat; a tunic; three pressed white shirts; and, perched on the top, a pair of black gloves for ceremonial duties. What those duties would be, I didn't have a clue, but I couldn't wait to get back to my room and try the lot on.

With the uniform came a price. Each morning we were told to present ourselves in full gear for inspection – which meant boots had to be polished, collars nice and crisp and shirt sleeves ironed with a crease you could cut your finger on.

I'd done many things in my life by then, but ironing wasn't one of them. I must have been wrestling with the ancient Hotpoint for half an hour when the only other bloke older than me, the old Para guy, came over and took it off me.

'It's painful watching you, mate,' he said with a laugh and then whizz, whizz, fold, fold and, two minutes later, he had my shirt pressed to pass any inspection. 'It's not all bayonets and bombs in the army, you know.'

There was one other garment handed out that day: a red tabard. With different classes starting every week, the whole college was divided into those on their first five weeks, those on their second and those on their third. As a beginner I got a red one, which would stay with me until the end of June – assuming I lasted that long.

Every morning at 8 a.m. sharp we all had to congregate on the parade ground beneath my dorm window. That's when we got to show off what we'd learned in marching practice; or, as I thought of it, bumping-into-each-other practice.

Sgt Butcher was the fella in charge. I can still hear his voice now, yelling: 'Lip, lip, lip!' – i.e. 'Left, left, left!' – for what seemed like hours on end. We used to march everywhere as a group. He was wasting his time with me, though. It didn't matter how many hours we spent swinging this arm one way, looking another way, walking a third way – I could not get it. When I've seen my boy, Robbo, march with his unit, it's like poetry in motion: his arms are the right height, his legs move at precisely the same angle every time and the whole squad is synchronised like clockwork. I, however, was less a soldier than a centre half – I turned the wrong way once, and brought down the whole row in front of me.

But, because I liked the old-fashioned way of policing, I grew to enjoy the pomp and circumstance of the drills, even if I was hopeless. A few years later it fell off the syllabus and the Met was heavily criticised for being the only force working the 1984 miners' strike who didn't march. But if they'd had a squad of officers like me I could understand why.

Luckily, no one was ever thrown out of Hendon for not being able to walk in rhythm. But there were other physical tests that did carry that threat. Every week we had a fitness test and, like the written exams, if you fell below a certain level you got one more shot at it and then you were given the old heave-ho. Despite my footballing days, physical exercise doesn't come naturally to me – it didn't help that the physical instructors were younger than I was. I remember once we had to do a headstand over a vaulting horse. All the 18-year-olds were having a go, some of them managing it. Eventually, the instructor pointed at me and said, 'You want to have a bash, old fella?'

Cheeky bastard.

I had a go and, after a lot of huffing and puffing, I made it. But the truth was I was nowhere near as fit as the rest and they all knew it. In the ambulance service you might be lugging people around all day, which obviously requires a bit of muscle, but no one was timing you.

If I didn't up my game I could be in serious trouble. But when was I going to get the time to train? Every night was spent head down in the law books, accompanied by the sound of my colleagues stumbling back from the bar. That only left the weekend – so what little time I had with Tina and the kids on a Saturday, I now had to spend dragging my carcass around the local running track. Lap after lap after tedious lap I'd do, followed by sit-ups, press-ups – basically all the things I've always hated.

Somehow I managed to reach the targets required, physical and written. Around 82% seemed to be my average mark in just about everything which, for someone who never took any exams at school, I was actually pretty pleased with. The cut-off grade was 70%, so I cleared that with room to spare. As for all the recruits regularly posting scores of over 90%, I tried not to worry. We all have our strengths, and crafting essays just happens not to be one of mine.

Along with reading.

And marching.

And ironing...

By the time we reached the end of August, I was marching in a blue tabard to denote the second third of my time. Only the yellow one to go, and then it was all over.

So, seven weeks in, was I any happier? No. At least once a week I made the decision to quit. And yes, it was always on a Sunday afternoon. Things got so bad one week that I found myself on the pay phone in the halls of residence. I had a stack of ten pence pieces and two numbers written down. The first was my brother's.

Barry listened to my problems then cut to the chase: 'Look, little 'un' – he always called me that, right to the day he died – 'you never worked at school so now is your chance to put the hours in and make something of yourself. In the long run, it'll be better for your family.'

I don't think I liked that answer so I rang the other number. Annoyingly, Mum said the same thing: 'You get nothing worthwhile without sacrifice,' she said. 'I'll back you all the way but if you really want to do this, and I think you do, just knuckle down and it'll be over before you know it.'

I knew they were both right. Maybe I just wanted to hear I wasn't being a bad dad. No matter how much mortgage I was paying off by being at Hendon, was it enough to justify the pain I was causing my son?

Come to think of it, was it enough to justify the pain caused to me? I remember once I called the lift to go to the fourth floor and this copper in a yellow tabard standing next to me just sneered in my face: 'Fourth floor? You could walk up there. We've got to go to the tenth.'

Like my other lift episode, I could have said some choice words as a reply. But that's not how the police works. More than anywhere else I've come across, it is an organisation built on hierarchy: you start at the bottom and you go up. Much like one of the lifts I kept having trouble with. Age, gender, race, inside leg measurement: all irrelevant inside the Met. It's a pyramid structure, pure and simple, and if you're higher up the food chain then you get to call the shots – and everyone below listens.

Which was why I bit my tongue at the yellow tabard. Yellow trumped blue, simple as that. And I wasn't one to cause waves. Not back then...

Ask anyone from my time at Hendon to describe me and, if they remember me at all, I bet they'd say: 'Old Driscoll? Quiet bloke, kept himself to himself.' Funnily enough, that's how most serial killers are described by their neighbours as well ... Yet, ask the same question to anyone I've worked with since and they'll laugh in your face: 'Quiet? Clive? Are you joking?' But that was the policeman I was trying to become: serious, diligent, putting work before pleasure.

In 17 weeks I didn't once go down to the building's bar or join the rest of the lads in a jaunt out of the compound. I certainly didn't let the boys from the CID course get their claws in me – their nights out were legendary, even within the college. I'm sure I heard a whisper or two about me but I didn't care. The end was in sight. I just wanted to get there.

Hendon is like a goldfish bowl. Or a prison. In fact, depending on your mood, it could be all things to all men.

Considering the Met is supposed to operate in the open air – in the wild, if you like – I was surprised that none of our training took place anywhere except inside the walls of the Peel Centre.

For example, when it came to showing us around a police station, they just opened up the west wing and there was a fully operational nick, accurate down to the toilet bowls. In there we could practise every aspect of station life.

A lot of our training was role-play and the fake nick featured heavily. I remember having to capture and process an assault suspect. I made the arrest, marched him to the 'police station', introduced him to the sergeant in charge of arrests and booked him in. The custody sergeant took the 'erbert – as he referred to all dopey villains – from me and he was charged.

That was only part one. After that I attended a full-scale replica of a court. In there I swore on the Bible, gave evidence, answered questions from inspectors playing solicitors and watched and waited as the chief superintendent – playing the magistrate – considered his verdict.

Twelve weeks in and we finally got to step outside Aerodrome Road. The first I knew about it was when I got back to Hendon on the Sunday night. If anything I was in a worse mood than usual because, while the rest of the country would be enjoying a bank holiday the following day, I'd be stuck there, in Mordor. But finding a note pinned to the notice board piqued my interest:

'Full uniform, parade ground, 0700 hours.'

What's that all about?

It turned out to be a day out like the ones enjoyed by thousands of other Londoners. Except this one held the possibility of violence.

The Notting Hill Carnival has been running in west London since 1966, when Caribbean and London Free School hippy groups combined to produce the capital's largest outdoor festival. These days you can't see media coverage of the weekend without seeing photographs of bobbies on the beat dancing with colourfully clad Jamaican women, but back in 1979 dancing was the last thing anyone had in mind for coppers. The Saturday was fun, Sunday was thrown open for kids, but the Monday was the perky one. That's when you needed to have your wits about you. Perfect, then, for a bunch of over-zealous, inexperienced trainees.

The bus took us all round west London and dropped us in Ladbroke Grove, just south of the Westway. Piling off, there was a buzz of excitement in the air.

The inspector in charge lined us up and put everyone straight: 'If you get back from today without a brick hitting your head, consider yourself lucky.'

I didn't know if he was joking or not, but from that point on I was no longer on a school trip. This was an exercise in survival.

Just walking through the thronging crowds was an experience. You could have cut the atmosphere with a knife – given the looks of some of the revellers, maybe that wasn't too unlikely a scenario. The mood in my own team was markedly different as well. I'd seen life and death, violence and pain and all points in between on the ambulances. Suddenly all the motor-mouths, egos and Big I Ams in my class were silent. They were out of their depth and they knew it. And so was I.

We were walking along in single file – not even pretending to march, thank goodness – and I dropped my gloves. My lovely black gloves, there on the ground with the abandoned beer glasses and God knows what else. I turned around to pick them up but I hadn't got more than a couple of feet before the old inspector said to the others, 'Grab him!'

He thought I was legging it! The deeper we got into the heart of the festival, the more I could appreciate why.

It was early in the morning but the crowds were already substantial in number and unfriendly in character. The 1970s, even the tail end, weren't the most racially enlightened of times and the police force and minorities had form, that was a given.

Nor was the festival the multicultural extravaganza it is today. Anyone watching the scene would have seen a sea of black with a thin line of white and blue injecting itself into the mass. We literally were the only non-Caribbean faces – which said as much about the diversity of the police as it did about the makeup of the carnival.

I'm proud to say I was one of the few not twitching at every lilting heckle and insult. In my last job I'd been verbally abused and physically manhandled by drunks, druggies and all sorts while trying to help a victim. This was nothing. Still, I was interested to know what the master plan for us was. You don't take 30-odd fresh faces to a racial melting pot without a plan.

When we reached All Saints Road all was revealed. We were to stand two arm lengths apart and ... that was it. Just stand there. All day. 'Filtering' they called it. It was essentially a way of breaking up the heaving mass of the crowd. Imagine a stream splitting to go round a rock in the water. Those rocks were us. These days they use horses. In 1979 they had other dumb animals.

Even as we got into position I thought it was a cock-up. In fact, I didn't think: I *knew*. There was this mass of humanity, a sea of bodies swilling our way, many of them antagonistic, and all of a sudden you've got this line of police officers standing there, exposed to the world. We may as well have been in the altogether, that's how exposed every one of us felt.

Remember, this was long before the days of riot gear being handed out willy-nilly. We had our usual ''Ello 'ello 'ello' outfits on, black gloves included, and that was it.

Seriously, what hope did we have?

One lad, smoking something so sweet I could have put it in my tea, came up to me while I was getting into position and shook his head. Then, in the thickest patois I'd ever heard, he said:

'What are they *doing* to you, officer?'

Even the pot-heads were affronted on my behalf!

And yet ... this is the weirdest thing. Once we were all in our places, lined up like telegraph poles across the street, a strange thing occurred. The crowd, once a solid and amorphous mass, started to stop, break up, and go round us. Whereas I had fully expected to be flattened by the onslaught of off-their-face party-goers, something in our defiance or our uniform or their docility just made them split up and go round.

It's working! It's actually working.

I learned an awful lot that day. Not least that a group of people is far more brave – and more threatening – than individuals. I remembered being told that in one of our tedious lectures but, seeing it in action, right in front of my face, really rammed that lesson home harder than a hundred teachers or textbooks could have explained it.

The other thing I learned was this: it felt *amazing* to be called 'officer', even if it was by a pot-smoking teenager. He didn't know I was a student. To him I represented the Met and, for all my doubts, to be recognised as that made me feel a million dollars. If I'd needed an incentive to pass the rest of the course, that was it.

But not everything was so positive. A school near All Saints Road had been cleared for the police to stand down, get a cup of tea and recharge the batteries before going back out. While I was in there I saw two coppers – proper ones, not trainees like us – drag a young man in from the carnival and, basically, start to hammer him. I didn't know what this bloke had done but nothing deserved that beating.

Without thinking, I started to go over. My sergeant stepped in my way. 'As you were, Driscoll.'

'Sir, that's out of order.'

He nodded. 'Just get on with your own work. Make sure what you do is right.'

As it turned out, the human punch-bag got up and walked out, so he couldn't have been hurt that seriously. But the whole episode sat very awkwardly with me. I had signed up to stop bullying – not turn a blind eye.

'As much force as is necessary' was the phrase trotted out at Hendon. A police officer can pick up anything they like to defend themselves as long as they can justify it as 'as much force as is necessary'. And no more than that. So, if you are sitting there and I pick an ashtray up and hit you over the head with it, the police officer arriving at the scene will say, 'Hold up, Clive, why did you do that?' But if I was standing there with a knife or bottle in my hand or I was kicking out and spitting, then 'as much force as is necessary' is whatever it would take to bring me under control.

It's a bit subjective, I suppose, depending on whether you are the one being attacked or just watching. If it's your honest belief that there is a gun or a knife, you are allowed to respond accordingly. It might turn out to be a bloody ice-lolly – and we've had a few of those over the years – but if, at that moment, you are acting honestly and correctly and you think it's the right thing to do, then most courts will accept that.

Two men pummelling an unarmed reveller, though? That was a different story.

By the end of our shift I was a different person. Police work was no longer theoretical. It was practical. We'd been out on the streets, in a powder keg environment, and we'd coped. We'd had a taste of being the real deal and, mostly, we had liked it. If any of us cocked up now before the final tests we'd be gutted.

The final days came and they went. I wore a suit or a uniform as required. I filled in all the test papers. I answered all the questions. Then I waited. If I managed my average of 82% I would be OK. But this had been an exam. The pressure was greater. Anything could have happened.

But it didn't.

I scored 83% – a nudge above my average – and I knew I'd done enough. The four months of sacrifice, hardship, misery and, OK, a *lot* of learning had been worth it. I was proud to be a police officer.

For the passing-out ceremony my mother and my wife travelled up to see me stomp around the parade ground with the rest of my year before I was called up by the commissioner to collect my stripes with a 'Well done' and a handshake. If I could have bottled that moment I would have – I'd never felt so proud. I just wished I had a father who wanted to be there to see me.

But that didn't matter. Not that October day. The only thing I cared about were the words of the commissioner. He'd called me something that I had dreamed of being for as long as I could remember.

He'd called me a constable.

CHAPTER THREE

Where Can I Buy a Dress Suit?

Whoever's running this is an idiot.

Not what you want to be thinking after one day at work, but the evidence was pretty strong.

Following the first Sunday night spent in my own bed in four months, I got up that October 1979 Monday morning, peeped in on the kids, put on my uniform and, for the first time ever, felt like I deserved it. When I looked in the mirror I swear it even fit better now I was qualified.

Still, I was only on probation and there was a long way to go. A bloody long way as it turned out.

All the way back to Hendon, in fact.

It was a joke really. The Met breaks everywhere down into sections and I lived in Sutton, which was part of the 'Z District'. At the time this was the biggest, including Sutton, Croydon, Wallington and Mitcham, going right down into Epsom and out to Banstead. So I knew I'd be posted somewhere south. In order to find out where, I had first to report back to the Peel Centre.

I must admit, turning up as an officer felt a bit better than turning up on a Sunday night in my civvies, but the first sight of those towers sent the same chill down my spine. When I saw the group of kids wearing red tabards, I had nothing but pity for them.

It was good to see the rest of my own class again – or the survivors, at least. We'd started with 40; there were 25 waiting to be shipped out. That's how hard the course was. The staff had to take a lot of the credit or blame – depending on how you looked at it – for that. And they weren't any easier on us now we were qualified.

'Driscoll, over there.' A sergeant with a clipboard pointed to one of three lined up Green Goddess buses. 'Johns, that one. Shaw, you're here.'

No niceties, no smiles, no joy. But that was Hendon for you.

I climbed on board with a handful of the others, then watched the world move slowly by as we backtracked down south.

Typical for a Monday, traffic was moving at a snail's pace so it was a good 90 minutes before we pulled up at Croydon. *Okay,* I thought, *this is where I'm being posted.*

No.

Croydon was just where another instructor read out where we'd be in Z District: 'Davies, Mitcham; Jones, Clapham; Driscoll …'

Where am I going? Where am I going?

'Driscoll, Sutton.'

For the love of God, I can see Sutton nick from my house. I could have bloody walked there!

But that's the police all over for you. There's a way of doing things and there's a type of person who will fight to the grave for the right to do them that way, however cockeyed, skewed or downright stupid those ways are. Efficiency? Value for money? Not words in the Met's vocabulary back in 1979.

I thought it would be back on the Green Goddess but I was assigned a uniformed constable in a panda car – so named because all police cars used to be black with white patches – to chauffeur me there instead. She's quite high up in MI5 now, but she started off as a taxi driver for Clive Driscoll!

The welcoming committee at Sutton was not exactly red-carpet standard. I was deposited with the desk sergeant who barely looked up – if he'd had a Len Deighton novel on the go I wouldn't have been surprised.

I introduced myself and, all puppy-dog enthusiasm, said, 'I got 83% in my exams!'

'I got 93.'

I think he warmed to me after that.

I was shown behind the desk and given my locker. Finally, I was ready to do some proper police work.

'Where do I go now?' I asked.

'Home.'

'Pardon?'

'You're on nights, son. Piss off till ten.'

So that was it. Thanks to the unseen geniuses in charge, I'd left my house at half past seven in the morning and got back at three in the afternoon. In between I'd had a magical mystery tour of London, been sworn at twice and done bugger-all police work.

But at least I was wearing my uniform.

Luckily I was used to doing nights on the ambulances, so strolling over to the station for ten o'clock wasn't exactly a hardship. The biggest problem was being so excited during the day that I hadn't had a chance to catch forty winks.

The night-desk sergeant was Bill Wheeler, a much cheerier soul than his daytime counterpart. He showed me the station and told me that I'd be helping out at the desk for a few days until I got to know my way around. My probation period was two years. There wasn't exactly a rush to fit everything in.

At eleven, when the shift officially started, he told me to put my coat on.

'One of the area car boys is running late so you're taking his place.'

Get in! But all I said was, 'That's fine, sir.'

Brian Ferguson wasn't a character from *Dixon of Dock Green* but he could have been. An old boy, one of those quite happy to remain a constable all his serving life, he had a pipe in his mouth when we were introduced and it stayed there while we got in the car and started driving around.

What a lot of people might not realise is that police stations at night are like the *Marie Celeste*. I'd say Sutton ran a skeleton staff, but it was skinnier than that. There was Bill Wheeler on the desk and Brian Ferguson – with a rooky for co-pilot – out in the only area car. If the calls came in with a nice gap between them then we stood a chance of dealing with them. If more than one came in at the same time …

Fergie was nice enough. If I could have understood everything he said through clenched teeth it might have been easier, but he was calm, seemed happy in his lot and showed me the ropes. One of the things I had to do, he said, was log our job descriptions in the car's notebook so we knew where we were going. But when the first crackle on the radio came in, he just said, 'I know where that is,' so I left the pen alone.

No sooner had he docked the radio, than whoosh, he put his foot down and flicked a switch on the dashboard.

The second the blues-and-twos lit up the night I caught him flicking me a glance. It took a second to realise he was waiting for me to be impressed by the blue disco lights strobing the roads. I think I mustered a smile but the truth was, I'd seen it all before.

My first crime scene was at Carshalton Football Club. Only a bit of low-level vandalism but, when you think I should have been counting paper clips, it was a pretty good introduction. We secured the property then, crackle crackle, call number two – a report of a scuffle in progress.

Once again, Fergie said, 'I know where that is,' and – zoom – off we shot. When the third call came in – a domestic dispute – it was exactly the same.

Call number four was a bit different.

'Panda ZT1,' came Bill Wheeler's voice. 'Reports of a 99 at the station.'

'What does that mean?' I asked.

Without removing his pipe, Fergie said, 'There's a brew on.'

Our tea break coincided with Fergie's real area car partner turning up so, sadly, that was the end of my outdoor work and time for the more mundane stuff that a probationer should have been doing, like filing, more filing, and making the next '99'.

Just before the end of my shift, Brian Ferguson came back in, carrying the car's notebook. 'I can't find any record of those first three calls we did tonight, Clive.'

'You knew where they all were,' I said.

'But you still have to write them down.'

I was so ahead of my time I had eliminated paperwork from the job!

If night times were a bit slow, day shifts on the counter were like a revolving door. It's hard enough when you're trying to learn the ropes anyway, but having a constant queue of people lining up for eight hours straight was a nightmare – because every single one of them represented some note I needed to write or a document I needed to check or a form I had to fill in.

Paperwork, paperwork, paperwork – not exactly a bed of roses for a dyslexic. And this time I couldn't get out of it.

Most of the time I had a sergeant alongside me. One day it was Bill Wheeler. When a little old dear came in and said she'd locked herself out, he said, 'I'm ever so sorry, my love, but I haven't got a policeman to help you.'

I was standing there like a confused paperweight so she said, 'What about him?'

'Ah, well, he's on probation so he's not allowed out of the nick.'

'But it's not very far and I'm cold.'

Eventually Bill caved in and said, 'All right, Clive, see if you can help her get in. But you have to come straight back.'

So off I toddled with this little old lady to her little old house and, sure enough, I managed to get a window open and climb in. She was very grateful but, even as she was thanking me, she was pulling on a big, winter coat.

'Are you going back out, love?' I asked.

'Well, of course I am, officer. I've got to take you back to the police station.'

She thought she had to walk me back!

When I wasn't being handheld by old ladies, there were plenty of other jobs for me to do. Some of them were quite iconic – but even the classics get boring after the twentieth time. It was one of my jobs to take fingerprints. What amateur detective, especially kids, hasn't dreamed of doing this? Then I got to help with the mug shots. If you've ever seen a villain's police photo, they're always holding up a sign with their charge number and name. It's all digitised now but in those days someone had to physically stick magnetised letters onto a sheet of metal. No pressure, then, for the dyslexic...

Some people obviously liked it, though. The next time I opened the letter board there was already a message spelt out: 'ALL COPPERS ARE BASTARDS.'

I assumed a prisoner had got hold of it while I was setting up the camera, but I suppose it could have been anyone!

By day four I had settled into a routine of sorts, right down to expecting the lady who used to bring a basket of doughnuts in through the back door every day. The only thing that changed was the relief – or shift – times. Nights, days, earlies, they threw them all at me. It was an afternoon shift on my fourth day, however, when I got a message saying, 'The guv'nor wants to see you in his office.'

I'd been expecting it. No one of rank had done an official welcome yet, so this was obviously it. Off I went but, before I reached the inspector's office, I found him in the corridor.

Completely drunk.

He was a lovely chap, Hugh Jenkinson, and would later prove himself a bit of a lifesaver to me, but he liked a drink. He was so pissed that the only way he could go forwards was by leaning at 45 degrees against the wall. It seemed to be working for him.

Until he reached an open door.

Jesus Christ!

Del Boy falling through the bar in *Only Fools and Horses* had nothing on this. The sight of your superior officer disappearing sideways, a slightly confused look on his face, is not something they train you for at Hendon.

Instinctively, I decided it didn't look good to have the inspector's legs sticking out in the corridor so I rushed over and dragged him into his office. Then I just stared at the phone, sick to my stomach. Who would I ring and what the hell should I say? There was no way I wouldn't get into trouble, I knew it.

I was still crapping myself, if I'm truthful, when I felt a hand on my shoulder and another uniform said, 'It's all right, Clive, we'll take it from here.'

So, I never did get my welcome. Not from him anyway.

Most of my first week was spent stuck behind the front desk trying to keep the incident book up to date as every morning at seven o'clock sharp, the superintendent, a man called True, would appear to check it over. He was an ex-naval man, which I suppose explained his punctuality and love of order, and he also liked a bit of military speak when you handed the book over.

'All correct, nothing to report, sir,' told him it had been a quiet night. Or, if you had a guest in the cells: 'All correct, one in for burglary, sir.'

He'd sign it off and you could begin your shift proper.

On the Monday of my second week he came in as usual, checked the books and then, about an hour later, I got a call to his office. This time it really did turn out to be my official welcome.

'How are you finding Sutton, Clive? Nice and close to home, isn't it, so you can still see a lot of Robert and little Bonita?'

I was seriously taken aback – and more than a little bit chuffed – that he knew so much about me. When he started to ask me about my beloved Fulham I would have walked over hot coals for him. After the arm's length frostiness of Hendon – and that is putting it nicely – to have a superior officer take such a personal interest in me was truly heart-warming. It gave me a real buzz for the rest of the day.

The next morning – Tuesday – it was me on the desk again, and because I wanted to acknowledge my newfound respect for him, I gave it the big salute and extra-naval, 'All correct, nothing to report, sir.'

I think I made an impression because as soon as he finished with the book he went over to Bill Wheeler and said, 'That's a nice young man. Who is he?'

Twenty-four hours earlier he could have written my autobiography; now he couldn't pick me out of a line-up. Was it possible the higher up you went, the more you looked on the lower ranks as faceless bodies? Within two years I'd know the answer – to my cost.

Sutton was a great place, full of good people. But human nature is human nature and so when a newbie turns up, certain people see that as an opportunity to have a laugh.

As a probationer, you have to do attachments to all the different police divisions. You spend time with every department and get a flavour of their work – or learn how to put the kettle on, depending on the senior officer. The idea is that, at the end of your two years, you can then pick an area to go into.

Nicknames are all the fashion within the police, as they are within any male-centric organisation (although the Met has changed a lot recently). The army, and football clubs, spring to mind. Is there a better nickname than the ex-Palace player, Fitz Hall – known to his team-mates as 'One Size'? The only difference in the police is that the names often aren't so friendly. The CID – Criminal Investigation Department, aka 'El Cid' – loves putting uniform down with 'wooden top' and 'lids' – describing the helmet and peaked caps that officers have to wear. Criticising outfits doesn't work the other way round – the CID doesn't wear uniform – so El Cid gets called 'bananas' because they're bent and yellow (allegedly). Then you've got traffic cops, called 'black rats' – because of the colour they wear, and the fact they'll apparently prosecute other officers like a rat will eat its young. The mounted division are obviously 'Piccadilly cowboys' ... I never said the names were clever.

Anyway, on my third week I began my stint with traffic. As they had this raw, straight-out-of-Hendon recruit on their books, what was the first thing they did?

Took me to a post-mortem.

How many recruits must they have put through that particular little ordeal? I was shown into a room and there was Quincy in his mask with a scalpel halfway down a bloke's chest. I could feel four pairs of eyes on me as the skin was folded back and the pathologist's hand reached for a drill. They were still on me 10 minutes later when the victim's vital organs were sitting on the outside of his stomach. I knew what traffic were up to so I didn't give them the satisfaction. When one of them had enough and said, 'Breakfast?' I slapped my hands together.

'I could murder a full English.'

On the way to the greasy spoon they really piled it on. I heard about this nasty accident where a baby was killed, another one where a school bus was totalled, a hanging where the head had fallen off – you name it, they told me about it, right up until my plate arrived in front of me.

It was as I tucked in that one of them caved.

'Clive, how can you eat after all that?'

'I used to work on the ambulances. I saw worse than that before breakfast, lunch *and* dinner.'

They were good as gold after that.

The testosterone-inspired challenges continued when I was finally let out on foot patrol.

The officers who pound the streets are called 'homebeats' because they pad around the base area. A lot of people turn up their noses against the flat foots but, like Brian Ferguson in his car, for a lot of people it is exactly the sort of policing they want to do. And they're damn good at it.

It was a night shift and I was put with Harry Heavy. A good bloke, a good teacher but a bloody fast walker. For three hours solid he marched me around the area, pointing out this villain's haunt, that dodgy building – all the hot spots and occasional no-go zones. But he did it all at such speed I could barely take it in. I'd never been so relieved to get the '99' call, but the second we got back to the station there was Pete Sulley waiting for me.

'You're with me now, lad.'

I'd thought Harry was fast but Pete was nearly running – and I'd been out for three hours already. By the time my shift finished I'd been dragged around by three different blokes and got blisters on my blisters – and then I had to walk home!

Dragging a newbie around is called 'puppy walking' – or 'puppy running' in my case – because you really do feel like a dumb, happy pup when you're out there. Harry was great at saying, 'What do you see, Clive?' when we hit a street. He wanted me to know every blade of grass we passed. I'd have to rattle off everything I saw, every person, every thought I had, and he would just nod. Know your surroundings, know your potential problems, know what you're going to do about them.

For Pete, however, it was as simple as 'Know where you are.'

We were in the middle of a road and he said, 'What street are we on, Clive?'

'I don't know.'

'Well, if you get into difficulty, how are you going to get assistance here?'

If I didn't know exactly which street, which shop or which house number we were outside, he'd chew my ear off. And rightly so. Being able to take in your surroundings without even realising you're doing it is an essential police skill. But then so was marching and ironing, and I was crap at those, as well.

I don't know what Harry, Pete, Bill or Brian thought of me, but after four weeks of being police I knew what I thought.

I'm not enjoying it.

The Royal Marines have a saying. 'Identify the enemy.' In other words, it might not always be the people in the opposite trenches. I have to say, around this time I felt the enemy was very close to home. Too close, if I'm honest.

My wife had never been impressed by my career switch but her family, and her mother in particular, hated it with a passion. To my mind it's irrational but a lot of people hate Old Bill, simple as that. Whenever I saw one of them, and it was most days, there'd be a load of digs about the police and how I had changed. That alone made me really consider whether I was doing the right thing.

The biggest threat to my new life, however, was myself. Ever since my first day at Hendon I had had this stereotype in my head of the kind of policeman they were trying to produce. He should be dedicated, quiet, unsmiling, a straight-up serious type of geezer. That just wasn't me. I could do it, I could be quiet and poker-faced for eight-hour shifts, but it was an act.

An act I could not keep up any longer.

At the end of my fourth week of probation I found Bill Wheeler alone by the desk and I said, 'I've given it a shot, Sarge, but this isn't me.'

'What are you saying, Clive?'

'I'm saying I want to quit. I don't want to be a policeman after all.'

This would be a bloody short book if that's where the story ended but, at the time, I swear it was what I wanted if only to please Tina and her family. I'd tried my hardest and I couldn't cope with it. I was a square peg in a round hole. And an unhappy square peg at that.

I had to work a month's notice, which I was not looking forward to. When the ambulances had learned I was quitting, the entire organisation seemed to turn against me, like I was some kind of Judas. The police, however, didn't do that. Maybe I wasn't important enough.

Business carried on as usual and, in fact, I started to do a few more interesting bits and pieces. This included being let out on my own. Maybe they didn't care about me any more because I was leaving, or they thought I was more experienced because of my age – maybe they were just short of staff – but I came in one day and the rota just said: 'Driscoll – beat'.

Well, this should be interesting.

I had all the routes from Harry and Pete in my head so I started off following one of those, then swerved up Sutton High

Street. Knowing that I was not long for the job gave me a bit of a boost, if I'm honest. I felt relaxed, nodding and smiling at passers-by, and I couldn't actually wait to do a bit of policing. Then it happened.

I saw a geezer clock my uniform. He was standing outside the post office and he kind of did a double-take. Anyway, he made up his mind and made a beeline for me.

Here we go.

I cleared my head and tried to focus on my training. I had the Theft Act, the Road Traffic Act, all the big ones ready on the tip of my tongue. Whatever this citizen's legal dilemma was, I was fully primed to have an answer.

He stopped about a foot in front of me and nodded.

'Can I help you, sir?' I asked.

'I'm desperate, officer,' he said.

Sounds serious.

'What is it?'

'Where can I buy a dress suit?'

Hendon really prepared me for that, didn't it!

I managed not to laugh. I even had an answer.

'I think Dunnes down there, on the left, should help you out.'

And that was it. My first professional engagement with the public. And, I thought, it didn't go too badly. I allowed myself a little smile and, strangely enough, I think I kept it for most of the day: after that, people were stopping me for all sorts of reasons and I found that I really enjoyed having a chat with most of them. Even the ones who clearly didn't like the uniform were worth a few minutes. As a dyslexic, talking and listening is how I prefer to get my information. And, as it turned out, I was pretty good at it. By the end of the day I really felt I was ready for anything – even my first arrest.

I was on my way back to the station, still buzzing from a cracking first solo flight when I came into Sutton Grove. If

I'm honest, I had virtually switched off for the day but I saw a situation and my instincts went haywire. I didn't know why, just that I would regret it if I didn't respond.

The situation was as innocent as simply spotting an ordinary-looking pedestrian coming towards me. Nothing about him seemed unusual except his reaction to seeing me; the second I stepped around the corner onto Sutton Grove he looked as if he'd died a thousand deaths. The blood drained from his face and, even though it was probably no more than a second before he regained his composure, my Spidey-sense began tingling.

Now, it could have been because he just didn't like the police. Lots of people don't. But again, intuition – it couldn't have been experience – said otherwise and so I decided to perform a 'Stop'.

I must have been acting on adrenaline because I don't remember any nerves. I said everything I'd been trained to, parroted it word-perfect to him, and asked him to empty his pockets.

They were stuffed to the brim with jewellery.

It turned out that he was a prolific burglar wanted for a spate of crimes in the area over the last few months. Even though El Cid swooped in and took the case off me, I was a bit of a hero back at the nick for a few minutes. I have to admit, it felt good.

Over the next few weeks I made some cracking arrests; the very next day I got a beauty. I heard a bit of commotion in the high street, and found a shopkeeper wrestling with a shoplifter.

I say 'wrestling' – the villain was an 80-year-old woman. It wasn't exactly WWE. She came clean, bless her, and took me back to her house which, I swear, made Aladdin's cave look a bit empty. What she had managed to get out of the shops you would not believe: tables, chairs, lamps – seriously large things, and hundreds of them. We filled two whole cells with her loot and half a notebook making an inventory. Another feather in my cap. Another reason to smile.

At the end of the week, Bill Wheeler came up to me.

'You look happy, Clive.'

'Well, I've had a good few days, Sarge.'

'Too right. I have to say, you're probably the best PC we've had here in my time. It's a shame you're leaving.'

'Yeah,' I said. 'It is.'

My next solo shift was on nights. Walking out and about in the dark isn't as much fun. For a start, there aren't as many people to keep you interested. And, by then, I was interested. Still, in my new, relaxed manner I usually managed to find someone to talk to.

One evening I came out of the nick and decided to walk around the A217. I was just near Sutton Cricket Club when I saw this old-style Jag driving towards me with no lights on.

Here we go …

I stepped off the kerb and did the old waving-it-down-with-the-arms, sighing with relief as the car slowed down. A bit like being a human filter in Notting Hill, you're relying on the other side playing ball. If this bloke had wanted to he could have put his foot down and sped past or even run me over. But he knew the rules. The driver pulled over and wound down the window, just as my training had predicted he would.

But that was when the rulebook went out the window.

'You've been waiting for me, haven't you?' he said.

'No, sir.'

'Don't lie, son, I know you have.'

'I can assure you I have not.'

'Oh. Well, you know who I am, don't you?'

Christ, you're not the commissioner are you?

As firmly as I could, I said, 'No, sir.'

'Well, you bloody should know.' This man was in a nice suit and trilby hat, and looked proper affronted but I still didn't have a clue who he was. 'You shouldn't be out here walking on your own if you don't know who I am. I'm Dinky Di.'

So you're not the Commissioner then.

'Look, I don't know who you are and I don't really care. Could you just put your headlights on please?'

I waved him on but he wasn't finished.

'You're obviously new,' he said. 'Do yourself a favour and go back to the nick now. Look at my collator's card. You should not be walking around on your own if you don't know who people like me are.'

I told him to move along as firmly as I could but as soon as he was out of sight I hightailed it back to the nick. Back then, every villain or hotspot was assigned a collator's card with all their details. There was an index card for everyone of interest and every case. The filing cabinets, labelled 'A', 'B', 'C', etc., filled a large room, as you can imagine. It's all computerised now, of course. I pulled out the Ds and sure enough there was Dinky Di. It turned out he used to knock about with the Krays and another bloke called Joey Pyle. A proper villain's villain.

Two nights later I was back out and I heard this *toot toot toot*. I looked around and there he was.

'You've read my card now, haven't you?' he said.

'Yeah, and you've found your light switch, so it's win-win.'

And off we went.

There were loads of old villains who used to live out Sutton way. Some of them had interesting names like 'Reg the Veg'. Others were more straightforward like The Jacksons. Maybe nothing rhymed with 'scrap dealers', which was their trade.

The Jacksons' collator's card made interesting reading so, one shift, I made it my plan to swing by their yard. It was all silent on the outside so I decided to wander round the back and have a peep over their wall. I'd like to say it was all above board but I did happen to take my top hat off – it's a bit of a giveaway if they spot it the other side. I found a fence to climb up and just as I got a foothold I felt a tap on my shoulder.

Rumbled.

It was one of the lads. He said, 'Can I help you, officer?'

'I thought I heard a noise in your yard. I was checking it out.'

'Of course you were.'

And I scarpered.

I had the rest of the nick in stitches reliving that one later. No one was judgemental, they'd all done similar, and the spirit of camaraderie actually made it funnier. I realised that was what I had been missing for most of the year. I hadn't had it at Hendon and I'd tried my best not to have it at Sutton. But hearing other coppers laugh and share their own stories and feeling part of something had a profound effect on me. So much so that I went up to Bill Wheeler afterwards.

Before I said anything, he said, 'You need to see Grimshaw. He's in charge of personnel.'

I nodded and found the sergeant at his desk.

'How can I help you, Clive?' he asked.

'It's like this, Sarge,' I said. 'I was wondering if I could withdraw my resignation papers.'

He clapped his hands together then stood and shook mine.

'That is fantastic news, Clive. You won't regret it.'

'I know I won't.'

The job hadn't changed but I had. I'd identified the enemy – and discovered it was me all along. 'New Clive' – the copper I thought Hendon wanted – had been a terrible mistake. So I was going back to the original, and the best. No more acting, I just had to be myself. Not the man I thought I should be, just the man I once was.

I just hope he's good enough …

CHAPTER FOUR

Throw 'Em Back Alive

It's funny how things turn around when you're enjoying yourself. In 1980, it was unheard of to get a panda course before your two years of probation was up, but I was put forward for one after 11 months. I must have been doing something right. The good news was it was a three-week course, so obviously very thorough.

The bad news was it was back at Hendon.

Hendon driving school sits just to the right of the college but it may as well have been inside because the drills were the same. You got up there for eight o'clock – at least I didn't have to live there – and the first thing you did was parade. Don't ask me why, and I hadn't done it for nearly a year, but that's how they did it.

About a week in, we were all lined up and, come 8 a.m., we still weren't ready to start, even though a chief inspector, an inspector and two sergeants were all there. Whispers started going around that the new chief superintendent in charge of traffic division wanted to know what he was talking about so he was coming to join our course. Hence the delay.

About a minute later there was a kerfuffle at the gate and an old geezer came bustling in. The inspector, the chief inspector and two sergeants clicked their heels and the whole company straightened up in salute.

Except me. 'That's not the chief superintendent – that's Old Gators!'

It was the funniest thing I ever saw at Hendon. Just because he was old, all the brass assumed that PC Gators was the governor. There were some right rages when they realised their mistake and, I'm sad to say, Gators took the brunt of it. Serves him right for being late, though.

The actual lessons were pretty routine: how to change a tyre, basic bog-standard maintenance, reversing, parking, nothing out of the ordinary. The cars weren't much better. Austin Allegros weren't even new back then. The biggest disappointment for most people was learning that pandas aren't actually allowed to drive through red lights. But I knew that from the ambulances.

Something else I already had a heads-up on was giving a commentary as you drove. Harry Heavy had made me do this on the homebeat so I knew what was expected: 'On the left-hand side I can see a man with a dog ... I see traffic lights in front of me but they have just changed to green so unlikely to change again before I go through ... There is a child on the pavement but he is being held by his mother so I'm ready to brake, although not expecting to ... I can see a bridge ... I can see a school sign ...' Basically, anything my eyes saw, my gob reported, while one of the two traffic cops assigned to us would nod and make the occasional note.

At the end of the three weeks I had to drive up to Mildenhall and then bomb back at the top legal speed while running through a commentary the entire journey. Yapping is, so I'm told, my forte and I happen to be pretty observant too, so I have to say I breezed that particular test.

Once you pass the panda course you are a panda. Simple as that. Daytimes could be a bit hectic, although at least there was cover. On nights it was just me, always on my own. If it was quiet, I'd cruise around some likely sights seeing what I could dig up. Other nights I'd be like the fire brigade, bouncing from one crisis to another.

The boys at the station would have a laugh when I was that busy, but I'd rather be haring around like a blue-arsed fly on the streets than stuck behind a desk all night. How many crimes were they going to solve looking at four walls? To this day a lot of people think that's where you do it. That's why they go for promotion after promotion to earn the right to never leave their office. I learned very early on that the best place to find the truth is out there, where the crime took place, where the witnesses are, where the perpetrators are leaving clues.

I really loved nights. You could do all sorts of things on those shifts. When I was swanning around in my Allegro, it was at a time when the IRA was still blowing stuff up, so I was on the alert for possible targets. When I passed a gasometer one night I thought, *That would make a bit of a bang*, so I pulled over, found my way over a fence and climbed up the ladder on the side. I learned three things that night. One, gasometers are a lot higher than they look. Two, because they go up and down they are coated in oil – and so was my coat. And three, there was no bomb.

Another night I passed the hospital and thought about a whisper I'd heard from an informant, or 'grass' as villains say. They were growing cannabis there, he said. But considering everything else he'd told me was a lie, I'd ignored him, or at least pretended to.

But one night-time, and with the radio silent, I thought I'd have a look. I parked up close to the wall, went up on the bonnet, then the roof, then over the brickwork. If I was any cleverer I might have been scared of security but luckily I'm not blessed that way. That's how I discovered the greenhouses full of weed.

A lot of panda drivers are happy to respond to the 999s, then use the downtime between emergency calls to have a breather. I hated that. I'm a simple man. The thrill for me, right from day one, was catching villains. At the start of each shift the sergeant would read out any particularly active leads. For example: there had been a spate of burglaries in so-and-so area; this bloke was wanted and was seen here; this club turned out at this time and last night there was trouble ... Again, you could ignore all of it if you wanted a quiet night. Or you could use that intelligence, listen to the whispers and the hunches, and poke around, see what you could find. Sometimes I got lucky. Sometimes I got very lucky.

As I got more comfortable in the job I started to go one further and began each shift with a visit to the collator's office. I would start with 'A' and work through any that caught my eye or were outstanding. *OK, he's a burglar, he's a disqualified driver, he's on the run* – I'd make a note and store as many of them as I could in my memory, then make it my business to have a look for them while I was out. If there was an area where something was happening over a period of time I would go and coast around there as well. Just on the off-chance. It sounds a long shot but I needed to be somewhere in between calls, so why not be somewhere with potential?

I collected a lot of my own information as well. Any opportunity I got I would pull over somewhere of interest, stick on my top hat – I never wore the flat one us officers were given at the time – and go and have a wander and see who I bumped into.

Having fiercely resented my dyslexia at Hendon, it was proving to be a real boon for me, as a panda. Give me a suspect or a witness and I could normally make them talk. There was no trick to it. I just like to chat to people, see what they know; I don't try to be clever or threatening. I might buy them a cup of tea or a bun, or tell them a joke – whatever it takes to put them at ease. Too many people hate the idea of Old Bill. I tried to make it as hard as possible to hate this particular one.

I developed quite a nose for crime solving and so when it came for me to join Epsom CID on attachment I was quite excited.

That is until I got there.

Most of them were ex-Flying Squad, the armed crime mob popularised in the 1970s show *The Sweeney*, and much too important to show the ropes to a 'wooden top'. It was going to be a miserable three weeks.

The thing about the rivalry between uniform and non-uniform is we all start at the same place. Every Piccadilly cowboy, black rat or banana in the Met went to Hendon and did exactly the same training as every wooden top. They all started as PCs, just like me, and went out to Sutton or somewhere else on a two-year probation. The difference is, they chose to move sideways – not up, regardless of what they think – into the horse division, or the motorbike lot, or CID.

Contrary to how it's portrayed on the telly (and in their own minds), CID is just another department in the police service. At the end of the day, a police constable and a detective constable are the same rank, same pay grade. It's just one is a CID officer, and one ain't; one of them wears a uniform and the other one can wear swimming trunks if he wants. And it is the same all the way up through the ranks. You can either be a detective sergeant or a police sergeant; a detective chief inspector or a police chief inspector – it's exactly the same, right until you get to the commissioner's office.

When a few of El Cid started calling me 'The Cockney Columbo' as a put-down I actually took it as compliment – which made them give up, of course. What I didn't like was the way uniform always came off second best in public. A PC might be the first at a murder scene but the suits from CID soon took over – and the poor sod who called it in was stuck outside guarding the door.

During my attachment, the only bit of action I got was after a grievous bodily harm case when I was sent to the dry cleaners to see whether or not anyone had come in trying to shift a bloodstain. That wasn't a bad shout, actually. I made a mental note to do the same if I ever had a similar case. On the whole, though, I was generally ignored by the 'real' detectives, so I amused myself by reading the crime reports and getting to grips with how cases had been solved, or not. Maybe there was stuff in the notes that could help me in the future?

My time at CID was a lost opportunity but at least it was an interesting division. With my next attachment at Community Engagement imminent, I was prepared to be bored. But it turned out to be exactly what I thought police work should be.

I would go into schools, meet local groups, talk through concerns and see what we – us and them – could do about it. This was right up my street. I was only on attachment there for a couple of weeks but, I was told, I was more use to a lot of the local action groups than the regular police liaisons.

'What have I done that's different?' I asked one bloke, genuinely interested to learn.

'You listened.'

Simple as that. Sometimes police work is just about giving people the time of day.

One of the other aspects of the community engagement programme was using sport to bring the community and the police closer together. Some coppers didn't like this bit but I jumped at the chance of arranging football matches between local youths and teams from the Met. It's an amazing chance for plods to be involved with young people in a non-confrontational situation – the odd silly tackle aside – and I have to say it had a profound effect on me. After my attachment finished I continued to organise police teams, and the Met 5-a-side tournaments have become legendary within the service. More importantly, to this day I still run a team called The Metropolitan Police – but the players aren't Old Bill. They're all inner-city kids, often from communities where the

Met aren't exactly regarded as friends. A lot of them have been in trouble with the law but, when they pull on that shirt and they score, there is no sweeter sight than seeing them slapping or even kissing that police badge.

If that isn't what police work is all about, then I'm in the wrong business.

I could have stayed on that attachment for ever. However, after the Green Goddess bus tour and Superintendent True forgetting me overnight, I had begun to realise that, at some level, in the Met every officer is viewed as little more than a pawn to be moved around a chessboard that happens to look a lot like London. Just because you like a particular job or you're really very good at it, that doesn't mean some unseen hand won't just scoop you up and plonk you somewhere else. It happened all around me at Sutton. It happened to me as well. Policing requires flexibility and pawns, or foot soldiers, are needed. Hendon had made no secret of that.

Even though I was panda qualified, and pretty good at it if I say so myself, because I was on probation I still had to help out on the more mundane jobs. Sometimes that was as simple as escorting prisoners to and from cells. At other times it was helping bigger operations.

Traffic lights were a big thing at Sutton: every so often the inspector would have a blitz on motors jumping red lights, especially near schools. He would send a team out and you'd have a couple of bodies watching the lights, with someone else positioned about 50 yards down the road. They'd watch for jumpers, hop on the radio, then you'd step out and flag the car down.

We weren't exactly hiding so you'd have to have been pretty stupid to do anything with an audience made up of PCs but, after about half an hour or so, the radio fuzzed and Harry Heavy said, 'Got one – the blue Escort coming towards you.'

Here we go.

Just as I'd done with Dinky Di, I stepped out into the road, flourishing my arms like a bullfighter and, once again, the speeding mass of potentially deadly metal pulled to a gentle stop in front of me.

I explained to the driver that he had been seen jumping the lights and – this was a surprise – he held his hands up. I took his details and told him he could probably expect a fine and points on his licence. It was up to the magistrate.

Normally that was where I would have left it. Then, a few weeks later, Sergeant Wheeler called me over and said, 'Remember that red light you caught?'

'Yes.'

'Good, because you'll be representing the prosecution against him at court tomorrow.'

'Why me?'

'You were there and you're the only one available.'

That was a turn-up. I'd done quite a bit of decent work, including arrests, but someone else had always waltzed in at the last moment and grabbed the case for themselves. Usually it was CID; sometimes, though, it was my senior colleagues who said they wanted to ease my workload. It meant the notch went on their belts – but it also meant they had to process the case through court.

Not this time, though. Bill Wheeler studied my face as I mulled the repercussions of his words.

Ask most people to list their greatest fears and 'public speaking' is usually up there. As a country we're not raised to enjoy it – whereas Americans seem to come out of the womb ready to deliver a speech. I don't know why that is.

Ask me to read in public and that's a different matter. Thank you, dyslexia. Ask me to talk – anywhere – and that's my strength. My super power, if you like. I'd spent my whole life compensating for the reading so talking was my friend.

'OK, Sarge, no problem,' I said.

'You're OK?' I think I burst his balloon.

'He's bang to rights. He even admitted it. What could go wrong?'

Famous last words.

I arrived at Sutton Magistrates' in good time. Was I nervous? Yes. Although we'd practised procedure at Hendon in their mock-up courts, the first time for anything can be daunting. Was I nervous about speaking in public? No.

I knew the facts, I knew the law and I knew I could handle it. What I didn't know, however, was that the accused was going to fight his case. The first inkling I got was when he strolled in with a barrister. Those boys aren't cheap and hiring someone just to plead 'Guilty' seemed a bit rich. So I knew something was up.

The magistrates got things going, then came my moment in the sun. I'd learned everything written in my notebook off by heart so I was able to recite all the facts of the case, including the crucial point where the motorist had confessed to jumping the lights. Nobody listening would have had any doubt that this was a certainty, a real stone bonker. And, I'd also like to think no one would have noticed it was my first time before the beak. I felt at home up there. I had truth and honesty on my side.

Then it was time for the brief to stand up.

Let's see what you've got, sunshine.

'Yes,' he said, 'my client did jump the red light.'

Thank you. Can we go home now?

'But,' he continued, 'it was in order to protect the children in the car behind.'

I beg your pardon?

I listened, absolutely gob-smacked, to what then came out of his mouth.

'The car travelling behind my client was speeding and too close to my client's Escort for his comfort. So close, in fact, that my client could see there were several children in the car. When the lights changed, he could have stopped – as he should have done – but he was concerned that the car behind would not have been able to respond quickly enough. There would have been a collision and that would have endangered the safety of those passengers. In short, my client acted in the way he did to save the lives of those children.'

I told the court that I didn't think this was the case. The barrister jumped on that.

'Did you see the car behind my client?'

'Yes.'

That was true. I would have seen every car, although I was only concentrating on one.

'Could you tell the court what car it was?'

'No.'

'So you couldn't say whether there were children in the car or not?'

'No.'

And that was it. I went from having a stone bonker, to being on the back foot, to being outmanoeuvred by a professional all in the space of a minute. The magistrates decided the accused was innocent and stopped just short of declaring him a national hero for saving those defenceless kiddies' lives.

The magistrates thanked me before I left, which I thought was odd. But I suppose I had played my part in justice, as they'd played theirs. The truth was, it was me who needed to thank them. They'd given me a lesson in there. It wasn't justice that was at fault that day, it was me. I could have won the case and I should have done – all I had to do was to remember the car behind. But I had been so focused on catching the bloke jumping the lights I hadn't seen the full picture. I would not make that mistake again.

As I skulked out of the building, I made myself a pledge: I would never, ever go into a courtroom again without having crossed all the t's and dotted all the i's.

Bad news travels fast. The second I stepped inside the nick I heard Bill Wheeler's voice booming out around the office: 'Here he comes, PC Throw-'Em Back-Alive Driscoll!' But it was the best training I could have had, and I am as sure as I can be that it was a deliberate act to send me in against a barrister knowing that if I failed we weren't letting a master criminal back on the streets. Bill Wheeler planned it all, I'm convinced: real court, real magistrates and, to my cost, real barrister. You can't buy that sort of training, even at Hendon.

While Bill Wheeler chose me to go to court that day for a reason, so many other times your name would get picked, virtually at random, for a job. If they needed 50 bodies they would pluck them from various stations. And that's all we were to the powers that be: bodies. It could have been me chosen or Harry Heavy, or Fred Bloggs from Wallington. Inside those uniforms we were anonymous.

While I never got to police the Notting Hill Carnival again, I was regularly picked to marshal the crowds down at Selhurst Park. When the command for *that* gig came through, I thought I'd died and gone to heaven. Be paid to watch a football match? Happy days!

OK, so it was Crystal Palace and, technically, we were meant to be watching the punters not the players, but even so. It beat watching traffic lights at three o'clock on a Saturday afternoon – yes, this was in the days when all matches took place then.

Unfortunately, what I had started to see at Craven Cottage – the aggression, the tribal divides and, frankly, the violence – was more than prevalent at Palace. Like most other grounds, there was no seating, just terraces, and nothing but good will to stop the fans from mingling with each other if they wanted.

The first time I went I was actually looking forward to the match – due to some team changes, goals were on the cards. And we were stationed at the back of the stand so I would actually get a good view.

As three o'clock neared, however, one of my more experienced colleagues alongside me said, 'Get ready.'

I looked at the Palace fans lined up neatly in front of me and the visiting opponents – Spurs, as it goes – minding their own business an arm's length away and shrugged.

'They look peaceful enough.'

Then the referee blew his whistle and it all kicked off. And I don't just mean the football.

Bang on three o'clock there was a roar from the whole ground and the section below me started to move. It was like a tidal wave of colour: one minute the crowd was chatting, drinking, eating pies, then, as soon as the match got underway, anyone near the Spurs lot steamed into them and vice versa. And it was nasty as well. Bits of wood, glasses, a couple of walking sticks came out of nowhere, and suddenly half the crowd was tooled up.

That's when we got the command.

It was 3.01 when we surged forwards. I hadn't seen a single kick of the ball but I felt half a dozen on my legs before I'd got three yards.

I don't think some football fans are the brightest bulbs, and definitely the hooligan element wouldn't illuminate anything. They only wanted to attack each other, so when we got in the way to separate them they got a bit confused. Somewhere in the back of their primeval minds they knew you didn't hit coppers, so they'd shout and swear and try to get past to someone they could hit.

As I said, not too clever.

It was like a gentlemen's excuse me with menaces. One geezer tried to leap over me so I let him have it with a shove. He went flying back into his mob and didn't return. The next one who came near me got a wave of my truncheon and, when he still kept coming, I yanked his hands up his back in the old 'hammerlock and bars' and marched him out. All the while we were yelling at them, 'Settle down! Get back! Behave!' and it was not making the slightest bit of difference. They were all buzzing too much. Hyped like greyhounds released from their traps.

It was a real bundle and I have to admit the police gave as good as they got. Was it heavy-handed? No question. But was it necessary? At the time, yes it was. We wanted to keep the fans apart and we would do it by any means necessary. Those were the orders and usually they worked. It took about 10 minutes at the start of every match, but having the wall of blue did seem to get a result.

As rough as it got, I only ever really got hit once – and that was by a copper. We were having some rough and tumble with a couple of away fans across from the main hub. When they tried to get away another officer threw his arm in an attempt to catch around the neck of one of them. The guy ducked and my nose was right behind him. *Crack.*

It wasn't just Crystal Palace that we got bussed out to. Chelsea was another regular stop. Were their fans any nastier than those at other clubs? Not especially. But did I take greater pleasure in throwing some of them out? You bet.

I remember one game where we'd managed to quell the initial storm and we were standing there, about 10 of us, when one of our lot dived into the Shed end. When I saw that my heart actually stopped for a second – this was not a crowd to mess with alone. Quick to react, the nine of us pulled out our sticks and, as one, took a step towards where he'd disappeared – just as he emerged again smoking a fag. He'd only gone in for a light!

I can't say I ever enjoyed policing matches; I saw enough violence at Fulham – and enough dodgy football. And I'm not sure it's what the police should be doing. Sorting out a disturbance is one thing, but these matches were like organised bun fights. You knew it was going to kick off, the FA knew it was going to kick off, the owners knew and so did the government. And no one's answer was: 'Let's sort out the grounds'; it was 'Send in the police.' It was a sad time for real football fans. It could all have been sorted by the Big Bods, but nobody gave it a thought.

Occasionally a few of us would be diverted to another problem area, usually a riot in a pub. That was another situation where you needed to be heavy-handed or you'd lost before you began. Lots of those pub scuffles ended with me giving evidence, and I was always honest. If I'd hit someone, that's what I said. If I'd grabbed hold of someone, that's what I said. If I'd put their arm up their back, that's what I said. I've never had anything other than the court say, 'That's fair enough in the circumstances.' But while I don't believe I ever stepped over the line, if someone from 2015 walked in on me or any one of my colleagues mid-ruck back then, I reckon we would have had a hard job explaining it. I never attacked anyone, I never hit anyone and the only time I struck anyone with my truncheon was to knock the knife out of his hand. But I did grab hold of people, I did get them in headlocks. I had raving monsters up against walls and I was heavy-handed, no doubt. But it was all defensive. Of course, there were occasions where I heard citizens screaming about the rights of the person I was trying to disarm but, nine times out of ten, I reckoned, when you asked people if we did the right thing, they said 'yes'.

Critics of the police – and there seem to be more of them than ever these days – don't always like to consider the alternatives to Old Bill acting the way they do in certain situations. But, as I always say, we do it so ordinary citizens don't have to.

And never was there more of a case in point than in April 1981.

CHAPTER FIVE

Welshmen Never Yield

The lowest ever attendance for a Crystal Palace home match in the top division came on 11 April 1981, a record that still stands to this day. Only 9,820 fans turned out to watch the Eagles beat Birmingham 3–1. It wasn't a bad game, as it happens, and with so few fans there was less trouble, too: safety in numbers is always a major factor in crime, and hooligans are as cowardly as anyone.

There was the usual amount of paperwork to be done for all the arrests but we were basically happy to have seen a match, got some fresh air and earned a bit of overtime in the process. We were just pulling out of the car park when a motorcycle officer flagged us down.

He boarded the bus and spoke to the sarge at the front, then got off. Funny. Then the sarge got up, stood mid-aisle and hollered, 'Change of plan, lads. They need bodies in Brixton.'

No one questioned why. I think most of us just thought, *More overtime. Wonderful*, then got on with our games of cards or reading newspapers.

It's about 50 minutes from Palace to Brixton on a Saturday, so by the time we were near there was more than one or two of us asleep. Suddenly, the brakes banged on and again, someone boarded the bus. His name was Ted – he's a mate of mine now but I didn't know him at the time. All I could say about him at that moment was he looked a mess. And he didn't sound right either.

'Don't go down there,' he screamed. 'It's all kicking off!'

What was he raving about? I looked out of the window. Very busy, loads of people milling around, but nothing untoward. How did this nutter get on our bus?

But the sarge was more reasonable: 'We have to get to Railton Road, so we can't stop here.'

Ted looked at him like he was mad. 'You're not listening. You'll be fish in a fucking barrel.'

The sarge thanked him for his help but said we had orders, which we did. Then he gave the nod to the driver, who went to pull away but stopped almost immediately.

That innocent group of people I had clocked out the window had suddenly grown more active. They were blocking the bus, stopping it from moving.

Maybe Ted had a point.

The driver leaned on the horn and inched forwards. It was like watching the sea move – our bus parted the crowd, but still it pressed in on us.

The further we got, the bigger the mob became and the more animated. By the time we reached Railton Road there was nothing short of mass hysteria outside the bus.

The mood inside had changed as well.

Looking out at a gentle swell of a human sea is one thing; watching them turn angry is off the charts. I remember looking into the eyes of the young men and women surrounding us and realising they had their own orders. Where from I did not know, but they were going to follow them to the nth degree.

The back window went in first. A typical coward's act: attack from behind. I hoped that would be the end of it. But then the side ones started to pop. There wasn't the safety glass you get today, and vicious little shards soon covered the seats and floors, while savage jags held on in the frames.

With the windows popping left, right and centre, we were sitting ducks; a second after the one next to me went, a brick came through and out the other side.

We were in the middle of a riot.

Without shields, without armour and without warning.

'We have to get off!'

Football fans tell each other apart by their shirt colours; as the boys in blue versus the Rest, there was a bit of that in Brixton that day as well. But, like it or not, in hindsight, there is no getting away from the fact that our two sides were as much distinguishable by skin colour as uniform.

It's something that makes reporting this incident in 2015 problematic. I've used the word 'coward', I've used the word 'mob', and I will use other pejorative terms to describe my fear as a young officer on the receiving end of that behaviour on 11 April 1981. Some people will jump on that as typical police racism; to them, I respectfully say that, when you're watching three blokes getting ready to spear you with a 10-foot scaffolding pole, the last thing you care about is the colour of their skin.

Colour, though, was not the reason we were being attacked. I would only learn later that the riot had been triggered by an incident the day before. Police had tried to assist a young black male, Michael Bailey, who had been stabbed. While they called for help, passers-by began to accuse them of ignoring the victim. When the police tried to move the man, a crowd of men appeared and tried to claim the body. The man later died from the stab wounds, and witnesses said it was as a result of police brutality. Word spread and, from that moment, anyone in uniform in the area became a legitimate target.

It wasn't the best idea to park opposite a building site: missiles in the shape of pipes, screwdrivers and wrenches began raining down as we got off the bus. I pulled out my truncheon, lifted my coat over my head and made a blind dash for it. What my coat would do against a flying masonry drill I didn't know, but it was all I could think to do when I had a head full of fear. The guy two ahead of me took a mallet to the temple. Someone else was pelted with nails. I thought about Selhurst Park. Back there, we'd kept nearly 10,000 rival herberts in check. How was this happening? But then football fans had their own rules. Their enemy was the other fans. This lot, from what I could see, had no other enemy other than us. Why? I personally had no idea.

To be totally upfront, I was terrified. We all were. Not one person on that bus had expected this. No one had seen the like before, either. What the hell were we meant to do in our lightweight summer uniform and top hats?

My instinct, if I had been running a squad of men that day, would have been to get them to shelter. But the geniuses in charge didn't think like that. We were pawns, remember? And in the game of chess, pawns are there to be sacrificed.

I was just following the bloke in front and so when he stopped so did I – right in the bloody middle of Railton Road! Talk about exposed. If you'd put an X on our tunics you couldn't have made us look more like targets.

I realised I was next to Hugh Jenkinson, the inspector in charge.

'What are we doing, guv'nor? Are we trying to keep them in front of us?'

He shook his head. 'They're already behind us as well.'

'So what, then?'

'Just get in line.'

If he knew the plan, he wasn't sharing. I did as I was told and became part of two very thin blue lines across the junction with Bramwell Road. There were no more than 50 of us against hundreds and hundreds.

What happened next would be down to them, not us.

What happened next was that a brick hit a homebeat from Wallington. Right on the head. The top hat would have protected an attack from above but this went under the back and knocked him straight down. While PC Hugh Arnold and another bloke dragged him away for attention, I made a beeline for a couple of dustbins and grabbed their lids for makeshift shields.

Bloody rubber. Just when you need tin ones.

Then we just waited.

And waited.

After that brick, nothing really happened. There was movement all around us, and we were utterly and comprehensively isolated. If they'd all taken 10 steps forwards we'd have been swallowed. But they didn't. We held a line and they held a line. The magic that had worked in Notting Hill was working again. I was bloody grateful but I didn't understand why. Maybe they did know the rules, after all?

An eerie lull descended. For about half an hour nobody did anything to us: some of the rioters were too busy looting the shops on either side of the road, which I thought was weird. These were their shops, their community. But it wasn't the time to make that point.

Apart from the scum marauding through their own neighbours' businesses, there were murmurings and shouts coming from above. When I looked up, the rooftops and shop fronts were packed with spectators. Every building I looked at had people hanging out of the windows just watching, like we were just another channel on Saturday night TV. Watching, laughing, enjoying themselves. And waiting.

Who would blink first?

Turned out it was us. I heard a shout from the end of the first line and suddenly a couple of PCs appeared laden with shields. The story goes they'd had to break into a van to get them. The

Met denies this, or that the van had been there all along. All I knew is they were flipping heroes for fetching them.

The weird thing was, while getting that armour might have made us feel better, it also signalled the end of the lull. When we'd been stranded, terrified, defenceless, the rioters had held back; the second we got a smidgen of protection, the moment they couldn't see our faces, it was as if the gloves came off.

We stopped being people. We were targets again. And they went for it.

Bottles, bricks, lighters, bits of pavement, whole tubes of scaffold – if it wasn't tied down, it was lobbed. For the first time I was grateful for Hendon: almost to a man, we adopted the Roman centurion shield formation: three linked together one way, two another, some over the top. As the homemade doodlebugs descended we were cocooned in our little pod. Shield or not, though, the impact of some of them really hurt. I wondered how the hell they got some of their weapons in the air.

That went on for about an hour: them bombing, us being bombed. 'Stalemate' the senior management team at Scotland Yard would call it. And maybe they were happy with that? Although we weren't making any in-roads into regaining the streets, we hadn't given up either.

I could feel irritation growing in the crowd, though. We could carry on as long as our shields held, in theory. Again, it was a matter of waiting.

The next blink came from them. It was a big one, as well. And it had flashing lights.

For a second I thought it was the cavalry coming through. Then I saw the 'erbs hanging off the ladders of the big red fire engine coming down Railton Road, and my heart sank. A couple of blasts on the siren and the crowd magically cleared. A few theatrical roars of the accelerator and then quickly so did we.

This is something else I still do not understand about the violence of that day. The stolen fire engine scared the shit out of us and we ran like schoolgirls to get out of its way. If the mob had been serious about hurting us, that was the time – when we were petrified, on the back foot and split up.

But, again, they halted the attacks.

The big red giant that had destroyed our defences and could have been used to finish us off just drove off. It was later found torched and battered.

I'm not saying the Queensberry Rules were employed by anyone, but credit where it's due. We could have been beaten far worse than we were.

Only when we were back in formation did things explode again. And I mean literally.

Straight out of that weird interval came the most violent situation I have ever witnessed. I saw something whizzing through the sky and I thought, *Here we go again.* Then it exploded against the shield of the guy in front and I froze.

Petrol bombs.

Tools and beer cans are one thing; actual explosions are a different matter. There was a massive cheer when the first one hit – the rooftop viewers were going crazy – but that just signalled the start of the onslaught. *Bang, bang, bang,* they thundered against the shields, and you could feel the burn coming through.

The clever ones were bombarding the ground as well, trying to get under the shields, going for our legs and feet. It's hard to explain the sheer temperature when one of those things blitzes a couple of feet away. It's like a punch with a hot glove. Throw in the noise and the glare and you're being screwed in all senses, on all fronts. And that is when you make mistakes.

I saw the brick too late. I was so busy jumping over flaming glass that I didn't notice my shield had slipped an inch. As the brick landed, most of the brunt was taken by the plastic but a concrete corner pounded my temple and the world, just for a second, went black. If I hadn't been wedged in against my mates I'd have gone down. As it was, I felt like my head was going to explode.

Adrenaline was surging through my veins but it could only keep the fear of becoming a kebab at bay for so long. We'd already been out there more than five hours. Just like our shields would melt eventually, so would our resolve. The only question was, which would go first?

For a 30-minute period it was as if the sky was raining fire. As quickly as you stamped out one furnace the next would light up and you'd take another step back. Move or burn, those were the options. At the same time, a group at the front started ramming us with scaffold poles.

The reports afterwards said it was a spontaneous action but I was there. It was as strategic as any incursion into Afghanistan. Someone was controlling the attack. They had to be. It was too efficient, too militaristic to be an accident.

And it worked.

Above the raging fury I heard every scream from one of ours as a Molotov cocktail found its way through a gap prised open by a scaffold pole. The lucky ones ran for cover. The less fortunate ones had to be dragged away.

And then a very surreal thing happened.

Above the din of bricks bouncing off plastic and bottles of four-stroke detonating around me, I could hear singing. Big, loud, belting out for all its worth singing. And it was coming from us, from the front row. I don't know who started it but it began to spread and, moments later, we were all singing. Then the banging started as we all began beating our shields with our truncheons.

And do you know what the song was?

'Men Of Harlech'.

Aficionados of Celtic history will know it as a song commemorating the seven-year siege of Harlech Castle in the Middle Ages. Aficionados of Hollywood, however, are more likely to remember it from the film it was used in: *Zulu*.

Again, I am aware this does not sit well in a book written in 2015. Especially in one written by a police officer. It's more evidence, people will say, of 'institutional racism' at a time when cultural relations are strained enough. And, to be fair, I think we could have sung the theme to *The Magic Roundabout* and, if we'd put enough welly into it, it would have had the same impact. But we didn't, and records will show that we were slaughtered for our song selection.

But do you know what? Even though we were in Brixton not Natal, facing young British-Caribbean youths, not African warriors, it had the same effect as in the film. Better in fact. We belted it out like we were singing at Wembley and the missiles stopped coming. The scaffolding was dropped. Every time we sang a line and beat our shields we took one step forward. By the time we got to the line 'Welshmen never yield!' we sounded like 500 not 50 and you could see the panic in people's eyes.

Jesus Christ, they must have been thinking, *this lot are mental!*

And they all took one step back.

It was 11.30 at night and we'd won a small victory. But then what? Where were the rooks and knights and bishops and queens to save us? We'd held our ground, put an end to the aerial onslaught and stolen back some territory. *Talk about after the Lord Mayor's show* ... No one knew what to do. We were so few in number it was a joke. It was only a matter of time before we started singing again.

After nearly six hours on the ground, there was a break in the crowd and the cavalry did arrive. Except they weren't rooks, they weren't knights, they weren't bishops or queens. They were more pawns.

'We're here to relieve you,' one of them said. 'There's a van waiting.'

And that was that. We lowered our shields and trudged home the way they'd come. The crowd parted and let us through with no resistance. When I looked back, I could see the new boys being swallowed by the amorphous mass.

And then I heard the attack begin again.

It was an odd way to visit Scotland Yard for the first time. But that's where the coach took us. We were unloaded into reception, shown up to the canteen and let loose on the roast chicken, potatoes, beans and chocolate gateau.

We were all in too much shock to even talk. It was a surreal end to a nightmarish day. I think I went onto autopilot. Only when a drop of my blood dripped onto the pressed red-and-white checked tablecloth did I snap out of my reverie.

I can't believe what they just put us through.

That's when I noticed the dozens of other officers milling around. They weren't war-torn, battered, bruised and bleeding; they didn't have jackets ripped, ties missing, burns everywhere.

Where the hell have you been for the last five hours?

It got worse. As I was staring into my empty coffee mug, a back hall inspector walked past my table then did a double-take.

'You, man, where's your tie?'

Before I could answer another voice called out. Another inspector, actually. 'For God's sake, these men have been on the front line. Give them some peace.'

The back hall uniform stared at the inspector, then back to me, then at the rest of us. 'Front line where? What's going on?'

That said it all really.

I learned soon after that those dozens, if not hundreds, of officers in the canteen would have run to Brixton if they'd known about it. I've spoken to many of them since and, without exception, as soon as they did hear that fellow officers were being exposed to that level of violence, there was only one place any of them wanted to be – by our side. But the Grand Masters upstairs didn't take that into account, just like they didn't take into account our safety. As the night wore on they did eventually put men on standby, and across Kent too, but those men were never deployed.

Why not has never been explained to me, or to the general public. The disturbances in August 2011 triggered by the death of Mark Duggan had worrying similarities. I spoke to an inspector in charge of a number of tactical support units ready to go with riot kits on board during that period. Just as in 1981, they were never deployed. In Tottenham and Brixton, many people lost their livelihoods, many businesses never recovered, members of the public were injured and sadly one was murdered. I cannot find a reason why, when we had sufficient numbers on standby, the command to prevent this destructive public disorder was not given. It doesn't make sense to me, and I'm still confused about it to this day.

On that day in 1981, as it turned into 12 April, my confusion and despair were only just beginning.

In hindsight, I should have known it was suspicious that the Met would feed us at the end of a shift, however life-threatening that shift had been. There was a reason they'd led us to the trough: we needed sustenance before going back out.

The canteen was full of officers who didn't even know about the riots. Throughout the city there were hundreds of coppers nursing kettles until their shifts ended. Yet none of them was being deployed.

It was us. Again.

'Did I dream the last seven hours?' I said to Hugh Arnold.

'If you did, then fifty other blokes did as well.'

But it wasn't a dream. It was a nightmare. And they were sending us back.

Once again, the crowds parted and let us through. The squad who'd taken over looked dreadful. To be fair, it was like looking in a mirror.

There was another impasse while we retook our positions across Railton Road. I was front row this time, on the end, thanks very much. But at least I could see where I was going now. Because I intended on going forward.

'Shields up!'

That was the cue. The moment our shields went back up the heavens opened again, the air thick with plummeting debris. I don't know if it was because we were exhausted, scared or the mob had got stronger, but the bombs hurt more this time. I, for one, wasn't sure how long I could last under another sustained attack.

I wasn't the only one at breaking point and almost as one we decided we'd had enough.

'Let's go!'

I don't know who said it but we all responded. As one we piled forward and we must have won about ten feet of road before the enemy – because that's what they were – responded. There was a chilling roar and about a hundred blokes steamed towards us, full tilt. They had sticks, metal bars and knives, and they were going to use them.

When they hit, they hit hard. I got my shield in the way but I was rocked sideways. My foot caught on a little garden wall and I went flying over it. One minute I was upright facing an onrushing storm of hatred; the next I was on my back between a gnome, a fishing pond and the feet of a smartly dressed West Indian OAP sitting on his doorstep with a cup of tea.

'Are you all right there, officer?' he asked, doffing his trilby in my direction.

'Er, yeah, thanks.'

Just another surreal moment in the craziest day of my life.

But I didn't care about me. Falling away had left the right flank exposed and, because of the chaos, no one had noticed. No one inside the shield defence anyway, but the mob had noticed all right.

I was still getting up when I saw the petrol bomb tear through the gap.

Boom. It went up.

Instinctively, I looked at the perpetrator, not the poor defenceless coppers. I saw him and I thought, *You're mine!*

All the training, all the drills at Hendon flew out the window as a primeval rage surged through me. A horrible red mist – of which I'm not proud – filled my brain and I just got up and steamed after this bloke. Of course, he legged it. He knew he was in trouble. Being part of a faceless mob attacking a faceless creature made of shields was one thing, but he had made it personal. He had shown his face. And I was determined to rip it off.

I tore through the crowds, never more than an arm's length from him, thinking, *Any second, any second ...*

Just as I was about to grab his hood, a hand yanked my arm hard from behind.

For the first time I realised how stupid I was being. I'd charged into enemy territory with the obvious intention of hurting one of theirs. Now I was separated from my pack I was going to pay the price.

Except the voice I heard wasn't one of theirs. It belonged to a sergeant from Croydon. 'Get back in line, Constable!' he shouted. 'Now.'

Still not letting go of my arm, he turned me around and started pushing back through the crowd.

To this day I don't know the sergeant's name, which is shameful because he took such a risk on my behalf: we were in the heart of the people trying to torch us, and I'd been irrational in leaving the others. He'd done it with a clear head.

But, yet again, despite everything that had gone on between the two sides, another sort of amnesty was in force. Not only did the crowd not hurt us, they actually let us through without bother. Or, at least, most of them did. We were back near the action – I could hear our lads being bombarded – when a bottle smashed inches from the sergeant's feet.

He took one look at the bloke who'd sent it over and shouted, 'Oi! What did you do that for?'

The boy just shrugged his shoulders as if to say, 'I don't know.'

We had almost made it back to the others when another lone wolf made a move. This time I was the target. I spun around and grabbed the person who'd hit me, and I have to admit I was surprised to see it was a young white girl.

Well, I'll be buggered.

The reports from those that called us racist for singing 'Men Of Harlech' never mentioned the white contingent spitting bile at us, hurling abuse and trying to end our careers. They also kept quiet about the large number of older Caribbean men and women, who worked their way through the crowds all night, grabbing hold of any kids they knew and dragging them back to their homes. Whatever was happening in Brixton that weekend, it was not as simple as a race war. I saw that with my own eyes.

I saw a lot of other things, too, that will live with me until the end. I saw a pub burn down. It was what was called a 'black pub' – no one white ever drank there. It was in the heart of the Brixton community but it was attacked by the mob, its owners were robbed, and then the place was razed to the ground. I saw a fire engine – driven by a proper crew – trying to get through the throng to save the owners of that building and their livelihood. I saw the mob say 'no'. And I saw that building burn until it collapsed.

By then dawn had broken and the heat had gone out of the battle. The elders had whittled the crowds down and tiredness had done the rest. At half-past five we were faced with the agony of our injuries and the futility of it all. But we also remembered who we were – even if some of the locals didn't.

I will never forget this to the day I die: we were standing in Brixton Road, shields leaning against a wall, waiting for our ride home. Suddenly, there was a crash of glass and a lad walked out of a shop carrying a telly. They weren't flat-screens in those days and he was struggling under the weight. Maybe that made him more stupid, I don't know. How else do you explain a single youth robbing an electronics store and thinking he can walk past 50-odd Old Bill?

It was a race to see who could nick him first.

I got home about seven and, as was my routine at that time, I took our dog out for a walk in Nonesuch Park. I remember I was still in half-blues, a lump the size of a golf ball on my head, but the sun was shining and just for a moment all was well in the world. When a little old dear said to me, 'Isn't it a beautiful day?' I even had to agree.

'Yeah,' I said, 'I'm just glad I'm here.' *And not in Brixton. I never want to set foot there again.*

CHAPTER SIX

Pounds, Shillings and Pence

Several men resigned after Brixton. Even more talked about going. They knew they were pawns, they just didn't like being made to feel like it. I will never judge them but it would take a lot more than mob rule – inside the Met, or out of it – to make me quit my beloved force. It had taken me a long time to get there: almost 15 years since leaving school. I wasn't going to just walk away.

Even so, if I ever went back to Brixton I swore it would be too soon.

Fortunately – or not – I wasn't going anywhere for a couple of weeks. A doctor took one look at my bump and signed me off. I was lucky to escape brain damage, he reckoned. But then, to echo the words of Mr Williams, my old footy coach, who would know ...?

Two weeks at home had its pros and its cons. The biggest pro was being around the children. We'd had little David by then. The cons were ... well, there was more than one. Tina and I were not seeing eye to eye over a lot of things. Money, mainly, but there was something deeper and it was becoming difficult.

The other con was being left alone with my thoughts. Thinking can be a dangerous thing for a policeman, and I started going over and over in my mind why we had been left as a unit to rot. The Met could have shut Brixton down if it had chosen to, saturated all of south London. They hadn't, and not knowing why really hurt. So much so that when I went back to the quack's a week into my sick leave he diagnosed me with post traumatic stress disorder (PTSD).

'Normally only soldiers returning from the theatre of war get that, Clive,' he said. 'What the hell have you been doing?'

'Don't ask, Doc. Don't ask.'

I had to tell him something, so I described the fear and the violence. What I left out was the growing sense of betrayal I just couldn't shake. Knowing the powers-that-be could have sent back-up but opted not to left a bad taste.

To this day I still have PTSD. It's not a massive problem, nothing I'd take sick pay on. But even just sitting here reliving it has brought me out in a sweat.

I can remember every detail of that day, and I don't think I'll ever forget it.

Funnily enough, though, what I remember isn't enough. In the clean-up, just like they did after the rioting of 2011, the CID pooled every photograph they could find of Brixton dwellers and stuck everyone who was there in front of them.

'Just finger the scum,' I was told. I wanted to but it was hard. I had been looking at the bricks and petrol bombs, not the faces. It turned out we were all as useful as each other. CID loved that, of course, as it just confirmed their opinions of us: 'Pathetic lids ...'

To rub salt into the wounds, when I finally went back on duty and was coming up to take my final exams to shake the probation tag once and for all, I got a new posting.

It wasn't a permanent transfer. As I've said, when there was a shortage in one zone they'd ship in replacements from wherever the dart landed on the board – or so it seemed to me. On that day I must have been double top, because I arrived at Sutton and then it was off again to ... Brixton.

My partner for the day was a stranger, a DC down from north London and one who hadn't seen the riots.

Even though I had been there, as I walked down Railton Road I began to doubt my own memory. Where were the crowds? Where were the blood-thirsty hordes? I could see the places where Molotov cocktails had been launched – and plenty of places where they'd exploded. I admit I felt sick standing there. Was it part of the force's health programme to thrust me back there as soon as possible? To get me back on the horse? Were they that clever, though, and did they really care enough?

Cars were bombing up and down the road so it was hard to get close to ground zero but I admit I was lost enough in myself to jump out of my skin when a voice boomed from behind me. Yes, it was Caribbean. Yes, it reminded me of the ranting I'd been subjected to. And yes, I needed to get over that association. But no, he wasn't threatening. On the contrary ...

'Officers, can you help us out?' he asked. He was aged about 35 to 40 – the right age for one of the rioters. 'We've got a bit of a dispute down here.'

'Down where?' the DC said.

The man pointed to a staircase, leading to a basement beneath a shop.

My heart was beating overtime. Palpitations were making me sweat. *But*, I told myself, *the riots are over. It's been a month. Everything is forgotten.*

So down we went, naively you might think, into an unknown outcome. The place was heaving – 40 or 50 guys were packed into a tiny area, the air thick with the aroma of ganja. There was a band playing in the corner and it basically looked like a pretty decent place to spend your nights – except it was two in the afternoon.

The dispute in question turned out to involve a punnet of tomatoes!

I said to the original guy from the street, 'How much are they?'

He told me.

I said to the aggrieved geezer, 'How much did you give him?'

He told me that.

'Why was it short?'

He told me that as well.

In two minutes it was all sorted out, with no animosity, and thank-you-very-muches flying all around. What did I expect? These were decent, normal people. They always had been.

As we walked back up the stairs, I wondered if I had dreamed my last visit.

Maybe that brick caused more damage than I thought..?

You take your probation exams in your nineteenth month and, just after Brixton, I was told I'd passed. Usually you still have to work out your full two years but because of my age and experience they tore up the L plates early and I was given my own full-time beat. No more being a dogsbody, no more attachments, no more being at the beck and call of whoever was running the station that day. I was a PC, pure and simple.

A lot of people would turn their noses up at being a homebeat – the young DC from north London I'd wandered around Railton Road with had been right snooty about it. But there is absolutely nothing wrong in my book with wearing a uniform. My hero wore one and it was his specific uniform I had in mind. And after the trauma of Brixton maybe I needed a reminder of why I got into the service so I really went for it. I got myself a nice fob watch on a chain that sat in my breast pocket, I requested to ride a bicycle and I bought an old-fashioned sit-up-and-beg. I had to shell out for it, too – the force is always trying to modernise and at that time they were big on panda cars and trying to get away from the dated image of coppers on bikes.

To be fully Dixoned up, however, I needed one more thing, so I found one of the older homebeats and said, 'Do you still have one of those capes you all used to wear?'

Luckily enough, he did.

When I left the station for the first time, one of the sergeants said, 'Bloody hell, it's Dixon of Dock Green.' He meant it as an insult but I could not have been prouder.

The station I left from that afternoon was Epsom, which was dead handy for me because we'd moved house. I only had to step outside my front door and I was on my beat. It had been sad to say goodbye to Sutton, but Epsom wasn't exactly the dark side of the moon. In the Met, you do have to get used to moving on.

At Epsom there was no shortage of characters. It took me a while to work out, but the lady who took our 999 calls there, Betty, appeared to be deaf. These days all emergency calls are centralised but back then, everything went direct to the local station and someone on the comms desk would patch you through.

I was standing at the counter on my first day and I could hear this *ring ring ring* and I looked at Betty but she was oblivious. She could work the plugs all right but unless someone was shouting, 'Betty, Betty – phone!' nothing got picked up!

Maybe the atmosphere at the nick set the tone because I can honestly say I have never been happier in the police force than during those days as a homebeat. I loved bombing around on my bike, sticking my nose in anywhere I fancied, chasing down my own leads, calling in on familiar faces for chats and generally keeping an eye on my area.

Which was easier said than done. My patch included a lot of difficult areas, like the Longmead Estate. Part of it's a golf club now but in 1981 there was a different atmosphere. There was nothing wrong with the majority of people who lived there but an element had turned it into a small crime hotspot.

A lot of people saw it as a 'no go' area. I saw it as a challenge.

I mugged up on all the underground characters they had cards for back at the nick and then hit the pedals. Nowhere was out of bounds for me, as on the bike I could get up on the pavements and up on the walkways.

My first sortie was pretty uneventful but I was happy to make myself visible so, the next time I wheeled around there, people gave me a wave and a few were happy to chat.

On my third visit my research paid off. I was watching a young lad park a new-looking Honda, pretty skilfully to his credit, and it was only as he got out that I thought, *I've seen that face.*

By the time he'd locked up I was standing next to him, which gave him a bit of a jolt. No one hears bikes coming.

I gave it the full 'Ello 'ello 'ello and complimented the lad on his motor. I think we spoke about the engine size, and by the time we got to top speeds he was completely relaxed. That was about to change.

'I don't suppose you have the paperwork for this lovely car, do you, sir?'

His smile froze and he turned to leg it. By then my hand was on his shoulder and that, believe it or not, was enough to make his body sag and the fight leave his body before my eyes.

It was his bad fortune that I'd recognised his ugly mug from the collator's files about a family of car thieves. And my good fortune that I'd spent the hours studying them. When the area car boys arrived to take him to the station one of them said, 'That was a lucky break.'

If I'd ever waited to use a famous quote, this was the moment. 'What's the phrase?' I said, knowing how cheeky I was sounding. 'The harder I work, the luckier I get.'

'Don't push it.'

'Fair enough, lads.'

It sounds a bit romantic but I swear it was the blue uniform that had all the power. I was just the skin and bones inside it. It didn't matter what was kicking off, nine times out of ten if I rode into the picture with the full cape, triple 'ellos and a quizzical eyebrow, everything halted. Everything.

I found myself across the border near Sutton High Street once and I could hear something wasn't right so I followed my nose. Well, my ears. There was a club underneath an insurance office and, by the sound of it, it had gone off. When I arrived, there were two gangs standing about throwing bottles left, right and centre. It had flashes of Brixton, if I'm honest, so it needed stamping on.

I'm sure some of them must have expected Old Bill to turn up to a bundle like that, but I don't think anyone predicted a copper on a pushbike, wearing a cape.

They literally all stopped when I scooted up. They didn't put down their bottles. They just stopped and stared.

There was a steak bar a few doors along, owned by Joey Pyle. His clientele were no shrinking violets but this wasn't their fight so they'd just been watching it all play out. When they saw me pull up, take my time to lean my bike against the wall and walk over to the crowd, I think they thought they were about to see some old gladiatorial entertainment. These herberts who had been trying to smash each other would tear me to shreds, wouldn't they?

If I hadn't been wearing the uniform, maybe they would have. Instead, I walked right into the centre of where the bottle war had been going on and looked for the biggest kid I could find.

'Where are you from?'

'Croydon.'

'Well, fuck off back there then. We don't need you here.'

There was the sound of, let's say, disgruntlement, but one by one they all started to drift away. The other gang started calling out, so it was their turn for the Driscoll stare next.

I can't emphasise enough how in thrall they were of the uniform. Just two of them could have ripped me apart; the lot of them working together could have made sure my own dentist wouldn't recognise me. But I was unarmed, I was firm and I was dressed like the Old Bill of their childhoods.

When they had all cleared off, I got a few nods from the lads at Pyle's. The funny thing is, although I recognised more than one or two of them from the collator's cards, they were old school, not kids. I genuinely think if one of the gang lads had turned on me the old 'uns would have waded in to protect me. There are rules in life, even for criminals, and attacking an unarmed policeman is just not on.

With the bike I could get about so quickly it was like having another area car; in fact, I took it as a personal challenge to race the four-wheel plods. They thought they were the Billy Bollocks, didn't they, so it was purely ego that got me pedalling. I lost count of the times they'd turn up on the Watersedge Estate – another notorious address on my list – and I'd be having a cuppa with a resident while a handcuffed suspect sat stony-faced on the kerb.

When the call was for further away I normally let them have it but, one night, it was a bit quiet when I got a report of a burglary in Banstead village. It said the suspects were still in the area, and Banstead was just off the main road so I thought, *I'll never get there before the car – it's a long way and it's all uphill for a start. But maybe I'll get lucky and bump into the suspect.* So off I went.

Thirty-five minutes later, I arrived at the victim's address, wringing wet with sweat. I had to lean against his gate before I could summon up the energy to walk in – I didn't want the area boys taking the mick too much. Worst of all, I'd had no luck with the burglars.

I knocked on the door and this nervous-looking guy opened it. 'Thank God you're here!'

That's how nice the British public are. How lucky the British police are to have them. We'd taken 40 minutes to respond to his call, the bloke we sent was a walking sponge, and he still said, 'Thank God.'

Of course, when the area car did pitch up, I made out I'd been there hours. Small victories ...

If I'm honest, I did stick out a little bit among the others. I got on famously with everyone and there was a solid social side at the nick, but because I didn't have a partner, I dressed a bit differently and I had a very particular idea of the kind of police officer I wanted to be, I heard whispers of 'eccentric' and 'loner'. Did it bother me? Not in the slightest. I enjoyed working on my own – the arguments were a lot more interesting, for starters.

I loved my work for what it was but some coppers – and I suppose this is true in all walks of life – liked to pep things up a bit. I was out one night when Roger Hastings, the area car PC, pulled up.

'There's a practical joke going down in Wallington nick,' he said. 'Fancy taking a look?'

Practical jokes sail a bit too close to bullying for my money but funny is funny and so, against my instincts, I jumped in the Allegro with Roger. When I found out about the joke, though, I regretted it. The victim in this prank was a female PC which, I'm afraid to say, for some of the lads, was enough to make her a plausible target.

Anyway, it was all going to go down in a graveyard next to a factory estate in their area so we parked up in the estate, clambered over the wall, then crawled on our hands and knees across a grassy area to get a front-row view.

The wheeze was this: Judith Harrington was to be told there was something suspicious in the churchyard. When she got there, a sergeant from Wallington was going to leap out from behind a gravestone dressed in full rabid-zombie-on-the-rampage gear, she'd nearly have a heart attack and we'd all have a laugh.

It didn't quite work out like that.

We saw Judith's car pull up, and we watched as she got her flashlight out and started kicking around the yard. Right on cue, the zombie leapt up but, instead of running, Judith fainted – and cracked her head on the way down. When the sergeant got to her she was covered in blood.

That wasn't the plan. Everyone was doing an impression of headless chickens but they managed to bundle Judith into a car and get her to hospital, toot sweet.

I felt a bit sick and Roger didn't look too chipper either, so we ran back across the field, jumped over the nearest part of the wall – and nearly landed on one of Croydon's most prolific burglars!

I had to feel sorry for the guy. He was just going about his business, robbing the factory, and we just dropped from the clouds because we guessed wrong about where behind the wall our car was. I'd recognised him immediately from the collator's cards, but a warehouse door swinging off its hinges, the boxes he was carrying and the non-likelihood of him having legitimate business out there at night helped a bit, too.

What I like about proper villains is that, even when faced with insurmountable evidence, they have an answer.

'My wife is about to give birth so I went in to use the phone.'

I didn't say it was a good answer …

Our con admitted to a string of other burglaries and eventually we got a commendation for that collar, so it was a pretty good night in the end.

Less so for the sergeant at Wallington. When he'd got to the hospital, Judith Harrington had been rushed to Emergency, and then the sister there had come back and dressed him down for 15 minutes like he was a schoolboy.

Bad enough his career was almost certainly over, but he was having to listen to all this in fancy dress.

Then, suddenly, the curtain around her bed was pulled back and there was Judith laughing her head off. She'd got a whisper about the prank and had taken fake blood capsules with her.

The whole thing had been a re-prank – even the sister had been in on it.

Despite being a bit of a lone wolf, what I really loved about the Job was knowing there was this entire operation behind me. Brixton had been a bit of an eye opener but day to day, if back-up was needed, back-up was given.

In 1981, some genius decided to open a pub right in the middle of the Longmead Estate. My Spidey-sense rattled off the hook on this one so, come turnout time on opening night, it was *Sefton Arms, here I come.*

To say the clientele looked like they'd had a drink is an understatement. Judging from the noise outside the red-brick building I expected to see one of those cartoon punch-ups, with the cloud with arms and legs sticking out. Everyone was blotto, and they were vicious with it. Perhaps I should have played it differently but, as I've said, nine times out of ten the uniform is enough to shut the noisiest bugger up.

This was one of those other times.

As the fight spilled out onto the road I gave it the full Dixon 'What's going on 'ere then?' – and they went for me. About five of the gang pulled away from the bundle and rushed me so fast I toppled over and landed on my back in someone's well-tended front garden.

For the majority out on the streets that was one taboo broken. A crowd gathered behind the five breakaways. They didn't look like they were worried about taboos or uniforms; in fact, I would say they looked like they could smell blood.

I could see where it was going so instead of trying to get up I just cradled my head with my arms and waited for the first boot to land. It seemed to take for ever, but when one started they all joined in, kicking at my head like they were taking penalties. Eventually someone called them off and they ran away. That's when I opened my eyes.

The look on the garden owner's face when I got up ...

'How the hell are you still alive?'

'I've got your green fingers and some very drunk idiots to thank for that,' I said. 'They weren't kicking my head – they were kicking your rockery!'

It was a lucky escape and I knew it. The next night was a different story: ten area cars, thirty bodies, five minutes of our particular kind of heavy-handedness and the cells from half the stations in Z district full for the night. They soon learned you don't want to take on a policeman unless you want to take on all policemen.

If only we'd done the same thing in Brixton.

Being a homebeat offered something for everyone. If you were so inclined you could just go around patting kids on the head and say you were helping the community. But that wasn't enough for me. I loved investigating. If I didn't have a crime to solve I'd be looking for one.

Apart from the Longmead and Watersedge Estates, my beat covered a lot of Horton Country Park. This is a lovely nature reserve now; in the 1980s it was still getting off the ground and it had an edge, especially at night, when a lot of drug dealers used it as their office, and drug users used it as their front room.

I was happy to use it to fill my cells.

A lot of my area overlapped with another homebeat's, PC Peter Westercott, so we helped each other out when we could. I'd be on his turf chasing someone and he'd be on mine, and we'd sort the paperwork at the end. As long as all the ground got covered, that was fine by us.

I liked Peter because he used a bike as well, which meant we could occasionally ride together or, on possibly one of the best nights of my early career, ride from opposite directions.

I was on the Longmead one night when a bloke I'd helped out before waved me down.

'All right, Clive,' he said. 'I thought you might be interested to know there's a man selling pounds, shillings and pence down the road.'

'He's what?'

He looked at me like I'd come down in the last shower. 'LSD, Clive.'

LSD – £/s/d. Of course. To be fair to Hendon, I think I might have been ill the day we did slang for drugs.

'Where's it happening?'

'The burger van in front of the watchtower. You can't miss it.'

I jumped on the walkie-talkie to see where Peter was. I preferred working with him to the area boys – nothing personal, just us bikers sticking together. It turned out he was five minutes the other side of the estate and so a plan was hatched.

We got in position, then I flew down the high street one way while Peter, in classic pincer movement, came in from the other.

We needn't have rushed. No one seemed to notice our arrival. In fact, even as I approached the van I heard one customer say, 'Hamburger, chips and two tabs.'

Bang to rights.

LSD was sold in little squares like stamps; wholesale, they were all stuck together like sheets of A4 paper. This burger van contained hundreds of them. What made me laugh was chummy in the chef's hat was obviously making a tidy income from his burgers and chips as well, because some of his customers genuinely only came for the food. I was standing in the van, at the window when a young mum called up, 'Two burgers, please. No onions.'

I was there in my full uniform, not an apron in sight.

'Do I look like I'm frying burgers, madam?'

She shrugged. 'Got any chips then, instead?'

I give up sometimes.

If we thought we'd struck gold with the hundreds of sheets in the van, back at the dealer's drum there were thousands.

Boxes and boxes and boxes of hallucinogens with a street value of more money than I would ever see. For years, Peter and I held the Surrey record for the largest haul of LSD – and we'd done it all on our bikes.

As I cycled back home that night, cape fluttering in the breeze, I thought of old George Dixon and his adventures. I was having quite a few of my own thanks to him, and I really could not have been happier.

CHAPTER SEVEN

Altogether Now…

Napoleon said he'd rather have a lucky general than a good one. Well, excuse me for correcting a military mastermind, but for a while I'd say I had a touch of both.

I owed the LSD victory to the tip-off, which was definitely a stroke of good fortune, no two ways about it; but that only occurred, I reckoned, because of the weeks and months of little chats and interventions I'd made on my beat. So many people knew me, so many people had told me their life's problems and, when I was able to, I'd helped them. Sometimes that help involved having a chat with kids about kicking a ball against an old lady's wall. Sometime it was moving someone's settee while I was asking them about a burglary. I like helping people: do one nice thing for someone and you'll get it back double. I've always believed that, and I think it works for me. That bloke on the Longmead would not have flagged down a panda car, I can promise you that. And if he hadn't seen me, he wouldn't have told anyone, and those tabs would have been on sale outside the watchtower for a lot longer.

But don't get me wrong: record-breaking drugs busts were not the daily diet for a homebeat. Sometimes it was a lot more dangerous.

I was on the Longmead again and, as usual, it didn't take me long to see something of interest. Was it an armed gang? Was it an international team of human traffickers? Not quite. As I swung down a residential road, I was appalled to see a large coal lorry parked, in my opinion, quite disgracefully.

Oh, the glamour.

I knocked on the nearest house and, from the state of the bloke's hands, I'd found the right door.

'Is that your lorry, sir?'

'Yes.'

'Can you shift it, please? It looks like a two-year-old's parked it.'

'Sorry, officer, I was in a rush. I'll get straight out.'

'If you wouldn't mind.'

I watched him do it then cycled on. No more than two minutes later, I got a radio call: gun fired on the Longmead. I got back and there, lying on his doorstep, dead, was the coalman.

Two minutes earlier and I might have been shot myself. Or I might have been able to prevent it. I wished I'd been given the chance.

After the coalman's murder CID swooped in with their trademark good grace. What names I wasn't called for neither apprehending nor getting a look at the shooter isn't worth writing. Still, they got their man. It turned out to be an inter-family argument gone wrong.

You can't always be in the right place at the right time, and that applies to criminals as well. I'd already apprehended a particular man three times, going back to my Sutton days, when I came across him again mid-job in Brunswick Road. There were no fisticuffs, he didn't try to run for it, he just climbed out of the window, walked over and stood next to me like a good puppy while I rang for a car. I tried not to handcuff people if they behaved – which I think he appreciated.

Because of the previous arrests we actually got on quite well. I was processing him back at the nick when, at a time that we were out of earshot of anyone else, he said: 'What's in it for me if I tell you who done four jobs in Upper High Street – and where the stash is?'

'If I'm honest, I haven't got a clue. But I know a man who will have.'

I went and found a DC called Mick Poyser. A lovely bloke, one of the best detectives I ever worked with, but sadly dead now.

'What you've got there, Clive,' he said, 'is an informant.' Then he gave me a clutch of forms and showed me how to fill them in – something that hadn't come up at Hendon. 'You write down the guy's name there, then you invent a name for him and put it over there.' He pointed to a box on the form. 'Don't show anyone then you stick it in this sealed envelope and it goes into the DCI's safe. The DCI is the controller, you're the handler and the mystery man is the grass. Whatever you do, never reveal his identity.'

Faced with conjuring up a pseudonym, I reached for the names closest to my heart – and came up with Maurice Cook, Fulham's former striker and one-time record transfer signing. Over the next few years several Fulham legends helped me out with information: George Cohen, Johnny Haynes, Rodney Marsh, Allan 'King' Clarke.

The other thing I had to fill in a form about was money. 'Maurice Cook' actually wanted to have his charge dropped in exchange for information. That never sat well with me so I said no, but how about fifty quid?

'Done.'

So Maurice went before the magistrate, took his punishment and was a very reliable source of titbits for years after – although sadly not for me. Mickey Poyser had told me to keep the identity secret but of course he knew. And, in true Metropolitan Police fashion, he swooped in and nicked Maurice Cook from me as his grass.

As for the original tip: solid gold. The burglar had buried everything on common ground. Tips, however, don't do all the work – they point you in the right direction and then you have to do the usual police legwork and build a case. In that instance, we got fingerprints from the buried jewels and tracked down the thief. On other occasions, you might still have weeks of work to do to get a suspect in front of a magistrate, but the informant can be an important starting point.

You always had to be wary of who was talking to you, though. Some grasses were just after the money. Others released information strategically so you took out the opposition. I had a problem doing a villain's dirty work, even accidentally, so I made sure I was hard on them as well. The best result for me was getting in the middle of a couple of sorts, ruffling them up and watching them bring each other down. I'd rather have people behind bars than being ears on the street if they are going to keep robbing.

I'd also have more respect for grasses if they coughed up information before they were arrested, like normal people do. You'd be surprised how much police work is helped by absolute strangers coming in to make a statement or phoning with a witness statement. Grasses like to wait until they're in your cells before playing the Good Samaritan.

A guy in for burglary one New Year's Eve was a case in point.

'Clive,' he said, 'I am on a racing certainty with a young lady at a party tonight. You have got to get me out.'

'Sorry, mate, it's up to CID, not me.'

'What if I give you information about two other burglaries? Would that open the doors?'

'I can't make any promises,' I said, but in my mind I was already adding another Fulham player to my all-star Driscoll Eleven. 'Tell me what you know.'

'OK – you know the sports shop and off-licence on East Street were both done over?'

'Yes, spot on. A lot of gear went missing.'

'Well, I know who did it.'

'Go on then.'

'Are you letting me out?'

'It's possible.'

'Right, well, the person who robbed those places ...'

'Come on ...'

'Was me. I did it.'

On my life.

He never did make it to that party.

Since the early 1900s, Epsom had been designated as some kind of hub for hospitals specialising in mental issues. The 'Epsom Cluster' as it was called included St Ebba's, Horton, Long Grove, Manor and West Park. Two of them were on my beat and the others were of interest.

St Ebba's I knew because I used to play piano there. Every Tuesday, without fail, my friend Graham and I would go along and entertain the patients. We'd do two hours and, I have to say, whatever was going on in the world or in my life, it was all forgotten for those 120 minutes. St Ebba's mainly housed mentally handicapped boys and girls, people who were put inside because society – in my opinion – was too embarrassed to deal with them any other way. I didn't think it was right but at least the staff was blinding to them and I loved to get them all singing and running around and clapping to 'The Grand Old Duke Of York'. It was such a kick to see them all happy.

There was one young lad whom I really used to have fun with. I'd be bashing the old joanna, Graham's behind me on the bass, and this lovely Down's Syndrome kid – about 13 years old – would stand the other side of my upright piano and dance like crazy. Every so often his eyes would glaze over and he'd get this almost spiritual look of happiness and, seeing that, my heart would be fit to burst. To be able to give another human being pleasure like that would make anyone's day.

After a couple of months of this I mentioned it to one of the nurses, who looked at me like I was mad. 'He's not dancing – he's masturbating.'

Suddenly the glazed look wasn't such a thrill for me any more ...

We only stopped playing there when Ebba's was due to close. Then, a few years later, one of the nurses asked if we'd play at her new job.

'We'd be ever so grateful – and we'll still pay you the fifty quid, if that's all right.'

I worked out we must have had about £6,000 stolen from us by one of the staff!

I had quite a few dealings with the hospitals. Sometimes, however, I was the one taking business to them. I was patrolling near Ruxley Lane one day and this teenager in a school uniform flagged me down.

'Oi,' she said, 'what are you doing about the flasher?'

'Who?'

And so she told me about this bloke who used to wait for schoolgirls going into a nearby school. He'd hide behind a hedge then leap out in the altogether.

The girls had told the school but the school hadn't told the police – they had told the council. So what did the council do?

They cut down the hedge.

Problem solved, wasn't it?

I told the girl I would sort it and, I'm pleased to say, I did. It basically involved finding a hiding place near the school entrance and waiting to see who turned up in a raincoat. I let him have one go to incriminate himself then nabbed him.

Sometimes you arrest criminals and you think, *You're a wrong 'un.* Right from birth you can see they've been trouble. But with this guy I was a bit out of my depth.

'You're not well,' I told him.

'I know!'

'Well, we've got to sort this out.'

To be fair to him, we went to the station and I got out the crime books and he went through them and pointed out all the flashing incidents that were down to him. 'I done that, I done that, I done that ...' Ticking off an unsolved crime always wins big brownie points with the sarge, so the teas were on him that day.

I then said to my flasher, 'I'll get you help.'

'You'd do that?'

I would, and did.

When we got to court I told the magistrate that I was committed to helping the suspect and so he was let out on condition he agreed with what I had arranged. I knew of a group called the Lucy Faithfull Foundation in Horton Hospital which dealt mainly, as far as I could see, with Catholic priests who'd got into trouble. I'd had a long chat with a psychiatrist there who said he could help him. I put the two together and, to my knowledge, there were no more incidents again.

The same can't be said for his brother, though, who was a prolific burglar; while one of them was whipping out his old boy, the other was whipping out car radios. I got to know him through the flasher and so, when I saw him actually walking away from a car, its window smashed, carrying a stereo, I was clapping my hands with glee.

As I've said before, the pros always have an excuse. His was a blinder: 'I found the radio on the ground and was on my way to hand it in to the police when you saw me.'

Priceless.

However, it was enough for him to avoid prosecution, which I took as a personal affront, and so I decided to follow him. People will criticise me for this but I actually let him smash another car's window – apologies if it was yours – just so that I could step out and say he'd been seen.

As I'd learned to my cost on my first court case, remove any doubt before you get in front of the magistrate.

I actually got on well with the burglar, as I did his brother, especially once he also coughed to a load of historical house-breaks, so I said to him, 'You're obviously a clever bloke. Why don't you do something legal?'

Soon after he came out of prison he started a scaffolding company, and I still see him for a chat every now and again. His son is a season-ticket holder at Tottenham (which is sad), but otherwise his life has been transformed. If I played a small part in it, I'm very proud. But that's what policing to me is all about. Yes, the Met can be an army if called upon, but at its very heart we are dealing with individuals: people who get hurt and people who do the hurting.

Being able to make a difference is why I loved being a homebeat.

Sex and mental health issues can often go hand in hand. This was never more forcefully brought home to me than when I was asked to go to Springfield Hospital to speak to a group of adult sex offenders. I kid you not, every single one of them was from St Ebba's. That's how successful the system was. There is a massive argument about keeping people locked away but, if you're going to let them outside, I think you have to support them. These boys became men and would not have known what they were doing. They would not have known it was wrong, I'm sure. But that was why I was there.

The thing was, they all took one look at me and thought I was there to play the piano!

It's very disconcerting trying to play the big, bad policeman and give a lecture when your audience starts clapping when you walk in. In fact, I nearly said, 'Here's a new one for you – it's called "The Sex Offenders Act". Altogether now ...'

The tragedy of how the system treated those Epsom Cluster patients wasn't just something I picked up on while playing piano. Horton patients used to wander the grounds and it was understandably difficult to monitor them all the time. Again, in my opinion, it's a balancing act. You can't just lock people like that up because they haven't done anything wrong – some people were in those places historically just for getting pregnant – but as soon as they were out of the hospital gates, which they were often, they were vulnerable. Some of the local kids were nasty to them. And then there were the adults ...

I was cycling past one day and I saw a car – an expensive one – pull over and the driver start chatting to one of the patients.

Now, you would be right to say that the patients were entitled to a social life. And you would be right as well to say that the driver might just have liked the look of her. But this lady, whom I later met and was perfectly charming, had her face scribbled in lipstick where she couldn't control her hands, had her stockings around her ankles and her dress on back to front. Call me judgemental, but not the sort of look that would make you stop your sports car and say, 'Hop in, darling.'

I scooted over and tapped on the driver's window. He was a fat bloke, balding, in a too-tight suit.

'I think it's time you pulled away, sir,' I said.

He just looked at me. 'What's it got to do with you?'

I said, 'Hello? Recognise the uniform? I'm a police officer. Now jog on.'

After that I made enquiries in the hospital. Apparently it was very common for drivers to come from miles around, pick up the patients – men and women – and give them cigarettes or booze in exchange for sex up on the Downs. And it wasn't just Horton. All the Cluster hospitals had the same problem. The woman with the stockings was actually very popular, so I was told.

Again, there was a delicate line to draw because the patients were adults and they were entitled to a sex life. But, after consultation with the hospitals, I decided that they were actually victims whether they knew it or not, and I had to do something to protect them.

But what difference can one man on his bike make?

I tried. Every shift I made a tour of the Epsom Cluster and spent half an hour chasing off the toe-rags soliciting there. It was the devil's own job. I'd clear Horton, pop round to Long Grove – and the same cars would be cruising around there.

One day, I was busting a gut outside Long Grove when this smart old dude in an RAF blazer said, 'You've got your work cut out there, young man.'

'It's a full-time job.'

He said, 'If you want, I could write down a few registration numbers from the worst offenders while I'm up here. Would that be any help?'

Retired military man, upstanding citizen, nothing better to do on a Wednesday afternoon. Perfect.

'That would actually be marvellous,' I said.

'Right-o. Now, do you have anything I could write in?'

So I gave him one of my spare notebooks and a pen and wished him luck. At least that was one hospital out of five I didn't have to worry so much about.

Later that day I went back into the station. The bloke who used to work the PNC – the Police National Computer, which had a register of all cars and owners – came steaming up to me waving a pile of papers. All of them had obviously been torn out of the book I'd given the old RAF chap earlier.

'Stone me, Clive,' he said. 'You seriously want me to run checks on all these? We've got milk floats, post vans, school buses. You want me to go on?'

Christ, I thought, *Douglas Bader's a bit keen.*

But I said, 'Leave it with me. I'll sort it.'

I cycled back up to Long Grove more in hope than expectation. My eager assistant would have long gone by then. But, as I freewheeled around the corner, I spotted him lobbing a brick at a speeding car.

'Oi, oi, mate! What are you doing?'

'I'll have you know I work for PC Driscoll,' he said, chest puffed out as if for an inspection.

'I am PC Driscoll – don't you remember me?'

It turned out that the old bloke was ex-RAF – but for the last six years he had been a patient at Horton Hospital. 'Mad as a march hare,' one of the staff later told me, on the quiet, which was a shock. To look at him, he was spot on: the tie, the blazer, the slacks. No one would have known he was an inmate. His doctor actually said she'd never seen him so alert so I decided that as long as he kept violence out of it, where was the harm in him continuing to 'help'? But obviously he wasn't the answer to my problem with the Cluster.

The next day I went to see Chief Superintendent Rideout. 'If we don't do something about this situation, sir, someone is going to be murdered. I'm on my own up there and it's not enough.'

He gave the green light for some extra bodies: the ones I picked were female and, they won't mind me saying, rather attractive. The plan was to dress them up as patients and get the kerb crawlers for soliciting. Once word got out we were cracking down, I hoped the pervs would go back to their lives and their wives.

There was only one problem.

The WPCs didn't get a single bit of interest all day!

But the problem was still there and it was about to escalate. Three days after I'd seen him, Rideout called me in to meet the murder team. A patient from Long Grove Hospital had been taken around the corner and kicked to death.

'Clive's our expert on the area,' Rideout said. 'You can have him as long as you need him.'

I was cut up that one of those poor patients had lost his life and I was determined to help. Then I had a brainwave. 'What if we had the registration number of all the vehicles outside the hospital around that time?'

'Well, that would be marvellous,' replied one of the smug El Cids, 'but unless you've got a magic wand, where are we going to get that kind of information?'

'Give me five minutes ...'

I went down to the front desk and, sure enough, there was a fresh stack of car regs taken by my RAF guy waiting to be thrown away by the PNC guy. I scrabbled through them and bingo: a dozen numbers from the time in question.

From that scrap of information, we tracked down every car and found the killer.

My mad old boy on the hill carried on collecting numbers for years after. Epsom nick would hand over stacks of books and he'd return them chocka with numbers. I'm happy to say we did get on top of the situation at the Cluster but to this day I still get stick from some people for deputising a mental patient.

But he did solve a murder.

There was a fair bit of luck involved, I admit, in nailing the Long Grove Hospital killer, but my instincts had been right. Without me waging a one-man campaign against the sex pests terrorising the patients, there would have been one more murderer out there. As a result of that, and what I'd done with the flasher, I was called in to see the mighty CID shortly after. A DS – Detective

Sergeant – called Mick Wickerson, who'd run the murder team, said he'd like me to work with them.

'Park your bike, son, you're joining the A Team now.'

That's seriously how they viewed themselves – just because they didn't wear uniforms.

'With respect, I'm very happy to be on my beat, thanks.'

'Well, I'm not,' he said. 'You're joining us, simple as that.'

And so off I went and, actually, they were a great bunch – Mick Wickerson especially.

I was in two minds about hanging up the black gloves and top hat, but the work CID did played right to my strengths: I got to follow clues, work evidence and meet a lot of interesting people.

After several months, Mick took me aside: 'You were made to be a detective, Clive. You need to become a DC.'

'That's good to hear – but I've just put in for Police Sergeant.'

He blew his top at the fact that I'd applied for a promotion in the uniform division – if I passed, he was going to lose me.

'You're wasting your life with the lids, Clive! Stay and do proper work.'

I passed the exams with 92% and, once again, it was time to move on. Even as he wished me well, Mick said, 'I will never forgive you for this.' Then he added, 'You'll be back.'

I will always remember that first day, going into Wimbledon nick, which was to be my new home for at least a year until my new probationary period finished. As soon as I walked in a PC – an old boy who was probably in his fifties – came straight over, took one look at the chevrons on my arm, and said, 'Good morning, Sarge. We've been expecting you.'

For all he knew I had been a sergeant for ten years. He didn't know those arrows were freshly sewn on.

In those days, the sergeant ran the station so it wasn't only goodbye homebeat and goodbye bike, it was goodbye fresh air as well. But I loved it. I just loved any kind of police work that got me in front of other human beings. Whether it was checking prisoners in, moving the troops around or dealing with citizens reporting their latest woes, every interaction gave me a reason to smile. Yes, there was a lot of responsibility: if one car hit another car in the police car park, it was the sergeant in the cack; anything missing from the safe or the property store, exactly the same story. Whether I knew about it or not, the system said I was in charge of everything, good and bad.

Leading a team and having a bit – a lot – of autonomy was great grounding. I can honestly say that in that entire probationary year I did not have a single day where I didn't look forward to going into work.

So what I did on the day my probation ended shocked everyone: I handed in my papers and resigned from the force.

This time for real.

CHAPTER EIGHT

Strap Him in the Morning

So, what did I do between 1985 and 1987? Well, I discovered a new hero for one. Because of the occasional word blindness I wasn't much of a reader, so Sherlock Holmes didn't enter my sphere until Jeremy Brett brought him to the small screen. Sherlock Holmes – now, *there* was a detective I could admire, and probably the first, as it goes. Since then I've read all his stories a dozen times. I liked him because he used his brain, he used his connections and, I suppose, because he was a bit of a loner at heart. All that mattered to him was the case: not his reputation, not his relationships. Justice was all. And when his tail was up and he said, 'The game's afoot,' you knew he was loving it, too. That love of the Job spoke to me. My only criticism of Sherlock was he played a fiddle instead of the piano.

As for the rest of the time, I was still tinkling the ivories three or four times a week for residential homes and the like over those two years. I also ran the youth club on the Watersedge Estate; I started helping Fulham out as a scout; I ferried patients to and from Horton Hospital and ran musical therapy classes there; and generally tried to put something back into the community.

So that was the 'what'. 'Why' I was doing it is a bit messier.

'The hand that rocks the cradle rules the world' – that's another phrase, although I don't know if Napoleon said this one.

My home life by the mid-1980s was a car crash. Tina and I were barely talking – I was almost scared to go home some nights – and a very large part of that was because of her mother. I don't particularly want to speak ill of the dead, but Joan Jones was a piece of work unlike any other I had encountered either side of the cells at Epsom nick. It was like she never got over the fact I was a copper (although she had a photo of me in uniform on her fridge – albeit with a crucifix covering my face) and if she could find an opportunity to hurt me, she would.

My Achilles heel, as everyone knew, was my children: so often I'd look forward to spending the weekend with them ... only to discover she was taking them away for the weekend on the Friday night. And Tina went along with it.

For the year I was at Wimbledon, I was the subject of a dozen spurious official complaints from Tina's mum – each one was as professionally crippling and utterly made up as the last.

Even the bloke investigating them admitted it. 'But,' he said, 'legally we have to pursue every complaint.'

It was a very unhappy time for me, and would lead to me leaving Tina.

I still think Joan Jones's behaviour was unacceptable. However, she was grandmother to my children and, out of respect to them, I do not intend to go into any detail over this part of my life. It would only bring back bad memories to all concerned. I have no doubt I made mistakes and those mistakes caused hardship and pain to Robert, Bonita and David – something I will never forgive myself for. Nor will I hurt them any more by talking about this episode further. They are such a big part of my life and I am so very proud of them.

And so, during 1984, I was not happy and I therefore took the second-hardest decision I have ever taken, after walking away from my kids.

I walked away for the benefit of the Job.

You can't ruin my career if I don't have one ...

I thought I would be gone for a couple of months; it turned out to be two-and-a-bit years. Eventually Tina remarried, I began proper contact with my children again and I also found a new partner, Anne, to whom I am proud to still be married today. Without her, I wouldn't have my two incredible boys, Thomas and Harry. They're both big lumps now, but what I wouldn't trade for a minute with any of my children as kids once again. I've said it many times but I would give everything I own, every penny I've earned, for a few moments with them when they were small. Particularly Robert, David and Bonita. I missed out on so much of watching them grow up. I love seeing my young grandchildren playing but I regret missing it first time round.

When I was sure the coast was clear, I decided to reapply to the force. After such a long time away, my friends tried to dissuade me.

'You left as a sergeant – you're going to go back with the homebeats and the kids.'

'I don't care,' I said. 'The happiest days of my life were as a PC.'

The mugging-up for the written tests was as hard as I expected; the physical examination was a lot worse. Doing a programme designed for 18-year-olds when I was 36 years old took everything I had, and then some. Finally, we had a medical, where you had to stand naked and touch your toes so the doc could check if you had piles.

They knew how to make you feel special at Hendon.

After the last test had been done, everyone was seated in a large hall. A bloke with a clipboard came out and started calling people's names and asking them to go to a different room. When he was finished, there was only about a third of us left.

I was gutted. All that hard work and I'd flunked it. Why did I even leave in the first place?

Then Clipboard said, 'Congratulations, boys and girls, and welcome to the Met.'

Get in …

Before we left, they got me to sign some forms and said someone would be in touch with a start date.

I couldn't wait.

When the call came, however, I was a bit annoyed at how slack the Job had got.

'Hello, Sarge, we'd like you to start in two weeks' time.'

'OK.' *But do your homework, son – I'm not a sergeant any more.* 'Where am I going?'

'Do you have a preference?'

'Well, I have unfinished business at Wimbledon. Epsom was cracking, Sutton is a marvellous place …' In the end, I rattled off a dozen stations where I'd be happy to accept a post.

The guy rang off – calling me 'Sarge' again – and said he'd be back in touch within the hour.

Forty-five minutes later he was back on the line.

'Hello again, Sarge.'

'Listen, Constable – I was a sergeant, but now I'm not. I'd appreciate it if you called me by my proper title.'

'Sorry, Sarge, but you are a sarge, Sarge. I've got the form in front of me – you signed to join back at the same rank.'

Did I really? I later found out that I was the first person who'd ever left the Met and returned at the same rank: they normally make you rejoin at PC level to make a point. But I had mitigating circumstances, I suppose – they knew I had left only to protect the Job.

Having sorted that out, there was still the matter of my posting.

'OK, Sarge – if you don't mind me calling you that – I'm pleased to inform you that you will be reporting to' – a clunking of clipboards – 'Brixton! Have you been there before?'

'Oh, yes,' I said. 'I know Brixton very well.'

And it still gives me nightmares.

A lot of things had changed in the Job during my time out; some major, some less important. The biggie was the introduction of the Police And Criminal Evidence Act (PACE). This was an attempt to balance the powers of the police with the rights of the public, so it looked at fresh rules for stop and search, arrests, detention, investigation, identification and the amount of time you could detain a suspect for interview. All pretty healthy, really. A lot of the Job moaned about it but there was nothing unreasonable in it, in my opinion. You could still do everything you could before, it just required you put in a bit more research or effort first.

A smaller change to the system also came as a result of PACE. When I was a sergeant at Wimbledon I ran the whole nick, including the custody suite. Now with all the prisoner rights, each station had a designated custody sergeant. Guess who got that job?

It could have been quite a nice little operation but at Brixton, the cells were in the bowels of the building. They were so deep, in fact, I never knew what on earth was going on at land level. If someone came in soaking wet I knew it was raining, if they came in wearing a shirt and shades, it was probably sunny. It was grim and, for the foreseeable future, that was where I was going to stay. I used to say to the prisoners, 'At least you're only going to get two months. I'm here for a year.'

The plus side was that it felt a little bit safer than when I was last standing out on Railton Road. When I looked up now I just saw concrete, not hundreds of plummeting petrol bombs. Although if I closed my eyes ...

The only times I got a glimpse of the sky was if I covered another relief. I was happy then, ridiculously. I would drag the old boneshaker out of the garage, clip on the cape and hit the road.

Watch out, Brixton: Dixon of Dock Green is here.

Virtually everything was the same as at Epsom – the only difference was the magnifying glass in my breast pocket. You can thank Mr Holmes for that. It might sound weird, but the public absolutely loved it. They have an image of the police in their minds just like me, and when I whipped it out to study a crime scene I could almost feel them relax.

It's OK, we're in the company of professionals.

Yet again, I got a massive kick out of racing area cars to calls. And, yet again, wherever I went, the uniform did the work of 10 giant police officers standing behind me. Even the shoutiest gangs turned it in when I arrived.

I swung onto Myatts Field Estate one night and found a group of youths, all big units, getting a bit animated. When I pulled up ''Ello 'ello 'ello-ing' even as I dismounted, they stood back, stared at their shoes and didn't murmur. And that was when I saw the gun on the ground. No one admitted to whom it belonged so I hooked it up with my pen and bagged it for evidence. When I then suggested the lads would have to accompany me to Brixton nick, they all just swore and waited patiently for transport.

Again, I put it down to the mystical powers of the uniform. I believed in it, and so did they. At any point one of them could have upended me and dumped me in a bin. Instead, they all just took their medicine. Nice boys, as it turned out.

As was often the case, it was sometimes easier to get on with villains than so-called allies – even a fairly green copper could usually appeal to the better nature of hardened criminals if you were in the full blues. The infamous Freddie Daly tended to do whatever I asked, usually with a smile. And Ralphie Irving, a big old lump, was causing traffic chaos one day by parking in a bus stop. I just rolled up on my bike, tapped on the window and before I could speak he said, 'Do you need me to move, officer?'

'If you wouldn't mind, sir.'

Sometimes, though, I had more than a car to contend with. There was a legendary Brixton guy who used to drive a tank around – a massive yellow tank, with caterpillar tracks, a giant gun – with a picture of a big pig in my beloved uniform painted on the side. He hated Old Bill with a passion, goading the area cars and the homebeats. He was a very intimidating fella. The first time I saw him, he was coming down the centre of Loughborough Junction.

Well, this is different.

I pedalled to about 20 feet ahead of him, then pulled up and stood in the road next to my bike. I had no idea about the braking power of a Sherman but I hoped it would be enough. Of course, that was assuming he would even try to halt.

The tank got bigger and bigger as it bore down on me and I'm pretty sure I closed my eyes at some point – when I opened them again I fully expected to have to dive left or right. In fact, I found myself looking up at the barrel of a bloody big cannon.

'Overcompensating for something are we, sir?'

'Fuck off, pig.'

I met the guy dozens of times after that and, although the tank got the occasional respray, that was pretty much typical of the conversations we had. He thought he was some kind of urban warrior but the truth was he annoyed everyone with his tank: pretending to break down and making everyone queue behind him.

Still, I counted the days when I ran into him as good ones. At least it meant I was above ground.

On another occasion in Myatts Field Estate, I didn't find a gun, but I did find a shell case – because my partner had been shot.

I didn't often go out with anyone else, partly because I was a loner and partly because I found people were more likely to share their life stories if they weren't outnumbered. Some DIs didn't like it, especially in Brixton, but I was comfortable. On this occasion I'd met up with a PC called Stevie and we were nosing about, as you do. We'd heard a bit of a commotion so turned a corner to investigate, just as the crack of a gunshot sounded.

'Christ, Stevie! Did you hear that?'

'Heard it? I felt it.'

When I looked back at him, he was touching his face where he'd felt the pellets from the shotgun pass.

Among other things I learned that night, the most telling lesson was how not to trust some of the media. This is the quote that Stevie gave a newspaper: 'I would expect the full weight of the law to be brought against the shooter.'

This is what the paper wrote: 'STEVE SAYS: HANG 'EM HIGH.'

Journalists, eh? I must say, I have worked with some very professional people who are a credit to their profession and the public, but some of the others – even when they're on your side, they're not on your side. It's their agenda or nothing, however big the smiles – or the lunch accounts. Identify the enemy ...

I did the journey to the centre of the earth most days for a year. Then, one day, an old face – Mick Wickerson, the DS from Epsom – brought a collar down. He was a detective inspector now, and he could not stop laughing that I was on the custody desk.

'You're not going to solve any murders down here, Clive, are you?'

'I might have a clue about the next one. *Sir.*'

He told me, once again, that I was wasted in uniform. More than that, he promised to tell the chief superintendent, a top bloke called Bert Aitchison. True to his word, Mick somehow swung it that I was allowed to go up for fresh air and work under him in CID.

Once again, it was uniform back in mothballs, and civvie suit here I come.

It was good to have a champion in Mick Wickerson, especially one who recognised I was too good a detective to be a costumed babysitter to ne'er-do-wells. And that was before he knew I'd been studying Sherlock Holmes.

But he hadn't just plucked me from the depths out of the kindness of his heart.

The police had never reclaimed Brixton after a second period of riots in 1985, triggered this time by the accidental death of Dorothy Groce by police hunting her son on a firearms charge. Murders, assaults, you name it, the numbers were sky high in SW9. In particular, they were being mullah-ed by 124 burglaries a week. Someone needed to get a grip of that.

'Think you can do it, Clive?'

'But I'm a uniform sergeant.'

'Well, now you're an honorary DS.'

I was put in charge of the burglary squad with a 'real' DS called Bubsy. Coming into a new team – especially fronting it up – can be tricky if you're replacing someone who didn't, let's say, want to leave the post, but the results of my predecessor spoke volumes: volumes of crime. The rest of the team, to be fair to them, were willing to give it a shot under me. They didn't like the bad figures any more than the brass did.

We all hit it off immediately. Bubsy was a great lad but was ex-Flying Squad and like all Sweeney Todd you needed a dictionary to follow a word he said. On my first day he came up with an action plan unlike anything I'd ever heard: 'Righto, Clive, diddly donk, bosch bosch, I'll tell you what we're going to do – we'll have a walk down the big house, we can see the face, cop a W, then we'll go down and spin him. And I'll tell you what, I reckon a right result's on the cards.'

I got the hang of it in the end. The chief superintendent never did. I remember another ex-Flying Squad, DS Birdy, sticking his head round Bert Aitchison's door and saying, 'Oh, guv, just to let you know, chummy's ducked his head and we're running him up the road.'

Bert just stared at him, then me.

'If I may, sir.' I translated: 'The robbery suspect has been interviewed in accordance with PACE, he's been charged in accordance with law and is now being transferred by police vehicle to court where he may be applying for bail.'

Easy, really.

As if Birdy and Bubsy weren't hard enough to understand, we were occasionally joined by another ex-Flying Squad called DC 'Daisy' Glenister – when he wasn't being plucked to front up a bigger CID job. He was an excellent officer and his colourful *bons mots* when he did make an appearance were always worth hearing.

On one collar: 'Clive, you've taken the dairy right off the top! We'll lay him down overnight and strap him in the morning. Crack on, my son.'

Obvious when you think about it.

Apart from Bubsy (a detective sergeant) and me (a police sergeant), we had eight DCs. But, like Birdy and Bubsy who came and went, any of those boys and girls were liable to be stolen with no notice. If there was a murder, someone would wander in with a clipboard and say, 'Right, I need a DS, I need three DCs, I need someone to do the card system,' and people would just disappear. My team of 12 could be half a dozen if there was a murder on – and, in Brixton in the 1980s, we were getting six or seven a year. This turnover had its advantages, though – it hadn't taken me long on the burglary squad to realise one DC was as wet as a bank holiday weekend in Scotland, so when the brass hooked him for a job I was actually happy.

Another time, Mick Wickerson came over and said, 'Clive, who is this bloke, this DC?'

I had been in Brixton about two years by then, but had never heard of the DC in question. I said, 'He's not our CID.'

'So why do I keep signing his duty statements then?'

A bit of digging revealed the DC in question had been acquired by Flying Squad for a series of robberies six years earlier and had never come back. Nobody on the team remembered him it was so long ago, but every week he still submitted his duty statements to his original department and somebody signed it – as well as the overtime.

We made some cracking progress on burglaries. One collar alone coughed for 280 jobs. Just having him locked up overnight took a one-man crime wave off the streets for 24 hours.

It helped that the team really responded to my way of working. One DC, a great lad we called Taff, clocked up his hundredth burglary clear-up while I was there. In fact, we were able to split them up and submit them over three weeks so our figures looked good for longer.

A lot of sergeants are happy to sit behind a desk all day, especially if they're got a big team working for them, like I had. But that wasn't what had got me noticed, so why stop? And, more importantly, it wasn't what I was good at. These days I see a lot of young sergeants and inspectors whose whole ambition in the police is to never leave their office. One inspector said to me: 'I don't go out any more. I'm a manager now. I could take my skills and manage Sainsbury's.'

Well, I couldn't. Unless someone's murdered in the bread aisle, my skills and Sainsbury's are not a natural fit.

But what I can do is talk to people, listen to them and put two and two together. You'd be surprised how rare a commodity that is in the police. I don't think Hendon teaches that terribly well, which doesn't help. The 'them and us' attitude that some in the Job have starts there, and they never get over it. If they did, they'd see it actually makes solving the odd burglary a damned sight easier. I wasn't quite as prolific as Taff, but I certainly tried to lead by example. I honestly believe the style of management in the Met stifles the amazing talent at their disposal. Some of the DCs and DSs, PCs and PSs are quite outstanding.

So, why were we so much more successful than other teams? Sometimes it was because we approached things in a more intelligent way. Sometimes we went where others weren't prepared to. Other times it was just hard work that got lucky.

One of the first burglaries I dealt with personally taught me a lesson. I went to a house and the whole place had been stripped bare: no carpets, no curtains, no furnishings. There was a little lad sobbing, 'Our telly, our telly,' so I said, 'It's going to take a while but we need to make a list of everything that was taken.'

Once again, the lad said, 'Our telly, our telly.'

'Yes, all right, son, but what else?'

'Nothing else,' the mum said. 'They only took the telly.'

That was an eye-opener for all sorts of reasons – but, number one, I got to see how some first-generation immigrants were living behind closed doors. It was explained to me by a second-generation lad: 'Remember, Sergeant, when you're used to living in a mud hut, just having four walls and a roof over your head is a step up. Many people have never seen curtains, carpets and cushions before.'

'But they've never seen tellies, either, and they soon get one of those.'

'You can't stand in the way of progress.'

What I didn't know about cultural differences I made up for in street nous. It didn't take me long to track down the toe-rag who'd stolen the Sony 32". He was a local druggie

– not a breed of criminal known for covering their tracks. Unfortunately, he'd already flogged the set by the time I found him: it was worth about £500 and he'd got a tenner for it. And given that little kid a harsh lesson in life in the process. A very typical story in inner London.

A lot of our burglaries were drug-inspired. In the 1980s, Brixton was known as the drugs capital of London. The users took what they could, then either sold it way under market value or traded it for a wrap, or whatever. When you're an addict, your bargaining power is limited so the deals were always shocking. Just as bad, from a practical policing point of view, was the amount of paperwork those cases took up for virtually no reward. It was a time when magistrates believed in rehabilitation punishments rather than incarceration and so, even with a guilty tag, chummy would be out on the streets before I'd got back to my desk – and back in three more times that week. The irony was, if we hadn't been so successful I wouldn't have had so much paperwork.

It was around then that I decided to forget the small fry and go for the big fish. Section 22 of the Theft Act says it's a crime to handle stolen goods. More importantly, clause b. says anyone guilty of doing so could get up to 14 years. Now that was a stretch worth filling in the forms for.

Handlers, fences, market traders who liked things off the backs of lorries: we targeted them all. If the outlet disappeared, surely the rate of burglaries would go down as well?

It did.

I'm not sure I would have worked that out if I hadn't been out and about myself. In fact, I'm not sure the so-called 'managers' back at the nick would ever have reached that conclusion.

Another lesson I learned that also had a massive impact on our arrest rate definitely came as a result of being hands-on – because it was actually a burglar I was arresting who taught me it.

I was marching him back to the car when I said, 'It was a bit risky, wasn't it, robbing the house next door to the one you'd just done?'

'That's normally the safest place to be,' he said.

'How do you work that out?'

'Think about it – if you get a 999 for a burglar alarm you tear up the streets, you tear up the garden, you tear up all the parks and bushes looking for the villain. When do you ever go and search other houses?'

He was absolutely spot on, and it changed the way I approached all burglaries from then on.

'Still,' I said, 'it didn't do you much good tonight.'

'Nah. *Bastard*.'

Brixton had such a problem with crime and not just drugs. As well as the burglary squad, there was a separate robbery team. A robbery is where you use violence to steal: if someone walks over to you and grabs your phone, that is theft; if you are holding it and he punches you on the nose to get it, it becomes robbery. Section 8 of the Theft Act.

Late one Friday night, nursing my tenth coffee and wishing I was out doing scene visits with the lads, a call was put through from the CAD – computer aided despatch – room.

'Sorry, Clive,' the operator said. 'You're the only one here.'

He flicked a switch and suddenly, on the other end of the line, was the plummiest voice I had ever heard. Still have ever heard, in fact. But it was what he said that got my attention: 'My name is the Right Honourable Philip Harvey,' he said. 'And there has been a murder.'

'Right!' Papers were pushed aside, coffee gulped and I grabbed a pen.

But before I could ask a question, His Right Honourableness said, 'What rank are you?'

'I'm a sergeant.'

'Well, that's no good. I need to speak to a superintendent. Minimum.'

'If you don't mind me saying, sir, it is Friday night – where am I going to find a superintendent at this time? I will come round, but please don't touch anything before I get there.'

'Very well.'

Mervan Road is slap bang between Coldharbour Lane, Effra Road and Railton Road, in those days the Bermuda Triangle of crime. A murder there did not exactly surprise me. But the geezer who opened the door did.

From the outside, Number 82 was a narrow little place – not social housing but nothing special. Inside it was like Doctor Who had dropped Buckingham Palace in there. Time Lord technology.

It's bigger on the inside ...

'Thank God you're here, Sergeant. This way!'

Now, you don't just turn up to a murder on your bike. Not in Brixton. I had Homicide and the full range of hats bombing in there too, trying to cover all possibilities before I got to the bottom of what had gone on. By the time Lord Harvey led me up the stairs there was a queue behind me.

We reached a first-floor drawing room, which really showed how posh he was, and the lord stood back. He was in a bad way. Understandable, of course.

'It's in there. The body's in there.'

This was where my expertise ended, but as I walked into the room there were some things even I couldn't miss.

It's a fucking rabbit.

I don't believe it.

And it was. The murder 'victim' was a fluffy bunny. Sad, I grant you, but worthy of six uniform, four CID and me on a Friday night? In Lord Harvey's world, apparently so. And he'd have had the commissioner there if he could.

I thanked the murder team and said, 'I think I should be able to handle this from here.'

Lord Harvey's world, it turned out, was not a place I was too familiar with. There were pictures around the room of him as a kid next to the old king, and he even said they were related. He also said he owned all the airspace over Switzerland: if you wanted to fly a helicopter out of Zurich, you had to pay him. Did I believe him? Looking at the luxury pile he was living in, it wasn't that far-fetched. If anything, the most unbelievable aspect of his life was what had led to the 'murder' of little Snowy. He had befriended a Hells Angel, as all members of the aristocracy do, and left him to look after the house while he toured Europe in a converted horsebox. This man had turned out to be not so Angelic and had sold all the lord's furniture to fund wild parties.

'Prostitutes and drugs, officer – in my house!'

I could well believe it. On the table, next to a giant candelabra that would have made Liberace jealous, was an elaborate pipe still stuffed with a white substance.

'We'll get this tested,' I said.

'I don't think that will be necessary, Mr Driscoll. That's a candle snuffer.'

I think his lordship would have let the furniture go but the fact that the Hells Angel had killed, skinned and eaten most of his rabbit had got him thirsty for justice. He gave me a list of numbers he'd found in the house in the man's handwriting and I said I would follow it up.

I'd been out of my depth alone on a homicide shout, but tracking stolen items? That was something I could do.

The first number I rang was answered by a woman. 'Hello, who is that?'

'Sorry to bother you, ma'am. My name is DS Driscoll. I'm on the burglary squad at Brixton.'

'Oh, the burglary squad?'

'That's right. I wanted to ask you a few questions.'

'Has someone been naughty?' Her voice was rather odd – low and breathy.

'It does look that way.'

'Have they been very naughty?'

This was getting weird. But that's the lottery of phoning people late at night.

'I wanted to ask if you have ever been to a party hosted by...', and I proceeded to give details of the man in question.

'Who did you say you were?'

I told her and she said, 'Can I call you back?'

I gave her my number and a minute later my phone rang.

'I checked your number with Directory Enquiries. You really are burglary squad, aren't you?' the woman said, although it wasn't so dreamy-sounding now.

'Well, I did say that.'

'Do you know what number you rang?'

'Well, yours.'

'It's a fantasy line. Men ring it at all hours pretending to be whoever they like and I pretend to like them for it. You're the third Old Bill I've had tonight!'

How was I going to explain *that* number on my phone records?

Through that woman I found the man I was looking for in Cologne, where he told me that his lordship was a nasty piece of work and had had it coming. Maybe he had a helicopter in Switzerland, I don't know. But he told me where every single piece of furniture had been sold and I got the entire lot back, right down to a tiny little Masonic ball.

But that wasn't the last I heard of Lord Harvey. A few months later, I responded to a call on my police radio. The last voice I expected at the other end was his.

'Is that you, Mr Driscoll? I have tied myself to an old oak tree to stop them cutting it down.'

Eccentric does not begin to describe it.

For all its bizarre origins, The Case Of The Murdered Rabbit had led to another successful win for my burglary squad. We really were flying. So much so that Bert Aitchison came in one day with a clutch of files. They turned out to be our numbers for the month.

'You've got a way about you, Clive, I'll give you that,' he said. 'But I think you're wasted here.'

'I'm not going back to the custody suite, am I, sir?'

'Not unless you annoy me. No, I've got a proposition.'

I was all ears. To have the chief superintendent come to me like this was an honour.

Bert said, 'Look, Clive, the police have lost Brixton – you know that and I know that. But there's a chance to win it back and I'm betting on you to do it.'

'Sir?'

'We need a community squad. You love a joke, you love a laugh, you love talking to people.'

All of that was true – and it was great to be recognised for it. To think how I'd fought to be someone else at Hendon, and when I started at Sutton …!

'What I want you to do,' he continued, 'is go out into the pubs and clubs of Brixton, make friends among the people, win their confidence, listen to them, learn what they want from us and then do your damnedest to deliver it. I'll give you a team, I'll give you a budget and I'll give you the freedom to follow whatever leads you see fit. Just bring Brixton back into the fold.'

'Crikey, guv. Anything else?'

'There is, as it happens. We're *personae non grata* in Lambeth Council. Make appointments, make in-roads, make friends. Get the council talking to the police. It's a joke if we can't do that.'

It was a big speech and a big shock to me. It sounded all a bit too good to be true, if I'm honest. A small part of me even wondered if it was an elaborate prank. But I was definitely interested – especially if the other option was returning to my subterranean bunker.

'Where do I work from?'

'You get your own office.'

'I hate being indoors. Do I have to spend much time there?'

'If you do I'll move you myself.'

'Then you've got yourself a deal.'

CHAPTER NINE

Just Make It Better

Bert Aitchison wasn't joking when he said we had lost Brixton. Because of the riots in 1981 and then again in 1985, the idea that the police were an extension of the Conservative Party had developed and there was deep hatred for the Job. So much police work centres on talking to people – whether it's victims, witnesses, experts or suspects – that if you're getting the cold shoulder by the entire community, solving or preventing anything becomes an impossibility. In Brixton, it had even got to the stage where victims of quite serious crimes would not dial 999. People had completely lost faith in the system. Even hospitals wouldn't talk to a uniform. If you wanted to be a criminal in the late 1980s, Brixton was the place to head. If you couldn't grow your drugs business there, you were using too much of your own gear.

How the hell was one man and his team supposed to make a difference?

To give myself the best possible start, I decided to swot up on other places that had been 'lost', or at least had wandered off for a bit. First stop was Tottenham. One of our own, PC Keith Blakelock, had been murdered and near decapitated on the Broadwater Farm Estate during the 1985 riots. Having been in Brixton in 1981, I could see how that was always on the cards but I wanted to see for myself where the trouble had begun, how it had been handled and how the community had been repaired – if it had. During this time, in fact, I visited every single place where the Old Bill had had a serious bundle: St Pauls in Bristol, Lascelles Road in Birmingham and Granby Street in Liverpool.

The riots in Toxteth, Liverpool, had been on a par with Brixton and that area, if I'm honest, was the only place where I felt actually uncomfortable – even though I wasn't in uniform, I'd had nothing to do with the policing up there and many years had passed since the trouble. Scousers are slow to forget. As soon as I set foot inside a club on Granby Street, a small woman came flying at me with a pair of scissors.

How does she know I'm Old Bill?

She didn't, but I was wearing a tie and that was what she objected to.

Snip.

'It's a bit of a custom round here, like,' she said, almost smiling, as she pinned it to the wall alongside about 50 others.

All previously belonging to undercover coppers, I assumed.

My initial response when I'd seen the scissors had been: *She's going to take my head off!* That was how far Granby Street had fallen off the grid. I'd just assumed she was going to stab me because locals and coppers did not get on.

I learned a lot about the different cultures everywhere I went. Outside London, only Birmingham, with its high levels of Hindu, Pakistani and India citizens, had real experience of ethnic conflict, most recently in the wake of the recent publication of *The Satanic Verses.*

One Indian community leader I met was very keen to talk on that subject: 'Have you heard the title of Salman Rushdie's new book?'

I'm not a big reader ...

'Buddha's A Fat Bastard!'

That tickled him and, I have to admit, me. But on a serious note it showed how one man's offence is another man's humour and vice versa.

On the back of the research I was doing, Bert Aitchison told me he was going to recommend me for a course. It was called Building Community Relationships, which, to be fair, sounded helpful. What I really liked about it was that it was targeted at the upper echelons of the regional forces.

Imagine their faces when a lowly DS strolls in.

The course was four weeks long and for a lot of that time we would be based at Chesterfield nick, but with field trips and studies all over the region. The other men on the course were all decent enough and only pulled rank on me about a dozen times. A day. Each. I knew they were serious because they all came from the places I'd visited: there was a chief inspector from Merseyside, a DI from Birmingham, one from Bristol, and one from every other hotspot. And there we were, all thrown together in Derbyshire.

Bearing in mind it was a course teaching how to get along in diverse communities, I was appalled at how many prejudices and assumptions I came across – and they were just the ones aimed at me.

Day one, and I was in the briefing room, having been told we'd all be going out to study the effects of the police on a place called Shirebrook. It would be a very good case to study: it had been badly affected due to pit closures, and was not a million miles from Nottingham, an area where there had been real aggro with the police during the miners' strike. Some of the things that had gone on wouldn't have been out of place in a gang flick. Nasty stuff, from both sides.

The door opened and a senior officer walked up to the bloke in charge and said, 'Whatever you do, don't let the Met man go anywhere near the Workingmen's Club. You know what they're like.'

I was sitting two feet away from him. I heard every word. When he'd gone, I asked, 'What's that all about?'

'We know what you Met lot are like with a drink.'

Seriously? On a 'getting along' course?

Shirebrook was an old mining town decimated by the closure of the pits: when they went, that was the end of life as the town knew it. For generations the whole town had depended on pit workers for everything: bakers, builders, cooks and cabbies – everyone owed their livelihoods to the cash put into circulation by the miners. With the tap turned off, the place was a ghost town.

Bearing in mind we were on a fact-finding mission, and the mission was to investigate inequality, I couldn't help noticing it started right at Shirebrook nick. It was a typical, snoozy village outfit that probably saw as much crime in a month as Brixton got in an afternoon. And because of that, they didn't get the resources we had. This was highlighted when we realised that, when they knew we were coming – all the inspectors and chief inspectors, supposedly, from the big metropolises – they had ordered new chairs and tables for us. You know how the Queen thinks the whole world smells of fresh paint because everywhere gets tarted up before she visits? It was like that – although only in the public areas. I don't know about Her Majesty, but I like to wander off. When I went into the custody suite I saw them hide the buckets that they used to catch the rain dripping through the roof.

So, even the police were affected by the missing mine money.

Shirebrook still had a population, and there were shops, but the people looked unhappy and the shops were either boarded up, drab or empty. But there was a bar, opposite the police station as it happened. The sign outside had seen better days but it was undoubtedly the working men's club.

Well, well, well …

Shirebrook had put on a show, and I had found it very helpful to hear what had worked and what hadn't when it had come to policing disenfranchised locals through difficult times.

No question, I'd be putting a lot of it to the test in Brixton, thank you very much.

But then they went and ruined it: 'Right, you've got one hour for lunch. There's food in the canteen but, if you do go for a wander, on no account go in the working men's club.'

'Not this again,' I said. 'Just because I'm Met doesn't mean I get special treatment.'

'I'm not just talking to you, DS Driscoll. If any officer steps one foot inside there will be serious problems, which I don't want to deal with.'

If you think I'm taking that rule back to Brixton, you've got another think coming.

Even if the club had a supposed reputation back then, the idea of there being a 'no go' area for coppers was abhorrent to me. Unnatural, even. Once you start saying there are places police can't go, you may as well hand over the keys to the prisons because you've lost the game.

As soon as we were dismissed, I headed straight across the road. To my eyes it looked like every other northern working men's club – miserable. Inside, there were about seven old men, grey from the lack of fresh air in the smoke-filled room, all sitting quietly nursing their halves of bitter. If depression had a face, they were wearing it.

I walked up to the bar and said, 'Hello, mate, I am DS Clive Driscoll, Metropolitan Police Service' – the full formal intro. I continued, 'We're up here doing a study on Shirebrook and I understand there is a bit of ill-feeling between the police and the locals—?'

Over to you …

The barman spoke without looking at me. 'We've no ill-feeling for the Met,' he said. 'You were what you were when you came up. You had jobs to do and you did them. It's that lot over there, across the street, who pretend to be your mates and then stab you in the back, who we won't forgive.'

I said, 'Sir, can I buy you a drink?'

'You can have one on the house.'

The barman proceeded to tell me some horrific stories about the local police operation during the strikes. As the weeks had turned into months, the miners' families had been starving because there had been no money coming in. For the police, however, it had been overtime city. And they had let the strikers know it.

'I saw men, friends of my father's, stand outside this club waving £50 notes at the miners. Taunting them because they were earning. And now look at the town. We're all fucked. Even them.'

I thought back to the buckets and nodded.

I don't think there were any winners in the whole episode, but the barman sharing the story with me, a copper, was a small step in the right direction. And when the door opened again and the rest of my course came gingerly in, he was just as generous.

He even had a few words of advice: 'Judge people as individuals, not groups,' he said. 'There's nothing wrong with individuals.'

'Blimey,' I said, 'you should be running our course. That's more sense than I've heard all day.'

As we left the club, I still had a drink in my hand. Before I could spin back to return the glass a chauffeur-driven car pulled up opposite. Inside was the same senior officer as before – the bloke who *was* running our course – and the one who'd told me to stay away from the club.

Everyone else dived back in the pub – the cowards. But I just raised my glass and said, 'All right, guv? Cheers.'

The lesson about judging people not groups stuck with me. I'd already been tarred by the Met's so-called reputation once: on day two it happened again.

I was being driven around by the local area car in Chesterfield. And the second I had stepped into the panda the driver had said, 'I don't like the Met.'

'Why is that?'

'Because you're all bent, you all take backhanders. You give us all a bad name.'

It's fair to say the next few minutes were quite quiet.

We were going down a country road when all of a sudden he spun off to the left and we bumped our way down a track to a farm. Wordlessly, he got out of the car and went into the farmhouse, coming out two minutes later laden with massive bags of vegetables. He put them in the boot and off we went. About 20 minutes later, he was loading up with four trays full of eggs and a load of bacon. The boot was full by this time, so they went on the backseat.

I said, 'What's all this for?'

'It's for the lads at the nick. The farmers give it to us to keep us on side.'

'You can't get that in a brown envelope, can you?' I replied after a pause.

It's all about perception, isn't it?

The best bit of the course, without question, was when I was given a family to shadow. The father was a mechanic and the mother was a housewife – they'd come over from India just before their two daughters were born.

Being embedded with them for two days taught me more than the rest of the month with the instructors.

For example, it taught me about my own prejudices. It makes sense that different cultures do things differently, but when the family ate their meals with their hands I had a problem doing the same. Then I thought, *You eat fish and chips like that, Clive, don't you?* and so off I went. I even got used to sitting on the floor.

The kids were angels. My heart went out to the younger one when she told me, 'I hate it when I get called "Paki" – I'm from India!'

At the end of the course I met a social worker who had accompanied a busload of Shirebrook kids on a trip to the seaside at Blackpool. This was a massive treat for them because, without money, none of them had holidays. As it turned out, in fact, none of them had ever even left the village.

They were only about two miles into the journey when they apparently started saying, 'Are we there yet?'

'Is that the sea?'

'Is that the beach?'

In a similar fashion, I knew some Brixton estate kids could go a whole year without seeing the Thames, just 20 minutes away. It wasn't much different, really.

As for everything else I had learned, I couldn't wait to put it into practice.

Bert Aitchison wasn't wrong about me being given an office, although he wasn't totally truthful either. I did have a couple of inches to call my own but it wasn't exactly prime real estate. If you came in the nick's back gate and you looked to the right, there was a stable. If you looked to the left that was my office.

The police horse and I used to look at each other, me thinking, *What do you do all day?*

And the horse probably thinking, *A little bit more than you, actually.*

This horse was the Met's champion but he was lazy: he refused to go out in the rain, however much his rider cajoled him. He reminded me of the best homebeat I ever worked with, PC Bob Lister. He only went out in the dry as well.

At least I had that over the horse – if I'm honest, I was very rarely in.

The bike was, once more, a godsend. I started sticking my nose in places again, usually the type of haunts where white faces, particularly ones wearing blue helmets, never went. I don't know if people were scared of me or amused by my cheek, but I went everywhere and I got the same reaction: usually there'd be a 'Fucking pig' or a 'Fucking white pig' within earshot, but people tended to do as they were told.

On one occasion a young woman swore at me so I said, 'What have I ever done to you?'

She said, 'I hate the police.'

I said, 'Funnily enough, I've just got back from visiting police stations up north. Would it make you feel better to learn they hate us too?'

In the early stages of my community squad work, I wasn't really looking to do any tidying up – that would come later. To start, I just wanted to get the lie of the land; I wanted to check out the nooks and crannies of the area so that when I did start yapping to people I would know where, if not what, they were talking about.

Often, just being a presence in certain situations is enough – little scuffles or deals stopped when I arrived. It was cleaning up the streets in tiny steps. Or, in my case, tiny pedals.

You'll only get so far on the streets, though – the real gen is inside, in the clubs and pubs. That's where people open up. Not always about stuff you want to hear, but you can't win them all. When I discovered a place called the Domino Social Club on Coldharbour Lane, I knew I had my starting place.

Forget race and nationality – what old fella does not like to share a yarn over a jar?

I was bang on, as it goes. I'd had a positive feeling about the Domino. There were other haunts, but they had made me pause a second on the threshold before opening the door. So much was riding on me not getting bottled when I went in, it had to be perfect.

Apart from the first visit, the Domino was a great place for me to start. It wasn't an auspicious beginning: I went in and everything stopped, like in an old Western – I just needed the ol' saloon piano to get a bullet from someone and that would have topped it off. Even though I wasn't in uniform, I've got an Old Bill type of face, I'm convinced of it, so there had been no point dressing up. In any case, that would have defeated the object. I was there to a) show that the police can go anywhere, and b) show we wanted to listen.

I went straight to the bar, about 20 pairs of eyes on me. I said hello and introduced myself, of course, because it's the polite thing. Then I clocked the barman and I said, 'I fancy a game of dominoes. Who's your best player?'

A bit of competition opens negotiations very quickly, I find. By the end of the afternoon I'd had about 40 games, lost most of them, but I'd reached out to a section of the community that I don't think had ever spoken to a copper, let alone played board games with one. I didn't get anyone to talk, not that time, but a little seed was sown.

When I left I said I'd be back and no one took particular umbrage at that, and so a couple of days later I returned. Once again, I left with spots in front of my eyes. But the old men and women were starting to open up. Another visit, I reckoned, and one or two of them might even have started to trust me. I hoped so, anyway. I was enjoying myself.

The Coach and Horses was one of Lloyd Leon's establishments. He was a local councillor – later Lambeth's first black mayor – which added to the sense of oppression when I walked in. But, as in Shirebrook, I didn't believe there should be places where police were afraid to go. And, sure enough, over time, the Coach and Horses became another place – like the Railton Arms and dozens of previously 'no police' boozers – where I would sit with a newspaper and drink, and people would know they could find me. If they just wanted to say hello or fuck off, it didn't matter: in between all that, I'd meet someone who had a problem. And that, if you don't mind me saying, is what I was there for.

One of my first chats was with an old boy who lived in Calidore Close. It was a block of flats off Ednymion Road and, even from the outside, it wasn't the sort of place anyone dreamed of living. But this grandpa had bigger problems. His daughter lived there and she was being hassled by men looking for prostitutes.

'Why are men looking for prostitutes there?'

'Don't you know nothing, boy? Calidore Close is full of them.'

'Leave it with me,' I said. I folded my newspaper and headed out to see if my bike was still there – never a given. It was, though, so I jumped on and headed back to the nick with a mission.

One of the flats in Calidore Close, it turned out, housed a brothel you would not have sent your enemy too. Prostitutes aside, it was nasty. The beds were places that dogs would have thought twice about before settling down – dirty, wet, stained, filthy – and the blokes who went in were exactly the same. We had the pleasure of housing an Irish lad overnight in the cells once. He'd already soiled himself when we picked him up and then he vomited in our custody. No sooner had he been let out, however, he'd headed straight over to Calidore Close.

And they'd let him in.

I spoke to dozens of neighbours over several days. They all complained about drunk blokes shouting and swearing or, worse, urinating up against their doors before going in next door. Noise and smell were other factors. A lot of the women going to and fro were harassed by drunk punters thinking they were prostitutes; one or two had been physically threatened for not putting out. It was a dangerous place.

I decided to pay the flat a visit. I knocked on the door and went in, as a matter of courtesy, to let them know I was, in all honesty, going to get them shut down. I made sure the punters who were there knew I'd seen them, and that they were to tell their friends I'd be watching. I told the women I could help them out of that hell and I told the pimps they had to shut down their operation or face the consequences.

They all told me to fuck off.

In a situation like that, the law is not as clear-cut as it could be. For a start, being a prostitute in itself is not illegal. Visiting a prostitute is not in itself illegal either. Visiting a prostitute who has been 'forced', visibly or not, *is* a crime but honestly, without a girl coming forward, that claim is dead before you get it to the courts. Even something as apparently nailed on as running a brothel when the entire neighbourhood knows that's what you are doing is a slippery one to hold. Without a client or a girl to corroborate the suspicion, you've got nothing. The clients won't talk for obvious reasons.

As for the lasses, I could not find a single girl to testify against her boss. Even if he was beating them, he was probably their supplier of charlie or other essentials, so they were unlikely to want that tap turned off, whatever the cost.

Some jobs have you banging your head against a wall and this was one of them. I could see the crime going on right in front of me. I could see the girls being victimised and, on a much wider scale, I could see hundreds of innocent Brixtonites suffering as well. And I was about as much use as a glass hammer.

I needed to box clever. But how?

Then it dawned on me. The place was a cesspit, and if I couldn't get the pimps on trafficking or running a house of ill-repute, I could get them on their poor housework. I managed to persuade someone at Lambeth who didn't hate Old Bill to send in a hygiene team and they found insects, rats – you name it.

'No choice,' they said, 'but to evacuate the building while we fumigate it.'

I managed to make sure that the fumigation took long enough that they never opened for business again. It wasn't the outcome I'd planned and those pimps and clients were still at large, but I'd answered the call of the community. Calidore Close was now a lot safer. I'm still proud of that today.

My triumph with the rat catchers didn't exactly make front-page news, but enough locals heard about it to start coming to me with their own stories of soliciting blighting their lives.

I got a complaint about another group of girls operating out of Acre Road. It was the same story: other tenants were living through hell as a result of the unsavoury clientele. I decided I'd stick my head around the door but this time it wasn't so straightforward – Lambeth Council, in its wisdom, had started installing security doors in blocks of flats, which was top-notch for keeping out aggressors but not so handy if you're the police trying to have a snoop around the walkways.

When I buzzed a few of the flats something about my tone gave the game away.

'You're Old Bill, I can tell.'

'No, I'm not. I just want to come up.'

'You're lying. Fuck off.'

I never claimed to be the greatest actor but Richard Clark, a young lad on the team, reckoned he was. He was also black and his colour, he said, would be like having a skeleton key to any of these door locks.

'Stand back and be amazed,' he promised.

We all stood ready to charge the door as soon as it opened as Richie hit the intercom button. When a wary voice answered I nodded at Richie to go for it. I nearly wet myself at what I heard.

'Blud! It's me, Richie, let me in, schooldays ...'

It was the worst Jamaican patois I had ever heard.

'Jesus, Richie, if I'd wanted to hear Chalky I'd have given Jim Davidson a shout.'

The girls upstairs clearly were about as impressed as I was.

'Fuck off,' one said. 'I know you're a pig.'

Funnily enough, we never did get in.

Helping prostitutes who don't want to be helped is the devil's own job. There was one group who used to take their 'friends' around the back of Iceland. I don't know if it was for a laugh, but when I turned up one January night – it wasn't just the shop that was freezing – one of the girls thanked me for caring about her welfare by offering me a freebie.

I couldn't see how it was humanly possible, even if I'd wanted to. 'I can't feel my hands let alone anything else.'

I struck up quite a relationship with some of the women. Even though me turning up was bad for business, they appreciated the fact that I had their best interests at heart. When I got a few complaints about the streetwalkers at the top of Brixton Hill, I leapt on my bike and pedalled up. The trouble was, even in civvies I stuck out like a sore thumb and as soon as I got close they all jumped on a bus and went down to the high street. So, I turned around and freewheeled back down. By the time I'd got there, though, they were back up at the top of the hill again. The only way I caught up with any of them was if the buses didn't run on time – which in London is pretty much every time.

After my fourth trudge up the hill a lovely woman, a motherly type called Mary Malone, said to me, 'We're all grateful for what you're trying to do, Clive. If you don't caution me, you could come back to my flat—?'

I replied, 'Mary, after four climbs up this hill I can barely get my leg over this bike, let alone you ...!'

As much as I hated what Mary did for a living – mainly because of who she did it with – I had to concede she was an adult who knew her own mind.

Not everyone was that lucky, though.

Off Brixton Hill was a block of flats called Dumbarton Court. One particular apartment in there was done out exactly like the home in a Hollywood B-movie. I knocked on the door one day, and it was opened by a really sweet kid. Youthful-looking, but a lot of these women dressed young, so I was disturbed but not overly so. In any case, she seemed quite happy to see us and invited us in. I think she was bored.

'Do you want a cup of tea, officer?' she asked.

'That would be lovely.' It would give me more time to search the gaff.

I followed her into the kitchen and when she opened the fridge I saw that it was filled with nothing but Wagon Wheels. My kids loved those – which set the alarm bells ringing.

'Excuse me, love, but do you mind me asking how old you are?'

'How old do you want me to be?'

Oh, dear ...

She was 14 and had been working for who knew how long. Her pimp – her boyfriend she called him – had installed her in the flat and said the way she could prove she loved him was by turning tricks. At an impressionable age, she'd agreed.

I have to say she seemed happy. She wouldn't hear a bad word against her boyfriend and to this day I view her as one of my failures. I couldn't get him on anything – not even sleeping with her himself – and she wouldn't admit to a thing.

Not all prostitutes were so sweet, however. For a while there was a trend where a bloke would pick up a prostitute, be taken around the back somewhere by her and then, before anything had started, two blokes would come along to give the punter a right hiding. They'd do him over, take his wallet and walk off with the girl. The last thing the guy was going to do was report it – nine times out of ten, he was married.

Again, it was a concerned citizen who pointed me in the direction of all this. I just had to wait for the right night and then, as if by magic, a car pulled up, the tom and her new friend got all lovey-dovey ... before three 'erbs appeared with sticks – and we nabbed the lot of them.

Some of these women did actually seem to have a handle on their situation. I'm not one to judge, and if a person says they're doing what they want to be doing, as long as it's legal and it doesn't endanger anyone else, each to his or her own devices. But some girls you could see were not in control of their pocket money, let alone their future. I met one household of girls who all promised me they were there of their own accord but something didn't smell right – and for once it wasn't the soft furnishings. I discovered that, unless each girl turned six tricks a shift, she was beaten by the pimp. I told them all that I could help them – I could stop him touching them again and I could get them out of that sex trap. Not one of them stepped forward. So I did the next best thing and confronted the pimp. I told him that I was going to put him out of business because I don't like men who hit women.

'Who says I hit women?'

'Their black eyes and fractures are a pretty good steer.'

'Who says I did it?'

'If you didn't, then you should be stopping whoever did do it. Either way, I'm blaming you.'

'You have no proof.'

He was right, I didn't. Not on the record, anyway. And so I decided to act off the record just a little bit …

'You're right, I can't prove you touched these women,' I told him. 'But what I can do is check your bank accounts. I can check your numbers tally with Her Majesty's Customs and Excise. I can go all round your motor and make sure it's roadworthy and have it scrapped if there's as much as a scratch on a tyre. Let's not beat around the bush – if I hear of one of these women so much as cracking a toenail, I will have you.'

The pimp stared at me. 'Yeah, yeah, talk the talk, policeman.'

I wasn't sure I'd got through, but the trouble with his girls stopped.

Is that sort of action in the Hendon handbook? No, it's not. Do I feel guilty about making threats to a member of the public? In this instance, no, I do not. And I would do it again. In fact, I did. Many, many times.

Bert Aitchison had been very clear in a very vague way: 'Do what you need to in Brixton, Clive. Just make it better.' And that was what I was trying to do, one incident at a time.

Getting to know an entire community wasn't going to happen overnight. Getting to know the major players, however, could.

There were plenty of characters in Brixton in the late 80s. Some were villains, some wanted to be villains, some were just annoying. There was a family called the Irvings who came up on the radar very early on in my fact-finding days – and then kept surfacing again with disturbing frequency. Ralphie Irving was the bloke who liked to park his car in bus stops. There was a mob of them and, rumour had it, they were the number-one gang in Lambeth. They were massive, fingers in all sorts of pies, but, like there often is with these families, the mum was a real matriarch who ruled with a rolling pin of iron. If I came across one of her kids up to no good I'd drag him back home and let her deal with it.

There were plenty of families I helped like that. I ran across a load of trouble once and saw one young kid who looked out of place among the rest of them.

'What's your name, son?'

'Adrian.'

'Where do you live?'

'Endymion Road.'

'How old are you?'

'Eighteen.'

'Of course you are. And I play in goal for Fulham.'

'All right, I'm fourteen.'

I didn't like the idea of a kid that age out on the streets on his own. Not in the company he was keeping. There were area cars bombing along to sort out the masses so I said, 'Right, Adrian, you and me are going for a little walk.'

And I marched him home.

His mum, a woman as large and as loud as she was amazing, gave him what for and me a smothering hug for bringing him home.

That was my first introduction to 'Big Marie'. I got to know Marie well over the years, through Adrian mostly, I'm sad to say. I'd call in for a cup of tea which she'd make with condensed milk that was so sweet you couldn't swallow it. I think that was just her way of making you choose to have a glass of her special punch instead. I don't know what she put in it, but one cup and you were happy for a week.

Every few months over the next couple of years I would find myself delivering Adrian to his mum, either on foot or in one of the cars. Let's not be naïve; he mixed with the wrong people, he was involved in fights, skirmishes and sometimes there were knives involved. But throwing the book at kids isn't right in my eyes. Half the time their parents don't know where they are, so if I could put them all together I thought that might be a good start.

I don't know if it was luck or experience – we'd have to check with the Little General – but more often than not I used to turn up just as things were about to start. You would have this massive shouting and hollering going on in the richest, thickest Jamaican patois, and I would roll up, the Cockney Columbo, and say, 'Woah, lads, the world is too full of aggro for you lot to carry on. Turn it in or you're all nicked.' Then I would see Adrian and some other lads who I knew and say, 'Right, boys, you're coming with me.' Not once did Adrian kick up, and not once did the opposition gangs kick up, funnily enough.

Unfortunately, I couldn't always get there in time to save him. When he was 19 Adrian was shot at a club in Wandsworth. The fact he'd strayed off my beat doesn't make me feel any better about not preventing it.

Big Marie was destroyed by that, of course. The worst thing was, she knew who did it. They told her they'd done it. She told me and I told the murder squad but there was no evidence. The dozen or so witnesses in the club just disappeared off the face of the earth, or lost all power of recollection, when the murder team came calling.

It didn't make much impression in the papers or on the news. I don't recall seeing even an inch in the press. I was surprised at the time. But, I realised, that was the lot of black lads where the media was concerned. A white boy gets offed, it's 'Hold the front page'; a black lad goes the same way and people acted like it was some sort of comeuppance – as though all black kids were gang victims waiting to happen. Adrian made poor choices but he was a nice kid and he did not deserve to die.

The media could have done a lot more to bring the boy's murderers to justice, I felt. And could the police have done more too? Were we guilty of leaping to the same conclusions about the value of a black lad's life? I know I wasn't, but how could I be sure about other policemen working Adrian's case? In light of what was to come, it makes you wonder.

There's no doubt that race relations are not helped by this sort of crime, even if it is 'black on black'. One of the bravest things I think I've ever done is attend that boy's wake. Like the majority of places on Endymion Road, Marie's house was a typical three-bed terrace. Not small, but not designed for the amount of mourners crammed in. I don't think I'm exaggerating when I say there must have been 300 people in there. The body heat was incredible – and that was from outside. The place was already heaving when I turned up and, I admit, there were a few antagonistic faces in the gathered throng. I couldn't blame them. I was obviously police and I hadn't been able to save Adrian. Also, if I'm honest, there were quite a few faces who I'd had run-ins with for various reasons over the months. Suddenly the idea of stepping into that morass of bodies didn't seem like the safest idea in the world. But then one of Adrian's aunts saw me and screamed, 'Bring that man in!'

It was like I was sucked into the room. The crowd parted like the Red Sea – where people moved to I do not know – and I was inhaled by the crowd until there was a shove on my back and I found myself at the front next to Big Marie and the pastor, who was giving it the full fire and brimstone service.

As the only police officer there, and not a particularly welcome one at that, I'd felt a bit vulnerable at the back. Standing in the spotlight with the main speaker bellowing about the injustice of it all, I could feel dozens of eyes burning into me. Burning and, by the looks of it, measuring me up for a concrete overcoat in a couple of instances.

I was actually looking for emergency exits, if I'm honest, when the pastor slammed his hand on my shoulder.

Here we go, this is it. The end of Clive Driscoll.

Then he looked into my eyes and screamed, 'The goodness in this man!'

That was a surprise to say the least.

I thought, *Keep it up, son. I'm feeling a bit vulnerable here.*

The people that killed Adrian were nasty, no question. They had to be, because no one else would have got away with the way they taunted Big Marie. This was the woman who won a humanitarian award for saving a police officer's life but also had a conviction for breaking a police officer's arm. She's a force of nature, and the fact that her son's killers were still at large months later meant even she was scared, if not of them, then of their friends.

That, at the end of the day, was the reality of Brixton. And it was the reality of the community I was trying to make in-roads into.

I'm sorry, Bert Aitchison, but how am I meant to make that better?

Protecting individual families of Brixton was some of the most rewarding work I've ever done but it was hard – and, if I'm honest, it didn't look brilliant on paper. If I'd been judged on successful prosecutions you'd have to say my record against spousal abusers wasn't stunning. But, luckily for me, the police have another measuring stick called your 'clear-up rate'. That is to say, if you can show that you investigated a scenario fully, you identified a suspect, you found evidence and you can explain why you did not then proceed to trial, that counts as a 'tick' in your column. Basically, you're covering yours and the Job's arse to show you did everything possible.

Even so, when I saw an opportunity to help the wider community – and score an easy victory with the magistrates – I leapt at that. It should have been an open and shut case. A tap-in for Driscoll from two yards. Should have been ...

Again, it started with a citizen approaching me. Their house backed onto some land that the council had cleared to build on. Nothing had happened for a few months so a geezer with a skip lorry had taken to dumping his crap on the land. 'Fly tipping' they call it – you've probably seen the signs and wondered what it meant. When I looked into the business practices of the guy, he was charging customers £300–£400 to clear their waste and then dumping it on this open land, rather than paying to dump it in proper landfill sites. According to my witness, he'd been doing it two or three times a day for at least a month. Eighty-odd skips at £300 a pop with no overheads is pretty good business.

I looked forward to ruining it for him.

We set up a camera and filmed the bloke over a couple of days. We got another company in to quote for clearing the lot – the geezer offered his services, but I passed on that. £35,000 was the figure. I didn't fancy making the phone call to Lambeth Council to tell them the news – but at least I could say we'd stopped the problem. They had to be happy with that.

To this day I don't know if they were pleased or not, for the simple reason that they refused to talk to me. The whole lot of them, the whole massive machine that was Lambeth Council just wouldn't communicate with me. It started the first time I rang up:

'We don't engage with the police,' a sneering voice said to me.

'Calm down, I'm not investigating you.'

'I know.'

'I just need a statement about this fly tipper.'

'We don't engage with the police.'

'But he's dumped eighty loads of crap on your land.'

Silence.

'And he's made a fortune out of it.'

Still nothing.

'And it's going to cost you – and taxpayers – at least thirty-five K to sort it out.'

Tumbleweed.

'You've got to say something—?!'

'We don't engage with the police.'

I lost count of the amount of times I had that conversation with various different people. In the end, when it went to court, the magistrate said, 'Who is the victim here?'

I said, 'It's Lambeth Council.'

The very people I had been instructed to build bridges with. You'd have thought that this would be a good place to start.

'And where are they today?' the magistrate asked.

'They didn't want to appear.'

'Then where is their statement?'

'They didn't want to give one.'

'And they are aware of your investigation?'

'Yes.'

'So how can we be sure they are a victim at all?'

And with that he let the tipper off.

It was the most bizarre atmosphere to be working in – at the heart of it this mistrust that Lambeth Council had of the police. For the sake of politics, they did everything they could to keep us away. Bert Aitchison had warned me they weren't on our wavelength but I could not believe they would rather ignore such an expensive crime against their own property than engage with me.

But this was the era of local politics taking on central government. Lambeth was Labour and Mrs Thatcher was taking root at Number 10 with the police, according to the opposition, as her personal army. The use of the Met alone to fight flying pickets during the miners' strike seemed proof enough. We'd just seen the end of the council's leader, 'Red Ted' Knight and his so-called 'loony left' policies, but his successor Linda Bellos hadn't exactly gone out of her way to distance herself from them. Making inroads into Lambeth wasn't going to be as easy as I had thought.

And the more I thought about the council ignoring me when I was trying to help the people they were elected by, the more irate I got. No one likes to see £35,000 flushed down the toilet – and it wasn't even my money. Who did the council think they were?

The answer is, arguably, they were who the Job allowed them to be. In the early 1980s we were guilty of standing back in Brixton to avoid any conflict, political or social. The problem was, certain people began to realise that, with the Watchers looking the other way, they could get away with anything. In some cases, the police's decision not to interfere was a licence to print money.

I decided to make a few investigations into the council. They already weren't talking to me so what harm could it do? Some of the things I discovered were shocking. At a very basic level I found corruption. Money was leaking out of the place. Was that a shock? Well, every year they were posting financial losses in the tens of millions so, no, I wasn't exactly stunned to see one or two underhand practices.

No doubt certain people on the council were making hay while the sun shone. For years it had been the same on the streets. In both cases I was determined to call a halt.

CHAPTER TEN

What Is the Deal You Want?

I could, if I'd wanted, have had a very cushy couple of years doing my community work. There were no real targets so I couldn't fail to meet them; I wasn't even given any cases. No one ordered me to go after the pimps – that was my own initiative. A different person could have put his feet up and out-stared the police horse all day.

On the rare occasions I was at my desk it usually meant I was doing paperwork, something that I prefer to avoid to this day. I cite dyslexia as an excuse but it's as much laziness. Often, I would keep an ear out for the ringing of the phone in the CAD room on a busy day. Just as the operator was saying, 'Damn, we haven't got anyone free,' I'd wander over like the prodigal son and say, 'GBH in Myatts Field, you say? I'll handle that if you want.'

I picked up some cracking cases that way. There isn't an officer out there who doesn't like to cherry-pick the ones they know they can wrap up in an afternoon and I was guilty of that, too. It can't hurt the CV if you've got a string of clear-ups to your name.

One Thursday, on evening relief, I took over a case which changed the way I looked at things. For ever, as it goes.

It started with a kerfuffle at the front counter. I stuck my nose round the corner and it was like a refugee camp. Half a dozen kids in various states of undress, a woman and two giant black bin sacks were dotted about the place.

'What's going on out there?' I asked the desk sergeant when he came hurrying by to fetch a form.

He shook his head ruefully as he scurried past. 'Domestic violence.'

I listened as the sarge struggled to make himself heard over the rowdy kids and hysterical mum.

'I'm sorry, ma'am, but you'll have to wait. I'm on my own here.'

I thought about the stack of paperwork on my desk then looked at the sobbing family in front of me.

Sod it.

'Can I help you, Sarge?'

Other uniform met me in the doorway. 'Are you sure about this, Clive? Domestic violence is one case you'll never win.'

'You might be right. But I'm going to have a bloody good go.'

I knew it would be a lot of work for little success, but as I walked over to introduce myself I thought, *If no one will touch DVs, how do you know they can't be won?*

Listening to that woman's story, I felt more sick than at any crash scene in the ambulance service. I'd picked bits of bone and flesh off the underside of half a dozen tube trains but that never seemed to affect me as much as hearing how this poor woman, five foot nothing and skinny as you got, had been treated by her partner. If there was a worse type of bullying I hadn't yet come across it – and nor did I want to. You know my feelings on that.

It took a while to get the story because I had to take care of the kids first. An aunt stepped up to the plate at the first time of asking. It turned out the lad who was the father of all her kids had women and children everywhere, and he treated her like a piece of meat to loan out. It was a Thursday night and he'd been on the lash, and when he'd arrived back with a couple of mates, he'd woken her up and said, 'Fuck 'em, baby.'

She'd resisted so he'd beaten her. Then she'd complied. Then he'd beaten her again. He'd then gone out so she'd grabbed her kids and clothes for them and run to us.

Her only mistake was loving the animal who put her through this – because it wasn't the first time he'd dragged her out of bed to service a stranger. She'd been woken a few weeks earlier by her boyfriend with his teenage son from another woman.

'What's he doing here? It's the middle of the night.'

'Yeah, he turned sixteen at midnight and you're his present.'

'What do you mean?'

'You're going to fuck him and make him a man.'

What has had to go wrong in your life that you think that's any way to treat the mother of your children? To think that's an acceptable birthday gift for your son? For as long as I live I will never understand people. Not all of them. That night I came as close to losing it as I ever had.

The woman had done as she was told because she was scared. But, more importantly, because she loved him in her own way and he was the father of her children. She clearly meant nothing to the boyfriend but he was the world to her.

Not any more, though. Not if I had a say in it.

First I needed to get her and the kids sorted out for the night. I called over the desk sarge.

'Do we have a number for Women's Aid?'

'Yeah, here it is. Good luck with that.'

'Good luck? Why?'

'You'll see.'

I punched in the number, explained who I was and why I was calling.

'OK,' the rep on the other end said. 'Could you ask the lady to go outside to the phone box on Brixton Road and call this number?'

'May I ask why?'

'It's safer.'

'Who for? There's a bloke out there who ain't afraid to give her a smack. She's staying in here and she can talk to you from this phone.'

'That's not possible.'

It was like talking to Lambeth Council all over again – except there was a lot more at stake than fly tipping.

'Why is it not possible for the woman standing next to me to talk to you on the phone that I am speaking to you on already?'

'Because you'll record everything.'

I give up. Wood – trees – can't see one for the other.

'Why would I record this?' I said wearily. 'I'm in the business of helping people, not taking down their life story.'

'You're the police.'

And that was a massive problem, right there. These days Women's Aid and the police work hand in hand – as we do with Southall Black Sisters. But they were in their infancy then and they were already bitter against the Met. Brixton nick had no relationship with them whatsoever. They didn't even trust us not to work against the victims somehow.

I guessed it was the poisonous branches of the council reaching out into all similar organisations but it didn't make any sense to me. Just because certain members of the council were accusing the police of being an instrument of Tory oppression, why would even Tories not want to help a victim of violence and her kids? And why would these agencies put their politics before doing their jobs?

My second rude awakening came a few weeks later when we appeared at the magistrates' court. There she was on the stand.

There was her boyfriend across the room glaring at her. Up in the gallery were dozens of his friends and family.

I looked at my witness and noted how calm she appeared. I could relax. She knew what she was going to say and was comfortable with the consequences.

I soon found out why.

As soon as the woman got the chance, she denied he'd touched her. She actually said she'd cheated on him with another man and she didn't deserve him.

I couldn't believe it. She'd sacrificed her own well-being – her own life possibly – to keep that violent criminal out of prison. How terrified must she have been of him?

Sadly, it was the first of many similar cases for me. Over the next few months I made it my mission to track down the wife-beaters and, each time, despite everything, when push came to shove, they weren't prosecuted. Making the arrest was easy, getting the charge was a piece of cake, but persuading the women to testify in court was nigh on impossible.

It's hard to explain. However evil, however low these men were prepared to go to abuse these women, at the end of the day they were still the father of their children. Time after time the women said to me, 'How do I tell my son I sent his father to prison?'

'I'll tell him myself if you'll testify.'

Once I started looking into it, I realised that Brixton had a shocking problem with DV. I wasn't sure if it was a cultural thing or a poverty thing, but there was a sizeable underclass that thought it was OK to beat a woman. It was as if the men owned them – they could do what they liked with them. Like a car run into the ground or a pony sent to the knacker's yard.

I saw things during those domestic violence calls that you can't imagine. Horrendous things. It is a fact that, to this day, the worst injuries I have ever investigated as a police officer were, nine times out of ten, the result of domestic violence.

I saw women who had had red-hot irons held to their faces. Women who were locked under the stairs at night while their old man went out on the razz. Women who were subjected to the most invasive and damaging gynaecological examinations because their husbands were paranoid they'd been unfaithful. Women who had had Stanley knife blades slashed across the bottom of their feet to stop them running away. Women who were beaten into submission so badly that I had to wait days sometimes for a statement.

These were brutal, barbaric, inhumane acts of aggression committed by monsters on the people who loved them the most. And because it was filed under the heading 'domestic violence', it was as though it wasn't as serious as assaults on strangers. To me it was, though. To me, it was more offensive. What is worse than a man abusing the mother of his children – in front of them?

I was desperate to make the bastards pay but without the victims' cooperation what could I do?

The first thing I did was pay a visit to the guy who'd farmed his own girlfriend out to his son. He'd just been declared Boyfriend of the Year in court, hadn't he, so he was on top of the world. I put him straight with the same tactics I'd used on the pimps: 'You can stop hitting her or I will have you. What is the deal you want?'

'Bring it on, copper,' he said. 'I'm not scared of you.'

That was fine. At least we knew where we both stood.

About six months later I saw him again. This time he was in the dock on a charge of handling stolen goods – a fact. I'd caught him red-handed. When he got the chance to speak he started yelling at the magistrate, 'I'm only in here because I hit my girlfriend and he' – pointing at me – 'said he'd get me.'

'Is this true, Sergeant?'

'It is true he hit his girlfriend but it is also true he handled stolen goods.'

Most villains were a bit more sensible after they had got the old gypsy's warning, as it used to be called. The ones who didn't, I managed to get by other means. They call it 'zero tolerance' now. I just called it getting the worst of humanity off the streets.

Whatever their circumstance, I like to think I've given all of my victims 100 per cent of my efforts, every time – whether they've lost their keys, been mugged or had their car broken into. But, I must admit, when it came to assembling the cases against wife-beaters, on the rare occasions the witness would go through with it, I dotted the i's so many times I went through the page. Nothing was left to chance.

For a DV victim to proceed with the court case her pain had to be so great that the husband couldn't scare her any more. One of the worst cases I saw of this was where a man, a vile piece of work, inserted the business end of a claw hammer into his wife's vagina and just yanked.

And he did it in front of the kids.

You can imagine the damage that was done – physically and mentally. But that women was brave. She knew there was no going back, for her or the kids, so she went ahead with her testimony.

Despite three witnesses, the husband denied everything. In his sick mind, they'd all back him up because he was the loving dad. But one of the kids had actually called it in and the other one was determined to tell the truth, even if Mum lost her nerve. I promised them all that he wouldn't get away with it. Because he was so arrogant, he hadn't even disposed of the hammer. Once we matched fingerprints on the handle and her blood on the claw, he was done.

Did I celebrate just a little more when I saw him sent down? Not for myself, no. But for those poor kids and their mutilated mum, yes, I did.

That case was an upwards curve as far as learning went, no two ways about it.

I realised I had to do something more about domestic violence, than just respond when it was too late. The problem was with how DV was perceived – it wasn't just the police who treated it as 'low-level' crime: friends, neighbours, even the victims and their families all thought it was somehow OK, just 'one of those things' that people in relationships have to put up with.

That was wrong. Whatever they all thought and did, in my heart I knew it was wrong.

I refused to let these atrocities be swept under the carpet any more, so I went to Bert Aitchison and got the go-ahead to set up the Metropolitan Police Service's first domestic violence unit.

It turned out not only to be one of the first in London, but also in the whole country. Whatever else we achieved, I wanted the Job to know this was a crime worth taking more seriously.

Putting the team together was slightly more problematic than I intended – although not for me. The uniform chief inspector at Brixton was a chap called Brian Paddick. You might have seen him more recently on *I'm A Celebrity Get Me Out Of Here* or running as the Lib Dem candidate for Mayor of London. He's a bit of a legend, to be honest, and a great friend. But, at the time, he was juggling his workload with the petty grievances and whispers that being a gay police officer in the early 90s could bring – so it didn't help when I dropped him right in it.

We were interviewing for a police officer on the domestic violence unit and, ever the professional (and just to make sure I was getting sympathetic officers), I wrote out all my interview questions beforehand. Because there had been a spate of same-sex domestic abuse I made sure to include three questions about gay DV as well. Then it was time to meet the candidates.

Six officers made the shortlist: two women, three probably straight men and one openly gay man. I put the same questions to all of them and a panel scored their answers. When the results came out and we made our choice, we got a complaint from one of the straight males.

'That questionnaire and the whole interview was weighted in favour of hiring a gay man. It's Paddick's fault.'

Brian was immediately hauled before the local commander where he got absolutely ripped apart for overtly favouring gay police officers in positions of authority. But two things were wrong with that – number one: he hadn't even seen the questions I wrote, and number two: the person we'd hired was a heterosexual female.

Although a small team, we were very successful as a unit, especially with prevention. We really let all known abusers have the gypsy's warning, and because they were all cowards they'd usually behave. More than that, if we got a sniff of DV going on we would get there en masse, while it was still going on.

Only once did I make the mistake of going on my own. Like I said, the majority of the lowlife who beat women are cowards. They'd never take on anyone their own size. The problem was, there was no one else the same size as this bloke.

It was in a house converted into two flats. The downstairs neighbour let me in the main entrance and then I burst through the inner door to the upstairs flat. I could hear the women being belted so, dodging the large fish tank at the foot of the stairs, I sprinted up as fast as I could, yelling, 'Police, stay where you are,' as I went.

Talk about little and large. The woman was probably less than five foot; the bloke, on the other hand, was a giant, an enormous barrel of a man. He took one look at me and, instead of calming down, going into denial mode like they normally did, charged at me like a bull.

He may have been built like the proverbial outhouse but he was bloody fast with it. He got me around the waist and against the wall before I'd had a chance to react. The next thing I knew, he was constricting me so tightly it was just a matter of time before my ribs cracked and I passed out from lack of air.

I didn't fancy my chances. My arms were locked beneath his; my head would be useless against his muscled chest. Which just left my legs – and my brain. Which of them came up with the escape plan I'm not sure. But desperate times …

I managed to manoeuvre my weight onto one foot then, with everything I had, I shoved us both sideways.

Right down the stairs.

You have to be in a bad way to think that throwing yourself down the stairs is the solution, but I was, and it was. At least I knew it was coming – the giant wrapped around my waist was utterly caught out. We went piling down the 15-odd steps.

The fish tank broke his fall. His huge stomach broke mine.

It was the element of surprise that did for him because, while he was flapping around with the goldfish among the broken glass, I was on my feet first and managed to get chummy in handcuffs, just as the cavalry pulled up outside. By the time they'd come storming in, I'd filled a saucepan with water and plonked the fish into it.

Back at the station I was a hero. The local commander called me into his office to congratulate me on my work and various area bods sent me awards.

For saving the bloody fish.

I'd gone in, tussled with a gorilla, survived a fall down a staircase, probably saved a woman's life and stopped a few fish from dying in the process. And it's the fish that got me my commendation.

Someone, somewhere had a very sick sense of humour.

*

Domestic violence cases sickened me for all sorts of reasons – bullying was my pet hate in the whole world, of course. But the men who did it usually had children with their victims, and what sort of person doesn't care about the damage they're doing to their sons and daughters? The kids may not have been the ones physically abused, but the trauma of watching and hearing their mums being attacked will scar many of them for life.

Trauma does scary things to people: in some it can lead to depression and, in extreme cases, suicide; in others, it sets victims on a dangerous path of hedonism and recklessness – basically, doing anything to drown out the memories.

As a copper, I saw the effects of it all too often.

One of the other major problems I looked at on my community watch was drugs. Brixton was still the number-one place to go to for things to eat, smoke, inject or ingest. To be fair, 20-odd years later you can still pick up virtually anything there, but at least for a while the numbers went down, and my team has to take a lot of credit for that.

One of the biggest complaints I ever got regarding drugs in Brixton was from people at a club called The Fridge. The problem wasn't that people were dealing – it was that they were dealing crap! Only in Brixton would citizens wander into the nick to complain about the quality of illegal substances they'd been buying. What was I going to say? 'Well, madam, have you got a receipt for your ropey narcotics?'

I joke about *caveat emptor* and all that, but when I looked into it there was actually a serious, potentially fatal problem. Someone was dealing imitation ecstasy in The Fridge and people were not only not getting wired, they were getting ill. The problem was, because it all got ingested I couldn't do any tests to see what the fake drug was. So we had to get hold of some.

Which was where Operation Worst Undercover Idea Ever came in.

Now, hands up, full disclosure: I am not a natural undercover officer. Covert ops and me do not exactly go together. As I've said before, there's something about my face that screams Old Bill. I knew it, and so did everyone in Brixton. So how I ended up agreeing to front an undercover raid on The Fridge one Saturday night I do not know. Oh, and it was a primarily gay night as well. Did I mention that? I was told the place would be wall to wall with bodybuilders, sharp dressers and, to put it bluntly, body fascists. My physique was obviously going to blend right in.

Luckily, our biggest ally was the club manager. We already had a good relationship from the times we'd sorted out homophobic attacks on his clientele and our clean-up rate on same-sex domestic violence had helped them out a lot as well, so he was in our corner right from the off.

Now for the plan.

The undercover Met team was made up of three blokes and three women – one of them, Janet, is now head of the Black Power Association. The plan – and what it lacked in originality it made up for in simplicity – was that they were all going to be clubbers.

They'll hate me for saying this but the lads were all a bit … 'metrosexual looking' you'd say today and the women weren't your typical dolly birds, so it was a cover that no one would see through.

But then there was me.

I think it was actually The Fridge's manager who said, 'Why don't you be an electrician? We've always got those guys crawling over the place.'

Perfect. I got myself a toolbox and some blue overalls and, job's a good'un, we were ready to go.

I decided to get into position early. I'd done my research, including a few daytime visits. The place was dead at eight but by ten it was busy, and by twelve it was heaving.

The fewer people who saw me arrive the better so I got there at seven thirty. The first hitch happened about a second later, when I saw the security was being done by the Irving boys.

I clocked them and they clocked me. There wasn't one of the lads I hadn't had a dealing with and, if villains remember anything, it's the face of the Old Bill who put them inside.

I was about to turn on my heel when one of the Irvings said, 'Come to check the electrics have you, chief?'

'Ello, 'ello ...

'Er, yeah, I have as it happens.'

'Fair enough.' He flicked his walkie-talkie into life and said, 'There's a sparks outside. Let him in.'

Lovely lads, the Irvings – I've always said that!

Inside, the manager led me down a dark warren of corridors. Suddenly he stopped. 'Before you go onto the dance floor, do you mind if I show you something?'

'I should warn you I'm not a real electrician.'

'Nothing like that.'

He led me to a room with a leather-clad door. When he opened it I thought I'd gone back to the Middle Ages. I was looking at a mediaeval torture chamber – there was no other possible explanation for it. And there were two modern-day geezers in there getting tortured. In the altogether.

I was wincing just looking.

Whatever you've done, son, just confess. Nothing's worth that pain.

But, judging by the size and prominence of the man's erection, he was enjoying it. Very much. And that was the manager's problem.

'This room is very popular,' he said. 'But do you think it's legal?'

My eyes were still watering when we got to the dance floor. They nearly started up again when I saw where I had to go.

'We've always got workmen up in the lighting gantry,' the manager said, pointing to the ceiling. 'You're safest up there – and you'll have the best view.'

He was wrong about the safe part. Shinning up a ladder built for someone half my age and half my width didn't exactly make me feel warm and fuzzy. Even when I reached the viewing platform at the top, one look down and I nearly fainted. I'd never had a fear of heights before; maybe it was just the fact it was pitch black, 100 feet up – and surrounded by cages.

To both sides of me there were these large structures that looked like jail cells – if jail cells were ever suspended above a dance floor.

At least we'll have somewhere to put the dealer.

But I had a feeling it wasn't the dealer who was going to use the cages.

Like all tradesmen, I had a packed lunch and a Coca-Cola to tide me over while I pretended to work. Below me the club had started to fill up. Even from my crow's nest I recognised half of them from various other places and misdemeanours. Then I saw Janet and Co begin to filter in. I had to say, they blended in. Who knew they all owned such garb? But none of them forgot why they were there and I was proud to see them cover all points of the floor and all exits. With me up top and them down below, we were perfectly placed to pounce. If our dealer showed, he was going to be surrounded.

It was about midnight when I finally saw him: a slick-looking male in all the show-off gear. The real giveaway was the endless queue of friends desperate to talk to him – and the couple of man mountains giving them the once-over.

This is it, I thought. I'd let him make a few deals then we'd swoop. Whatever he was peddling, I don't want any innocents taking it.

I switched my screwdriver to my left hand – an undercover agent needs a prop – and went to pull out my radio to give the signal to go. But, all of a sudden, the music stopped, an almighty anthem started pounding out and suddenly five men and a women appeared on the gantry next to me. From what they were wearing – leather trousers, boots with white socks turned down and nothing on top in the case of the men (a tiny bikini for the girl) – I didn't think they had come to give me a hand with the wiring. For a start, the baby oil they were covered in would have been a shock hazard.

One by one they peeled off into the cages, treading over me as they went. At least it was dark.

It's all right, Clive. You're the sparks, you're there doing a job, you're invisible. No one's looking at you.

But then the music changed again. The houselights dimmed – and six bloody great spotlights hit the cages. I felt like I was flying a Lancaster and the searchlights were training out of a Second World War sky.

And there was me, gleaming like a snowman in the middle.

It can't get any worse, I thought, as the boys and girl started writhing like they had itches all over their bodies. But, a few minutes later, catastrophe. The beat changed again and, right on cue, all six of them whipped off their strides. And started simulating wanking.

It was one thing being lit up as if a Lancaster was flying overhead. It was quite another having a bloke tugging his old boy two feet from your head.

This never happened to George Dixon ...

And, just when I thought it couldn't get any worse, I saw Janet and the others pissing themselves with laughter.

First the riots, then the punch-ups, now cocks in my ears. What else was there left for Brixton to do to me? *Thank you, God, thank you, Bert Aitchison, thank you, everyone who has had a hand in me reaching this point in my life.*

I honestly half felt like jumping off the gantry.

In fact, I managed to crawl to a corner where the lights couldn't find me and I gave the command to pick up the dealer – if he was looking up like everyone else, the last thing he'd expect was a tap on the shoulder.

It worked, too. By the time I got back down he and his minions were cuffed and cautioned. Now all we had to do was get them out…

Some people saw an electrician. Some people saw a mature white gentlemen in a strictly gay zone. But a lot of the others saw six guests and a weirdo dragging away the man with the narcotic plan. And they weren't too happy about that.

As the resentment grew among the clubbers, we managed to get to the club's entrance. And that's when I saw a giant paw reach out behind me and block the exit to the ranters and ravers following me. It was the Irvings again and, thank their mum for raising good boys, they personally saw us into our unmarked car and away. Who'd have thought that a year or two earlier, eh?

Some people reckon I should have left the dealer there – when the clubbers found out he was selling fake gear they'd have turned on him. But I couldn't afford to take that risk. A few tests revealed his so-called party drug was actually crushed aspirin. The downside was we couldn't, therefore, do him for trading Class As. But we could get him for deception and endangering lives. And if I could have done him for embarrassment in the line of duty as well, I would have.

After all, what *inspector* should have to go through that …?

CHAPTER ELEVEN

Wood Made Good

I loved being a sergeant. But I liked the sound of 'Inspector Driscoll' more.

To be precise, it was 'Detective Inspector' that grabbed me. Another hero of mine, Sherlock Holmes, was a detective, albeit a 'consulting' one, and if it was good enough for him, it was good enough for me.

Despite not having taken any detective exams, most of what I'd been doing for the previous few years had been pure CID work, so it made sense to go down that route officially. Also, by 1991, I was 40 years old. I'd been in the force for 12 years. A bit of seniority might suit me.

The interview was a day long and unlike anything I'd ever done. I turned up along with seven others and we were asked questions individually. Then we were all given tasks to test our team-building skills. One had an imaginary minefield to navigate, one had a crowd-control situation. My task, if you can believe it, was to propel an egg five feet across the room without it breaking – using only bamboo sticks and a rubber band.

This will come in handy next time I'm in a riot.

It was the most ridiculous thing I'd ever done in my life. But I managed it – I got that egg safely from point A to point B. But that wasn't good enough for the board: because I hadn't involved the 'team' on a 'team-building' exercise, I was marked down.

'I was freeing up the team to do proper police work,' I explained.

That didn't go down too well, either.

And that was definitely a recurring theme of the day. My face just didn't fit but lived in hope.

Still, one of the bits of feedback I got from the board was that I could benefit from more leadership experience.

By coincidence, the Met was undergoing one of its frequent, if apparently random, transformations at the time. If there is an institution that spends as much time staring at its own navel and concluding it needs to reinvent the wheel, then I have not heard of it. All I knew was that someone must have been on a course about 'sector policing' because in early 1992 the memo came down that Brixton was being split up.

There were to be three 'sectors': Southern, Northern and Western (Eastern sort of overlapped). Each area had its own little group of police officers reporting to a sergeant, with a shared inspector somewhere in the picture. As back-up there was a relief group that papered over the cracks and took jobs when the sectors were busy.

This worked OK for a while but then they cancelled the relief shift and chaos ensued. Without any real coordination, what if Southern, Northern and Western sectors all decided to work day shifts for a week?

It actually happened and for a few nights Brixton was like the wild west.

The sector system was good for me, though, because I was put in charge of Western. Mark Warwick was the inspector in overall command of Brixton but the sector was mine to deal with how I saw fit.

We had some great jobs. Landor Road in Stockwell fell under my umbrella. It was a big drug area and oh, the hours of fun I spent there, usually with an old-school – and plain old, if I'm honest – PC called Bob Lister.

You get different types of PC at that age. Some are like the Olympic torch – they never go out. They'll hang around the station just winding down the clock until home time. Proper canteen cowboys. Others are overtime bandits, always making sure their final call of the shift nudges them over their hours so they can claim double time. Bob won't mind me saying he was the latter. Nobody worked longer hours. If there was an arrest going, he took it; if there was a collar to be felt at five to seven, he felt it.

I loved leading my own team after so many years as a lone ranger. Humour helped. Apart from Bob – or 'Scarecrow' as he was known, because he had been a farmer – there was Colesy and Giggsy and, just because her name was Jenny Carr and we weren't particularly imaginative or mature – Khazi.

Drugs busts kept our cells and our activity logs full. But I never forgot that I had got into the police originally to work with people, not narcotics. As ever, when I heard of a domestic situation coming through the switchboard that the PCs were too rushed off their feet to handle, I usually nabbed those for myself. This day was one of those days.

I knew before I got there that I'd probably be doing a '136' [referring to the law which can be used to admit you, against your will, to hospital for treatment for mental illness]. The call-out's details had been sketchy but, in essence, a registered mentally ill woman was standing in her kitchen with the gas of all the hobs on – but no flame. It was only a matter of time before she, her flat and the entire block went nuclear.

Legally, the police have no right to eject someone from their house unless they're committing a crime. What we can do, under the Mental Health Act, is move that person to a place of safety – for example, a hospital, or the nick – but only if they're in a public place.

This was a tough one, then. That woman was committing no crime. If she blew herself and her neighbours up, then maybe it would be a different story, but at that point she was just being careless.

So, what do you do? I'll tell you what 99% of coppers would have done, and what I intended to do that day: walk in, ask the lady to pop outside with me for a second, then nab her in the street. If anyone asked, she hadn't been in her home when I found her. The gas would be turned off, she'd get medical attention and no one would have a problem with it. It might not be strictly in accordance with Section 136, but it was common sense. Nobody died. Nobody minded.

This day was different. This was the day I found somebody who minded.

When I found the flat, the door was open, of course, to let the gas out, but the woman wasn't alone by the hob. There were two Lambeth mental health workers in there with her.

I said, 'Why haven't you turned the gas off?'

'It's not our flat,' one of them pointed out.

'Well, you don't mind if I do, do you?'

As I walked over to the cooker, one of them said, 'Yes, I do actually. She has rights.'

Here we go ...

'We can talk about that when I've made the flat safe and got her out of here.'

'You're not moving her. It's her right to stay in her home if she wants.'

'But she's a danger to herself – and others, at this rate. Since when have we allowed vulnerable people to hurt themselves?'

But they would not have it. In the end I turned my back on them and asked the lady if she'd turn the gas off. Which she did. Then, I asked her about a picture of an older woman on the wall.

'Who's that? Is it your mum?'

And she told me about her mum.

I asked her about her dad and she told me about him. I asked her about her friends and she told me about some imaginary people in her head. It didn't matter. She was chatting, she was smiling and she wasn't trying to kill anyone.

For about 40 minutes we went on like this and then I asked her if she'd like to go for a ride in my car.

'That would be nice.'

Coats on, windows shut, out we went. I think she only agreed to get me to shut up!

I scored that one as a victory; the mental health people saw it as police bullying. I really lost my rag with them: 'I'm as much for people's rights as you are but what about her right not to kill herself? What about her neighbours' rights not to have their two-beds blown to smithereens? Where's the common sense here?'

It was my second attempt at dealing with Lambeth – the third if you include Women's Aid – and again I found myself banging my head against a wall at their behaviour. But at least it was only blinkeredness and stupidity. No one was actually doing anything illegal.

Famous last words.

The police service never stands still. Criminals never do either. By 1994, the Provisional IRA was announcing a ceasefire while the IRA, the other lot, were firing mortars at Heathrow Airport. It was also the year Fred West was arrested for the murder of 12 girls and Tony Blair won the leadership of the Labour Party. Politics affects the police a lot more than it should. I'd only ever known a Tory government since I'd signed up. I wondered how Labour might change things.

In the meantime, in my corner of the world, in Brixton, the wheel turned full circle – or there had been another course. Whatever the reason, the Met switched Brixton back again from sectors to one complete area. When that happened, I hung up the uniform once again and moved back to CID.

I was still trying – and failing – to pass my 'inspectors' so the job change didn't seem like a demotion. I had been a sergeant at the start and I was still a sergeant. In any case, running the crime desk in Brixton didn't exactly leave you much time to worry about your ego.

Again, probably as a result of another course, the mid-90s were all about figures and graphics; in fact, if you were to ask me to put a date on when the Met became more interested in paperwork than police work, that has to be it. It wasn't enough that we were solving crime after crime – we had to show we were. The wall in the crime desk office had four sheets of paper pinned up showing every stat you could imagine:

Burglary – down 5%
Robberies – down 8%
Motor vehicle crime – down 4%
Telephone answering time – 90% before three rings
Letter answering time – 96% within a week

Everything was there in black and white and every week the numbers would go up or down as appropriate. Every Monday morning, out would stroll the DCI in charge of the unit, Peter Atkins, and with great pomp and ceremony he'd pin up the latest sheets of paper. It was a good gee up for the team, if I'm honest, because it's nice to see you're making a difference. But the person who really enjoyed the numbers was Ian Johnston (now Sir Ian Johnston), then the assistant commissioner for south-east London, who used to walk along the wall and go, 'Well done, lads, excellent work. Keep it up.'

Peter Atkins would later find himself named in the book *The Untouchables* as part of a list of coppers who allegedly weren't as scrupulous as they might have been during the Brinks Mat job, the so-called 'crime of the century in 1983', but I couldn't place him among this group of suspects; to me he was straight up, funny and direct. He either trusted you or he didn't. The first time I walked into his office, he had his feet up on the table, his hands behind his head and, before I got beyond hello, he said, 'Yeah, yeah, Clive, that's right, that's right, go with it, whatever you see fit.'

Which, I think, meant he trusted me.

Another bloke I really enjoyed working with was a graduate entry and he did like writing a report – a shopping list from him was like *War And Peace*. On day one on the crime desk he had a 40-page introductory dossier waiting for me.

'The DCI wanted you brought up to speed,' he said.

I had a flick through the file and I could not make head nor tail of it. I plucked up the courage and went in to see Peter Atkins, 'Guv, look, I've got this dossier but there are parts I don't really fully understand. Can you point out the relevant parts and I'll gladly do them?'

Asking my boss to read something because I didn't want to wasn't the best idea. I expected him to be more than a little put out. But this was Peter Atkins.

'No problem, Clive. Give me a couple of days.'

A week later I went back in.

'Have you had a chance to go through the dossier, sir?'

'I binned it, Clive.'

'Oh.'

'I think you know what you're doing or we wouldn't have taken you.'

I have to say, I'd always done well in Brixton but our clear-up numbers on the crime desk were superb. Ever since my first court appearance for that red traffic light I had always made a point of dotting the i's. No stone was left unturned by me or by anyone reporting to me. And so, even if we didn't get a case to court, I made damn sure we pushed it as far as we could and got the evidence that we'd done so. That way the Met could be shown to have done as much as physically possible – and the crime desk could get another 'clear-up'.

Without blowing my own trumpet too hard, Brixton nick topped the charts for the whole district every single month I was there. The DCI loved that and the more success we had, the more he wanted. In fact, the only time I ever saw Peter Atkins angry was when he thought we'd missed one.

He was going through the books one day and he suddenly started tapping the page.

'Clive, what's this?'

'Guv?'

'There's a case in here not cleared up. Innocent, guilty, waste of police time, I don't fucking care. Get it cleared up!'

It was the only time I ever got a bollocking off him. That's how important the numbers were.

You'd think people would be happy that so many crimes were being solved in Brixton. But that 'not seeing the wood for the trees' condition that the woman from Women's Aid had had shown was all around the Job, too. Other nicks got very suspicious – and jealous – when we kept turning in the best figures and, before we knew it, we had Complaints paying us a visit.

Someone within the Metropolitan Police Service – one of our own – had raised an official suspicion about us.

The Complaints people did not mess about. They camped out in our offices, went through every single document pertaining to every single clear-up since I'd arrived, and put yours truly's heart through hell.

And, of course, while all this was going on I wasn't out in the field notching up more clear-ups. I don't know who had complained but they knew what they were doing. Or so they thought.

Judgement day finally arrived. I was sitting at my desk, unable to do any useful work because of nerves, and I noticed the Complaints team starting to pack up. I'm normally good with people – I read faces a lot better than I read books, but I was stumped. The head Complaints bloke didn't look like his cat had been run over but then he didn't look like he'd won the Lottery either. I decided it probably wasn't good. The only question was: how far in the cack was I?

After an agonising few minutes, the team leader came over. He had one of my books open and he was pointing to an entry.

Oh Christ, what's he found?

Peter Atkins suddenly appeared at my shoulder. Whether to throw me to the dogs or put in a good word for me as I collected my belongings I couldn't tell.

The Complaints bod plonked the book down on my desk and said, 'You should be ashamed of yourself, Driscoll.'

Gulp.

'Sir?'

'There's a clear-up here you've missed.'

Oh, the sweet smell of relief! The Complaints bods had spent four days going through my books with a fine-toothed comb and the only thing they'd unearthed was a case where, in their opinion, it had already been cleared up and we hadn't chalked it off.

In other words, the opposite of what we were accused of doing!

'Sloppy bastard,' Peter Atkins said. But he was as relieved as I was.

Over two years Complaints visited three times. As I knew to my cost, if there was an accusation they were duty-bound to investigate. But it was insulting, and it really got in the way of police work. How could I pursue villains, leads or the truth while I was being audited? As the DCI said, 'It's as if you don't actually want us to solve crimes because we make the rest of the Met look bad.'

In 1995, Peter Atkins left on medical grounds. Before he went I said, 'About the figures you put up on the wall every week.'

'What about them?'

'Well, now you're going, I need to do them. Only trouble is, I don't know where you get the numbers from.'

'Oh, those,' he said. 'I make 'em up.'

DCI Atkins – the one and only.

When I wasn't dealing with Complaints, I actually solved quite a few crimes. Again, one of my biggest coups came as a result of picking up a random call from the main desk. It'd sounded interesting; more importantly, it had sounded fairly straightforward.

It turned out to be anything but.

A kid had gone missing. That was the gist of it. A couple of people had become suspicious that a boy they used to see on the Moorlands Estate had just disappeared. The final straw had come when his dad had had his patio re-laid.

This was 1995, the year Trevor Jordache was discovered buried under the patio in *Brookside* and a year after Fred West had done the same thing to young girls in real life. We were all worried about copycats. So, DC Andy Ryman and I drove round there.

When we strolled onto the estate the first thing we saw was a horse – inside a flat.

Anyone who knows the Moorlands knows not to be shocked by what goes on there. It's separated from the high street by the train line so there's a physical barrier between the council tenants and the more up-and-coming parts. Even so, a nag inside a flat – albeit a nice three-bed, ground-floor place – was a first for me.

We found the complainant and she told us that her kids used to play over the way with a boy who lived with his dad. The kids liked going there because the bloke made them cakes and fried food. Anyway, in the last few days the boy hadn't been there, although the dad still invited them in.

'It could be something, could be nothing,' I said to the woman. 'But we'll check him out. It's possible the boy has gone to stay with his mum.'

'I suppose,' she agreed. 'But I've never seen her.'

We strolled over to the given address and introduced ourselves to the bloke inside. He said his name was Michael Johnson.

'Pleased to meet you, Mr Johnson. I'm here to ask about your son.'

'Who, Terry? What's he done now?'

'Is he home?'

'No, he's with his mum for a bit.'

I looked at my colleague. It was just as I had suspected.

'Can I ask what it's about?' the bloke said.

'Do you have any pictures of Terry?'

'Of course. Help yourself.'

He waved his arm at the mantelpiece which was covered, I now saw, with snaps of a little lad in school uniform, in football gear, in the starring role of a production of *Pirates Of Penzance*, even. Being a football fan, the only one I really took notice of was the picture of him in a Scottish replica shirt. Heart of Midlothian, I assumed, judging by the sponsor's name on the front.

There was something that didn't quite ring true about the whole scenario but I checked the patio and it had been down at least a month. The boy had been seen several times since then, so he wasn't under there.

'All right, Mr Johnson,' I said. 'We're sorry to trouble you.'

'If I can help you with anything else, let me know.'

'Well, there is one more thing.' *The Cockney Columbo strikes again* ... 'You don't happen to have your ex-wife's number, do you?'

Apparently she wasn't on the phone which he admitted was weird but, 'What can you do? Women, eh?'

But here's the funny thing: she *did* have a phone number, because after about 10 minutes of my being back in the car, her number was found for me by the nick. They even had an address.

Half an hour after leaving Mr Johnson's, I was face to face with the ex-wife.

And, what did I learn? Yes, she had been married to him – much to her obvious shame – but that was about all he'd got right.

'We never had any children!' she said. 'I kicked him out because he was horrible. The last thing I would do is bring his children into this world.'

'So who is this Terry then?'

'Your guess is as good as mine.'

You might call it a cul-de-sac. I call it an opportunity to find the truth. If Johnson had never had children, who was this 'Terry'? And where was he now? Furthermore, if Terry wasn't his son and didn't live with him, why were all these kids from the estate going over to play at Johnson's house?

Alarm bells were ringing like crazy, but where to start?

The police computer threw up some good stuff. According to the files, we'd always known him as 'Budgie'. Michael Johnson wasn't actually even his real name: he'd tweaked it slightly before he got married, so his wife never knew about his prior conviction for indecency. It also meant he'd evaded any scrutiny that the Old Bill liked to keep on sex offenders, even back then. It was actually really easy to have the system over, because all he'd done was alter a few letters of his name and there we all were, chasing our tails.

I knew we were on to something but what had the bloke actually done? Baked a few cakes for Moorlands kids and pretended to be some kid's dad. No magistrate was going to throw the book at him for that, past conviction or not. I needed to find 'Terry' and get his story.

Now, this is where my hero Sherlock Holmes gets a shout. It was Sherlock who showed me how to look for the clues you haven't realised you've seen. I thought back to Terry. What did I actually know about the boy? He was an actor, he had blond hair and he wore a Hearts shirt...? I *knew* something was wrong about that picture! Who supports a Scottish team unless they really, really have to?

Elementary, my dear Ryman.

I obtained a warrant to get a copy of that photo. Luckily, Johnson hadn't removed it. Why should he? It was his son. Except that now he knew that I knew it wasn't.

I also got permission to pick up any other photographic evidence. There were a stack of home videos by his bed so I decided to take a look at those. It took a while, but soon I found some film of Terry talking in front of a window. By the look of it, it was a high rise.

Again, this is where Holmesian logic kicked in. Hearts play their football in Edinburgh. Terry was in a high rise. For my next trick, I decided to pursue tower blocks in Auld Reekie which had the same view as the one behind the kid.

These days you click on Google Earth or Streetview or any number of other online witchcrafty elements; back then I had to print out dozens of copies of the image from the video and post them to Scottish police with a pretty-please request that they identify the building from the background.

Which, they only went and did.

You don't often get to travel to far-away climes when you're on the crime desk at Brixton but one day I was trudging around the Moorlands Estate, and the next … I was in Edinburgh's equivalent.

Oh, the glamour.

Actually, to be fair, it was a lot worse. I knew that because the local cops showing me around refused to set foot in the place.

'If ye wan'ee gor in thur, fill free. But we're no gorn in wi-oot numbers.'

Which, I think, roughly translates as: 'You two are on your own!'

I looked at Ryman. 'You up for this?'

'Do we have a choice?'

'I don't think we do.'

So in we went.

I noticed something wrong with the air the second I entered a stairwell: it smelled of disinfectant. Obviously the place had been drenched with the stuff recently which, at the less salubrious end of the market, often pointed to something being covered up. It didn't seem to bother anyone else, though.

I'd heard about the heroin problem in that area but I didn't expect to see it so soon. There were people just hanging over balconies, propped up against steps, all physically present but mentally on their holidays. It was a massive problem in Edinburgh at the time. At least on the Moorlands the only horse problem we had was the four-legged kind.

I started showing Terry's picture around to anyone who looked like they might be able to focus, but the people outside were useless. Knocking on doors, I found a more with-it type of person. Sometimes.

'Are you the porleeeece?' one young Scot asked.

'We are. From London.'

'The porleeeece? From London?'

And that was all he was able to tell us.

His neighbour was a bit more lucid. She actually recognised Terry, as did her flatmates. Before long we were making our way up to his floor.

Even from the balcony I could see it was exactly the view from the picture. Whoever Terry was, he was definitely the one on Budgie's mantel.

It turned out that Terry was, in fact, Billy. He'd been down to London to stay with relatives near the Moorlands and that's when he'd met Johnson. But, he insisted, nothing had happened. His mum was in the room – he was only 13 – so I didn't push it. But nothing he said rang true, so I invited him down to the local station.

On the way down, it was obvious that we'd become a bit of a hit – word had spread, and, as you never know when a crowd is going to turn, I had sent DC Ryman on ahead in case he needed to bring in back-up. But everyone was as good as gold and, when I arrived at the car, there was Andy giving kids laps round the car park.

Once community officers …

At the station there was a queue for the interview room. I watched some exchanges from the window for a bit and, if I'm honest, I was a bit shocked by what I saw. The interrogator was screaming at the suspect: 'You're fucking lying! You'll burn for this if you don't start telling me the fucking truth!'

'Blimey,' I said to one of my hosts. 'What's she done?'

'Nothing.' He laughed. 'She's a witness!'

Jesus …

My interview was a bit gentler. In fact, it was probably the hardest one I'd ever done for the simple reason you can't just come out to a kid and say, 'Have you been buggered?' Instead, you have to be more tangential and say things like, 'Do you have any concerns?' or 'Has anyone ever asked you to do anything you weren't comfortable with?' I came at it from so many angles my brain was in knots by the end. But we got there. He admitted what Budgie had done to him – and told us the names of a few other kids we might want to talk to.

By the time we reached court, the case against Michael Johnson was overwhelming. He'd groomed and assaulted several children, including Billy and, as a result, he was sent down for eight years. Happy days.

I got another commendation for that result but, even better, I got an actual compliment from a member of CID.

The bloke was another 'Budgie', as it goes, Budgie Burgess, a DS.

'Not bad for a lid, Clive,' he said. 'In fact, you know what you are, don't you?'

'Do tell me.'

'You're a wood made good.'

High praise indeed.

But inside, I was actually quite touched.

As a result of that collar I was asked by DI Jim Brightwell if I'd do a secondment on the Child Protection squad.

'Not a problem,' I said, 'if it gives me the opportunity of such exotic travel again.'

But, it turned out, in the first case I was given, the exotic travel had already been done.

The week I started was, by coincidence, the same week in 1995 that my son Thommo was born. Seeing new life breathed into the world one day then tracking down someone who would harm kids the next just made the crimes seem even more abhorrent. When a young victim was brought in to see me by her parents, I was ready to rip somebody's head off.

Unlike magistrates and juries, the police get to work with victims. We see what they're going through and that does get to us. We're only human.

This was the girl's story: she had attended an after-school gathering at the local church hall, as she did every week because she and her family were devout Catholics, but on this occasion a trainee priest had sexually assaulted her. She told me in great detail what the man had done and was able to show a female DC her injuries. She named the man as well.

'You can't miss him,' the dad said. 'He's Korean.'

I tracked the accused down and discovered he had indeed been brought over from Seoul to train in Clapham. When I put it to him that that training didn't include abusing young girls, he denied doing anything. Of course. But the evidence was overwhelming. The CPS – Crime Prosecution Service – agreed and a court date was set.

That was when the fun started.

Up until that point I had no agenda with this man other than thinking he was dreadful for fiddling with this poor kid. It didn't bother me particularly that the perv was a Catholic priest. If you think about it, what better job is there for a paedophile? If you want to pinch lawn mowers, go and work in a garden centre. If you want to nick drills, go and work on a building site. Similarly, if you want to fiddle with children, go and work with them. If you're a paedophile, you don't get a job on an oil rig, do you? You become a teacher or a Scout leader or, in this case, a priest.

Thanks, Sherlock, but I didn't need your help on that one.

But, just because this priest was a criminal, that didn't mean all priests were. He was bad because he was a predator, not because he was a priest. It's the same with any religion: the pieces of work who shot the people who worked for *Charlie Hebdo* magazine in France weren't bad because they were Muslim; they were bad because they were cowardly murderers, villains in any language. Nothing to do with their religion.

You speak to most Muslims and they are lovely. They hate murder as much as anyone. It's the same with most Catholics.

They can't abide the things some of their priests get up to. In each case, the bad guys hide behind their religion when in reality they were always rotten.

Anyway, as I said, I didn't have a problem with the Catholic religion when I worked on that case.

But it soon had a problem with me.

No sooner had I logged papers with the court than I started getting visitors to my desk, all of a certain faith. One or two of them I knew from the station; others I'd seen out on jobs elsewhere. But whoever they were, they all had the same message: 'This case is poison, Clive. The kid's obviously made it up. Get rid of it before it gets rid of you.'

'But,' I said, 'apart from the priest, no one's made anything up. We have forensic evidence, we have circumstantial evidence and we have witness testimony. This is going all the way.'

I couldn't believe people I trusted were actually advising me to put my own career before justice for this poor girl. How could anyone who believed in the law do that? You don't get at the truth by hiding. Still, my more well-intentioned friends had a point. I thought I was taking on one man, and a nasty one at that. In reality, I appeared to be taking on the Catholic Church itself – and about half of it appeared to work for the police.

Somehow the case got to court. On the day, there were queues of high-ranking Catholic Church officials – the big boys – all covered with jewellery and cloaks. They filled up the first few rows of the gallery and, unless I was imagining it, only seemed to have eyes for the victim and her family.

The intimidation, I have to say, was scary. Whether the child was right or wrong – and they didn't know, because they weren't police – how can it be right to just wade in and try to destroy a young girl – a young *Catholic* girl at that? Her parents had placed their trust in the Church and yet here were members of that Church out to crush the life out of all of them.

Somehow the family stood firm, even when a top doctor was called upon to challenge the forensic evidence and call the original doctor a liar. Even when the mother was described by people she thought of as friends as 'evil'. Even when an expensive barrister called the girl a spiteful fantasist who had dreamed up the whole thing because she was sexually deviant.

Thankfully, the family stood firm.

When the jury returned, it was with a 'Guilty' verdict.

It should have been the end of it but the smear campaign on the family did not end there, and nor did the pressure from all quarters. The priest appealed his sentence and he was acquitted. There were rumours surrounding the case, but there wasn't anything I could do.

I started investigating the religion after that. After all, I'd been in the force for 15 years and yet I'd had no idea that Catholicism was so prevalent in the Old Bill. Some detective I was. I'd heard that Freemasonry was very common – and, full disclosure, I would later join that organisation. But it was the first time that I'd seen any kind of religious influence on any part of the police force and I could only hope that I'd seen the last of it on my career.

I assume it was coincidence but I was transferred very quickly from Child Protection back to the crime squad. That tenure didn't last, either. A DI called Jim Mould, whom I'd worked with on various attachments over the years, was now recruiting for a division called CO41.

'We need a good DS,' he said. 'Will you join us?'

Fair play, I thought.

And so, after nine absolutely cracking years in Brixton, I had to say goodbye. After a quite literally explosive introduction to the place during the riots of 1981, I'd grown to love the area and its people. And, I like to think, one or two of them had got used to me.

Maybe, for one or two, I'd even made a difference.

CHAPTER TWELVE

Horribly, Horribly Wrong

If I'd made a difference in Brixton, I hadn't done it sitting at a desk – the horse could vouch for that. Even the top brass had noticed I preferred to be out rather than in. An inspector once introduced me to a new team member and said, 'Don't expect to find him here much. Clive job-shares with a bloke who's not here in the morning!'

Where I was being moved to in 1995 was going to take some getting used to but hopefully I'd still have the same freedom to get out and about. Then again, maybe I'd have a nicer office in Scotland Yard.

Apart from a few field trips and that night at the canteen during the Brixton riot, I'd never been to New Scotland Yard, to give it its full title, for actual work. But there I was now, part of a large, quite modern, open-plan office on the tenth floor. And I couldn't wait to get out and about.

Jim Mould may have been the man to bring me over but I had the honour of reporting not to a DI or a superintendent but directly to Commander David Kendrick QPM. That was unusual, but then my post wasn't exactly straightforward.

CO – Commissioner's Office – 41 had a lot of balls in the air: sexual offences, child protection, domestic violence, the paedophile unit and a new one, rohypnol.

At Brixton there had been bespoke teams for each area; at CO41 I was responsible for the lot.

Not just that. Brixton was like a goldfish bowl – albeit one filled with piranhas. But at least the geographical area was small and I stood a chance of getting one of those piranhas on my hook. CO41, on the other hand, had responsibility for the entire greater London area. I'd need a fleet of trawlers to make an impression.

All police work is about using your time to the best advantage. Even so, keeping those five plates spinning was going to take a lot of effort and skill, and a fair bit of luck.

I learned so much from Commander Kendrick, but then I had space to. By then I had good working relationships with Women's Aid and other groups – I'd even had the appropriate people at Lambeth Council talking to me by the end. I also got some early results with paedophile cases and sexual offences which had to impress the commander, if not the taskmasters I shared the tenth floor with. But then, no police like to congratulate someone doing well. Not to their face, anyway. Or not without a joke.

Not all my work was hands-on investigation: for the paedophile unit I attended various presentations and gathered information for the DI, Bob McLachlan. One of my tasks was going up to Bristol to discuss Fred West with Chief Constable Butler. It made a change from physically collaring people, but the research I did arguably led to just as many arrests. I hope.

With so much of my success based on getting out and about and talking to people I was surprised when a conversation I had with one person had such a wide-reaching effect.

That person was a journalist for *Cosmopolitan* magazine. I was speaking to her about a new drug-related crime that was targeting women. The drug in question was called flunitrazepam, prescribed by doctors to combat stress, anxiety and insomnia. One of the side effects of an overdose, however, induced a sleepy, hypnotic state in patients before leaving them with often only a hazy memory of events. With potency like that, it was only a matter of time before people started using it for other means.

By then, it was called 'rohypnol', or 'roofie'.

If it wasn't exactly a drug created for rapists, then it certainly was a lovely surprise for them. Men were getting hold of this drug, dropping it in women's drinks in nightclubs and pubs, then forcing themselves upon the women – who would not only go along with everything, but would also often have very little recall of the act. Almost overnight, we went from no cases to being bombarded by them. And it didn't take the media long to hint at an epidemic, which was why I decided to use publicity and briefings to combat the problem.

I started doing press interviews warning women to be aware of accepting drinks from strangers and encouraging them never to let their drinks out of their sight. As a result of the *Cosmo* interview, I received dozens of calls about the drug, not just from Londoners this time, but from the whole country. One call was from a solicitor in York who wanted me to meet his client. It was out of my jurisdiction but Commander Kendrick gave me the OK.

'Anything that helps us shut this down in London, Clive.'

In York I met a woman whose story, if I was honest, sounded implausible. She told me that she had been drugged and taken to a room, which had been set up like a church, where men in robes with animal masks had tied her to an altar and raped her again and again. She also said she hadn't been the only victim, or the oldest – young boys and girls had also been there, and subjected to equally horrendous acts. Her descriptions of the masks and of the men's behaviour and the children were so precise I knew she believed every word.

I believed that she genuinely had been drugged, but the rest all seemed a bit *Wicker Man* to me. Luckily, sorting the fact from the fiction was down to the local Old Bill – local police were investigating the accusation and so it wasn't for me to judge. I was only there to learn the role that roofies had played in events.

What all my interviews with victims showed me above all was the ease with which rohypnol was obtainable. I decided to work out why.

Sherlock Holmes was a great believer in following the clues so where better to start than at the beginning, with the drug's manufacturers. So I set up a meeting.

It was a revelation.

I said, 'The drugs being used against women are yours, and chances are they must have been stolen. No legit patient would waste them. Can you tell me how many you've lost?'

'No, we can't.'

Although the manufacturers had put safety procedures in place, the drugs were shipped out to distributors in bloody big canisters. While the number of pills arriving seemed to be logged, what happened en route wasn't always so clear.

'How do you know that the number of tablets that leave this warehouse is the same number that arrives?'

'We don't.'

'Have you thought about weighing the canisters each end?'

'No.'

'Well, maybe you should.'

To be fair, the manufacturers were incredibly helpful, and keen to play whatever role they could in shutting down the black market trade and, together, we came up with a load of ideas for tightening their security. Within six months there was a significant slump in rohypnol attacks and not just in London. And all thanks to a set of scales.

One of the biggest differences between Scotland Yard and Brixton was the scale. In SW9, I'd see inspectors and superintendents, with the occasional visit from the assistant commissioner; on the tenth floor at the Yard, I saw everyone. Because it was open-plan, if a commander or chief inspector or someone of even higher rank needed a word and fancied stretching their legs, they'd wander down and stop by.

I was at my desk one day when I heard hushed voices behind me. People can whisper all they like but when they're passionate sounds tend to carry. It was when I heard the words 'Daniel Morgan' that my ears pricked up.

Morgan was a private detective who, in 1987, had claimed he had irrefutable evidence of police corruption, drug trafficking and various other crimes. Very soon after he was found in a pub car park in Sydenham with an axe in his head. Obviously people started doing the maths and there was very quickly an inquiry into his death. Which was inconclusive. There was a second one, conducted by Hampshire Police, which got a copper charged with the murder though he was acquitted. As far as anyone knew, that was the end of it. But, as I tuned in to the agitated conversation going on behind me, I realised that there was in fact a third, *secret* inquiry going on right then.

And, by the sound of it, it wasn't going too well.

I realised that being at my desk had its rewards. I liked knowing what was going on: identifying the enemy is easier if you have the full picture.

I only heard the odd snatch from the top brass on Daniel Morgan, but there was another water-cooler conversation topic that had everyone talking including, again, the big cheeses. Once again it involved accusations of police corruption as well as incompetence and racism. The reason everyone was exercised about it was because it wasn't directed at one particular officer or even a couple.

This time, the whole of the Met was under the microscope and, as far as I could work out, it wasn't looking too healthy.

It centred around a boy whose name I recalled from my Brixton days: Stephen Lawrence – a young black lad who had been murdered in 1993, not long after Big Marie's son was shot.

Once again, the accusation was that the police investigation had been less than ideal. So poor was the execution of their duties, in fact, that, despite five suspects being named by dozens of locals and witnesses, no prosecutions had been made. An inquiry, led by Sir William Macpherson, QC, was attempting to establish why.

At the start of it the inquiry, the atmosphere on the tenth floor was bullish. The Met had done as much as could be asked. Yes, it was unfortunate that no one had been found guilty of young Stephen's murder but the evidence just hadn't been there. Otherwise we'd have nabbed someone.

As always happens in a murder case, there had been a review about six weeks in, conducted by Chief Superintendent Roderick Barker. He'd gone through the reports and concluded that everything that could have been done had been done.

Lord Macpherson, with all due respect, said: Bullshit.

Not in so many words, obviously, but he tore into the Barker review, and Barker himself. The police investigation had been shocking. The only question left for him, he said, was whether that was down to incompetence, racism or corruption – or a combination of all three.

That was the day to be a fly on the wall of the tenth floor, I can tell you. Jim Mould and the DCI, Ragnor Tulloch, were deep in conversation when they were joined by several higher-ranking officers, including the assistant commissioner Ian Johnston. It was actually the AC himself who plonked down at the desk one along from me, face in his hands, and said, 'It's all gone horribly, horribly wrong.'

A few days later he appeared at the inquiry and made a public apology to the Lawrence family, on behalf of Commissioner Sir Paul Condon and the Met, for the investigation. He 'could not justify', he said, the errors made in the original investigation.

I knew very little about the case other than what I'd seen and read, which was not much. From the outside, the investigation team did seem to have been presented with some A1 evidence, wrapped up with a bow, but that's my opinion. You don't know the complications unless you're working the job. I'm sure if some of that team or Barker had a look at my work they might pick holes. But, even before Macpherson published his report, it did strike me that the Met had gone to extraordinary lengths to deny any wrongdoing – and then as soon as one bloke had said the opposite, they had held their hands up and gone, 'Yeah, it's a fair cop.' Either they had known beforehand that they were defending the indefensible or they should have defended their boys a bit more rigorously, surely?

If I'm honest, I'd started to question the decision-making at the top end of the Met. Whatever the truth was, somebody knew it and thought they could suppress it. And while it's all very well looking after your own – who wouldn't want a boss to fight their corner? – this was a murder case. There was a grieving family out there whose pain was exacerbated every time the police denied making mistakes.

And at the heart of it all was a young, innocent boy stabbed to death for no reason at all.

Not all police, it seemed, were the white knights I'd hoped we were. But that was all the more reason for me to really step up to the plate to try to become one. I'd made good progress on rohypnol and all the other specialist areas on my watch, and that was as a sergeant. Imagine what strides I could make as an inspector …

I applied to go in front of another promotion board. I'm not saying I'd practised with eggs and bits of wood, but I had put some thought into how I would approach whatever tests they asked me to do.

I'd been knocked back so many times that I decided this would be my last go. Nobody thought I would get it – the polite version was that I was too much of a maverick and a free thinker; Jim Mould was more blunt: 'I'm not sure your face and voice fit what they're after. Good luck, mate, but prepare for the worst.'

I knew the gods weren't smiling on me when there was a tube strike announced for the day of my exam. Getting to Victoria on time from Cheam was touch and go on an normal day – arriving for eight o'clock in the morning when there's chaos on the streets? *Maybe I should just camp outside ...*

I did the next best thing: I bought a lilo and, once everyone had gone home, I switched off the lights and grabbed a few hours under my desk.

The next morning, after a relaxing 10-minute stroll, I went in – and wasn't best pleased to see someone else from the tenth floor going for it. Mikey wasn't my cup of tea as he liked to put on airs and graces and a lah-di-dah posh accent ... except that when he'd had a couple of drinks he spoke like me. I'm not a fan of people who aren't honest but, as long as they didn't give him a few pints, I felt his accent would probably swing the job his way.

On the plus side, at least I enjoyed the interview. It could not have been more different from the egg and rubber band assault course. For a start, the panel comprised a commander, a chief superintendent and a civilian. But the main difference was the tasks: I sat down and they asked me questions, proper questions, about policing: about what I'd done, what I'd do in this scenario or that, and what I thought could be improved in the Met.

Well, that's my specialist subject, isn't it? The time flew by.

When the results were in, Mikey and I were both called into the DCI's office.

'I'm afraid, lads, only one of you has got through.'

'Well, that is a shame,' Mikey said, big plum in his gob.

'And the person who is now an inspector,' the DCI went on, 'is you, Clive.'

Ah, well, I thought. *I did my best. It's just not to—*

'Hang about,' I said. 'Did you say me, guv?'

'Congratulations, Clive, and better luck next time, Mikey.'

Was it a wind-up? A mistake, maybe? I was out of there before he could change his mind.

I ran back to my desk and phoned my wife and my mum, both of whom could not have been more chuffed for me.

The second I hung up the receiver, the phone rang. I feared the worst: they were ringing to tell me there'd been a mistake.

Warily I picked up. 'Clive Driscoll—?'

'Just the man!' said a familiar voice. It was Gordon Briggs, another DCI at the Yard and a massive Everton fan. I'd taken him to Fulham several times. 'Clive, I wanted to be the first to congratulate you.'

'Blimey, good news does travel fast. Have you been speaking to my mum?'

'Now, I wondered – could you do me a favour?'

'Of course I can, guv. What can I do for you?'

'How do you feel about joining SO5?'

'Child Protection?'

'Yes. I've got a team that needs a DI – and nobody is better suited.'

'I'd be happy to. Where is it?'

'That's the problem, Clive. It's Lambeth.'

Just because you pass an exam in the force, it doesn't mean you are the new grade. That doesn't happen until you get a posting. Some people have to wait months until they can use their new title – and get the pay rise that goes with it. I had to wait approximately 15 minutes.

But Lambeth ... I'd left Brixton on much better terms with the council than I'd arrived – I would even say I had some supporters there. But the Job in general was still struggling to get a foot in the door.

Gordon Briggs said he'd send over the file on what was wrong with the police and Lambeth's relationship, written by the man I was replacing, my old friend, Jim Brightwell. I said I'd read it that afternoon. Actually it took a bit longer than that.

It was two feet thick.

If only Peter Atkins had been around to 'summarise' it for me.

Gordon Briggs said he wanted me to do with Lambeth what I'd done with the community in Brixton. The way I had done that was to speak to people and make sure everyone knew they couldn't get away with anything, so that's how I planned to start this time.

Who knew the can of worms that that would open? Or how quickly?

Joining Child Protection – or SO5 – meant another move, this time to Ambassador House in Norwood, right opposite Thornton Heath railway station. It was closer to home but I would miss hearing the top brass being put through the ringer. Still, given the choice of having a desk or being out and about, it was a no-brainer.

The day after Mr Briggs's call, he was due to have a meeting with Lambeth Council and invited me to tag along to get the lie of the land. It was meant to be a shadowing operation, with me playing second fiddle to the DCI, but it ended with me running to keep up – and not just because Briggsy always rushed everywhere like the world was about to end.

Everyone was very nice and congenial later, but it was like watching an opera when you don't know Italian. Suspects, witnesses, places and file names like 'Operation Progarda' and 'Operation Care' zigzagged across the table, and none of it meant a jot to me. The only thing I picked up for sure was that the Liverpool Police force was asking the Met for cooperation on Operation Care. Whatever it was, Gordon Briggs said, 'Absolutely, one hundred per cent, they've got it.'

Then, whoosh, he left the room like it was on fire.

Still a bit nonplussed and daunted by the amount of catching up I needed to do, I nearly didn't notice a woman hanging around after the others had left. She introduced herself as Libby Blake, someone from child services, and said, 'Do you mind if I have a word?'

I sometimes wonder what would have happened if I'd said, 'I don't have time,' or if I'd rushed out trying to keep up with Gordon Briggs. The short answer is, I'd have had a much easier life.

Libby's 'word' took about an hour. She started by saying, 'What do you know about John Carroll?'

As the answer was, 'Only what I've heard today,' she filled me in. Carroll had indecently assaulted a 12-year-old while working at an orphanage in the Wirral. He'd later moved down south to work at Angell Road children's home in Lambeth, eventually running it. During that time he'd had all sorts of visitors, including a paedophile, Steve Forrest. Forrest had abused a teenage boy there. While that was bad enough – Forrest also had AIDS. Carroll had left Lambeth over accusations of financial irregularities and returned to the north-west, hence Merseyside Police's interest in him as part of Operation Care. That was what Gordon Briggs had given his blessing for. But it was what Libby Blake said next that really caught my attention.

'Carroll was only the tip of the iceberg,' she said.

'Tell me more.'

'Speak to Anna Tapsell,' she said. 'She's the only one in Lambeth who'll tell you the truth.'

There weren't many positives to come out of my time in Lambeth but Councillor Anna Tapsell was, and is, a hero – to me, to the borough, but most importantly to the children who she tried to protect.

And what Anna told me was almost too horrific to process. According to her, children from homes in Lambeth had been farmed out to paedophiles and other sexual predators.

'Why has no one come forward?' I asked.

'They've tried,' Anna said. 'But they're up against some very powerful forces.'

She told me about a council worker called Bulic Forsythe. Apparently, in February 1993, Bulic had discovered pornographic pictures on council property featuring Lambeth care children and council members, and was going to expose the whole operation. He told a secretary in the lift that he was prepared to 'spill the beans'. That night he was murdered, and men were seen removing boxes from his house before the building was set on fire.

In 1995, another witness, a council worker called Sue Castle, had also gone to the police, with a story about her being raped on council property by local politicians and other known people. Shortly after her complaint, she'd opened her front door and a man had thrown acid in her face. When she had refused to withdraw her statement someone broke into her house at night, doused her bed with petrol and set it alight. Unlike Bulic, she escaped. But both cases made the papers, sending a clear warning of what would happen to anyone else tempted to 'spill the beans'.

'You need to speak to Sue,' Anna said.

'Yes, I think I do.'

The name rang a bell, in fact. I'm sure Jim Mould had been working on her case when I was at Brixton. There'd been something odd about it. What was it?

Of more pressing urgency was following up three other names an anonymous informant gave me. These weren't witnesses or victims like Bulic and Sue. They were *suspects*.

One of them was a Lambeth councillor. Another was a celebrity criminal. And a third was a member of the government.

That could explain why no one had come forward – and why those who had dared had found the police less than the white knights they should be.

But was it true? At that moment, in autumn 1998, I only had one witness's word. As evidence it was better than nothing, but none of it was provable and the witness was too scared to go public. To make it stick would require some serious digging.

I couldn't wait any longer.

If there was a wall of silence around the children's homes in Lambeth in 1998, I was determined to break it. I removed two officers from normal child protection work and tasked them with chasing any whispers about Angell Road or any of the other homes in the borough. For some reason, one of the DCs named the process 'Operation Trawler' – I accept it's not a good name for a child abuse enquiry. At the time I didn't notice, nor did any other police or social worker. If it offended anyone, I apologise.

Almost immediately Trawler struck gold. I managed to find someone who admitted they'd seen pornography changing hands on council property, which led to someone else saying there was a video doing the rounds featuring 'prominent' people engaged in sexual activities with minors.

In a situation like this, it can be tempting to rush at a case. In truth, if half the rumours of violence surrounding Bulic Forsythe and Sue Castle were accurate, then going off half-cocked would not work. If the sinister forces it had been alleged I was up against could make two allegations disappear, I had to be even more thorough than usual.

Not only did we find a lot of material but I managed to identify a potential pornographer behind the camera. You don't get better days as a policeman than when you get a result like that. When I tracked him down to his home in Wales he was almost boastful about what he'd been up to. In fact, after we'd searched his home from top to bottom and filled a car with all manner of disgusting and perverted images, he said, 'But you never found the good stuff, did you?'

The 'good stuff'? I would never consider myself a prude but what we had already bundled up was so brutal, barbaric and sickening it would turn the stomach of a dead man. If that wasn't the best – or worst – of the pervert's collection, then what the hell was left?

Even now I don't know if he was gloating just to take the piss or whether there really was something else we hadn't found. What I do know is that I've rarely been happier than when seeing him sentenced. To this day I believe he may have held the key to what had happened in Lambeth.

What we did find was pretty incendiary. There were recognisable faces in his pictures, both victims and perpetrators, and locations that could be traced; with more manpower I could see my trawling net closing in on a fair number of prominent and less well-known names. And I still had to interview Sue Castle – what other clues was she going to give me?

Before speaking to her I decided to research child abuse. I found an expert, a therapist called Dr Valerie Sinason. She was giving a talk on abuse of Down's Syndrome children when I met her. During our discussion, I mentioned the Roofie Foundation – a self-funding group aimed at helping victims of drug crime – and the rohypnol case I'd seen in York.

'That sounds exactly like Sue's case,' she said.

'Sue who?'

'Sue Castle. She was abused in a very similar way.'

Not for the first time I found myself saying, 'I need to speak to Sue.'

Not everything was going in my favour, however. Just as I really felt I was getting somewhere with the child abuse investigation, my boss, Gordon Briggs, was taken off the assignment. People come and go in the police all the time but when someone is as helpful and supportive as Briggsy, you really notice their absence.

Feeling I didn't have support back at Ambassador House amplified the awkwardness of every meeting with Lambeth. If ever there was a time to be grateful for being a loner, this was it.

At one particular meeting, however, I arrived in a fairly bullish state of mind. My investigations into the various suspects abusing children at Lambeth homes had produced a list of around a dozen names, and I was at the stage where I was prepared to share them. Confidentially, at least.

At the meeting was a representative from the Social Services Inspectorate and a member of Lambeth council. Only the chief executive and one or two others were higher up.

Before any Lambeth meeting, a set text was read out reminding everyone present of the confidentiality of anything discussed in the room. So, when the two men asked me for a progress report, I replied with full disclosure, including in my speech the complete list of names. I had known this was coming and had already spoken to my senior management team about it. It had seemed OK to pass all the names. It was a confidential meeting.

'These are all only suspects at this stage but I have reason to believe that further investigation will produce evidence that I can use to pursue court cases.'

Everyone in the room was happy; I left and my work continued.

One meeting I was called into was to discuss the boy raped by Steve Forrest. When I entered the room everyone else was already there, including the two people from the previous meeting and numerous people I hadn't met.

Three things became very quickly apparent.

Number one, the second I walked in, a couple of the gents around the table brought their fingers together in front of their faces, making what looked like quite odd hand signals. As nervous tics go, I'd seen worse, but it was odd.

But observation number two was the one to really set the tone. As the meeting started, any hint of the bonhomie of my first meeting, accompanying Gordon Briggs, was replaced by a cold wariness. When I got round to asking about the boy raped by Forrest, the atmosphere became positively arctic.

'Do we know if he contracted AIDS from Forrest?' I asked.

'No, we don't.'

'What do the doctors say?'

'They don't say anything – because we haven't told the boy.'

That was staggering.

'How can you not tell someone that the man who raped him had AIDS? It's the boy's right to know. Surely you can see that?'

'We don't believe it's in his best interests.'

'I'll remind you that I'm not only here on behalf of the Metropolitan Police Service,' I said. 'I'm here on behalf of the children of Lambeth – so if you don't tell the boy the truth, then I will.'

That kicked the hornets' nest.

'You'll do no such thing, DI Driscoll,' one of the men said. 'Or we'll have you removed.'

'Will you bollocks,' I replied. 'Pardon my French.'

I was prepared to end the meeting there and then but another man introduced himself as a solicitor and told me to stay.

'What's this about?' I asked.

'I want you to share with us your list of suspects,' he said.

I looked at the two men who had attended the first meeting. 'You both know the list. You tell him.'

'I'd rather hear it from you, Inspector,' the solicitor said.

I refused. I didn't know half the people in the room and the list just contained suspects at that point. It wasn't fair to reveal the names at this stage. Not to this group. Everybody is innocent until proven guilty.

But the solicitor insisted, reminding me of the commitment to confidentiality within those walls. And so, once again, I ran through my list of suspects.

When I left, I was not in the best of moods. I'd been shanghaied by people I was trying to help. Something wasn't right.

That was confirmed later when I asked for a copy of the file involving that meeting. Scanning through it, I was surprised to note there was mysteriously no record of my list – or of the argument involving Steve Forrest's victim. I spoke to two social workers, who confirmed there had been a further meeting to discuss the minutes. One of the original men present had gone through saying, 'Take that out … take that out … take that out.' What had been handed over to the police was very different to the version I lived through.

I don't know if the timing is relevant but the day after the meeting I received a very troubling phone call at my desk.

'Clive Driscoll?'

'Speaking,' I replied, still one eye on a file I'd been reading.

'A piece of friendly advice.'

I put the report down. All my attention was suddenly focused on the gruff voice on the other end of the line.

'What's the advice?' I said, standing up to make my own voice as serious as possible.

'Never mind about the Lambeth kids,' he said. 'We know where *your* children are.'

Christ. I apologise to you all because I exploded.

I said, 'I'll tell you where one of my children is, if you like. He's a Royal Marine. If you want to go and see him down at Lympstone, I'm sure he'll look after you.' Then I hung up and kicked the hell out of a potted rubber plant in the corner. It was all very well being blasé to the nonce on the phone, but Harry and Thommo were still very, very young. I had to treat it as a very serious threat. I reported it but was told it was impossible to trace the call due to the switchboard at Ambassador House. My team were very supportive for which I am still grateful.

Not long afterwards, Anna Tapsell rang. Something was clearly playing on her mind and it didn't take long for me to get it out of her. She'd had a visit from two Special Branch officers telling her to keep her nose out of the children's homes investigation.

'Clive, what's going on?'

'I don't know, but I've got a pretty good idea.'

I had several more meetings with council officials where I saw the same hand signals again.

Confused, I went to see a vicar I knew, a lovely man called Tom, who ran the church on Cannon Road in Wimbledon.

'I'm pretty sure the Freemasons don't do these signs,' I said. 'Is there any chance they belong to a particular religion?'

Tom only has one eye but it worked. He went over to his big bookcase and, after a few minutes of running a finger along a couple of shelves, dragged out a dusty old brown volume. He flicked through for a few seconds showing me a few pages of illustrations.

'Are those the sorts of signs you've seen?'

'Yes, they look about right.'

'Hmm, interesting.'

From what I could see, and from what Tom was telling me, these signs were almost certainly part of a secret Catholic organisation.

Many of these had been set up in the nineteenth century, designed to rival the growing power of the Freemason movement and they used these signs to communicate with other members. One sign could mean shut up. Another one could mean leave.

Suddenly it all made sense – well, more sense at least.

But, just as with the Korean priest case, why did it seem like some of the great and the good of this religion were helping out the bad ones? Couldn't they see that trying to cover everything up was worse than admitting the truth?

I was still talking with Tom when my phone rang. It was Superintendent Brian Tomkins.

'Clive, where are you?'

'I'm in Wimbledon, guv.'

'Great. Get yourself down to Barnes nick, could you?'

'What's this about?'

'I'll tell you when you get here.'

My head was still reeling when I arrived in Brian Tomkins's office.

'Can you tell me what this is about, guv?' I asked.

To me, he looked like he was under a lot of stress.

'I understand you have a list of suspects, Clive? Is that right?'

'Correct, sir.'

'Well, ... is it — —?'

And he named a government member.

'No, sir.'

'What about — —?'

And he named someone else.

Again: 'No, sir.'

He went through about a dozen names, all of whom suddenly seemed like prime candidates for Clive of the Yard to investigate.

Eventually he said the name on my list.

'That's the one I told Lambeth.'

'God, Clive, this is not easy.'

'What are you saying, sir?'

'I'm saying, it's all out of my control, but it might be time for a new challenge, don't you think?'

'I beg your pardon?'

'The investigation is over. You're being moved from Lambeth.'

Black queen takes white pawn. *Checkmate.*

CHAPTER THIRTEEN

This Could Be Our Belgium

The things I could say ...

With emphasis on the word 'could'.

Unfortunately, because my investigation was never allowed to run its course, I cannot legally name any of the people on my suspects list.

Obviously the Met couldn't just be seen to stop investigating when I was taken out of the equation. Instead, Operation Middleton was set up to take over Operation Trawler and to deal with the Lambeth situation. I was contacted by one of the team leaders and gave him a few steers.

'Thanks, Clive, but we're going in a different direction.'

They managed a handful of arrests over a decade. None of the major players from my list featured.

Did it hurt to watch those suspects carry on with their lives? Not as much as knowing the suspects were quite possibly continuing their predatory practices in the knowledge they had seemingly full protection from the law and the Met – if some of the stories I heard were true.

It's not for me to say anyone is guilty. That's the job of the courts. All I can say is that there was compelling evidence to mount an investigation against certain individuals and in each case, from what I have seen, it was never done.

I will never know what happened but a part of my confidence in the police service and government system will be damaged forever. In a strange way, that realisation helped me through the rest of my career.

There were articles in various newspapers about Forrest and the almost unbelievable decision by Lambeth Social Services not to tell the victim that he may have AIDS, and I hope with all my heart that young victim has now moved on.

Finally, 17 years after I was removed from the case, it's all started to come out. In the light of Jimmy Savile and Operation Yewtree, a lot of historic possible paedophile cases are finally coming to light. Sadly, a lot of the work appears to be being done by journalists and politicians, rather than the police. The *Daily Mirror* journalist Tom Pettifor has begun digging, requesting police and council files under the Freedom of Information Act – what he finds will depend on whether the files have been 'lost' – and the Labour MP Tom Watson has also been pursuing the story in Parliament.

And, as I write, the press are gathering information on the Elm Guest House in Barnes and the parties alleged to have taken place in Dolphin Square involving MPs and children.

For legal reasons, there is so much on which I cannot comment. What I can say, however, is that this could be our 'Belgium' and that the truth is out there – and getting nearer. If and when it does all come out, it could cause the biggest shake-up of our country since Cromwell. I must repeat again a principle I hold very dear: you are innocent until proven guilty.

A poor police investigation does not help anyone in the end. It certainly does not help the very brave and very kind acts performed by our police officers every day. Those just get brushed away and the focus will be on any suspicion of a cover-up or failing to do your duty.

*

During her visit from Special Branch, Anna Tapsell had been warned, in no uncertain terms, not to go near me if she knew what was good for her. She really is a hero. Shaken as she was, she never stopped chasing the truth or trying to protect the children. But things didn't end there.

At exactly the same time I was told I was being moved, I was hit with a '163' [an official complaint].

How could I fight to stay in the Child Protection Team when I was busy defending myself against a serious complaint from a 'member of the public'?

I have to say, Superintendent Brian Tomkins was a gentleman throughout our conversation.

'I'm really sorry, Clive,' he said, 'but the orders come from on high.'

So what was the complaint? That I had named councillors and ministers as members of a widespread sex ring operating in Lambeth children's homes.

I was interviewed on tape and answered the allegations. I think I left everyone open-mouthed when I said, 'Yes, I did name councillors and ministers and others as suspects in an alleged sex ring operating in Lambeth children's homes – for the very simple reason that I believe witnesses to be telling the truth. And this complaint is preventing me from acquiring evidence to bring those councillors and ministers to justice.'

The investigating officer said, 'I feel really grubby about this, Clive but we have to follow procedure.'

I couldn't help feeling that they'd got exactly what they wanted.

The tapes and records of this interview are now missing. It could be they were destroyed correctly after the complaint was warranted as needing no further action.

The irony of this incident has always been for me that I have never mentioned the names of suspects outside a confidential organised meeting or as a result of a complaints interview, as per the instructions read out before every Lambeth Child Protection Meeting. Yet my being '163-ed' was widely discussed.

The investigating officer wasn't the only one apologising. Simon Foy, the chief superintendent, wrote his commiserations to me when he left the post years later. It made me feel better, but did he know the charges were trumped up or blown out of proportion? If so, why did he – and everyone else – put me through it?

The case against me was eventually dropped – not that I was told at the time – moments after I was officially removed from Lambeth. I couldn't help feeling that it had been designed to halt my investigation long enough until other people were successfully put in place. I obviously had no proof but it was extremely disappointing.

And it worked.

I wish I'd never heard the phrase 'identify the enemy'. I was under investigation for doing my job too well, and the people who should have been championing my corner were the ones holding me back. The most terrifying thing was thinking there might be a very real puppet master pulling the strings and they were so far out of my reach. I felt genuinely scared, not only for me but for my family. Just a few short weeks earlier I'd thought I had a genuine chance of making an arrest that would end the torment of and bring justice for dozens, if not hundreds of innocent children placed in Lambeth's care. Yet, here I was, sidelined and neutered by people within my own organisation kow-towing to aggressive and unlawful forces above them, or so it seemed.

The Job had let me down, big time. I'd got into the police to fight bullies – and here they were within my own organisation. And the level of bullying that they were capable of was off the scale. It was a lesson I would learn from and never forget.

The weeks after my meeting left a cloud over me that I struggled to shift. My new posting should have made things better but it didn't. On paper, moving to an office on Nightingale Lane, just up the road from where I was born, should have brought me full circle. Working on Operation Trident, tackling gun crime and homicide, definitely should have got the old juices running. But I knew that was the point. It was a distraction. Someone, somewhere, had concocted the perfect job for me to keep me busy. And any other time I would have just swallowed it. Thank-you-very-much, head down, do my job.

But Lambeth had changed me. If I'd taken a suspect to court and lost, that would have been hard, but you accept it and move on. But being kneecapped before I could even speak to my suspect burned me up inside.

The Job could move me around all they liked but I would never, ever forget what they'd done to me.

I owed it to the public to give my new job my all, however. And so that is what I did. And, actually, I did have a bit of fun at first. But I found myself wondering how long it would be until someone or something would start to interfere?

It turned out, not very long at all.

You can't open a newspaper these days, especially in London, without 'Trident' being mentioned. As the police unit for dealing with 'black on black' crimes, it's a big deal. Back at the tail end of 1998 it was a bit more homespun, having been formed from Operation Dale House, an investigation into a series of Brixton murders. I knew all about that one, having been a DS in Brixton at the time. A group of men had come over from Jamaica, having heard the police had lost the streets of Brixton, and had shot people – for fun. They killed quite a few but the one I will never forget is Avril Johnson. She had been selling a bit of blow to make ends meet and they had wanted her clients – so they had made her kneel down in front of her kids and shot her in the back of the head. Total assassination. If we needed a reason to be present on the streets again, that was it.

So, Trident was formed and, luckily for me, they weren't above taking recruits thrown off other investigations. We had a little office in Mitcham police station, and from there six or seven of us took on the whole black underworld. That was the theory, anyway.

The very first job I did was a crack house down on Acre Lane. Our info was good and, based on that, we got a warrant and burst in. Suspect number one took it upon himself to leap through the window like he was escaping from a burning building.

'Aren't we on the first floor?' one of my team asked.

'Well, he's not,' I said. 'We'd better go and pick up the bits.'

Unfortunately for me – although fortunately for him – the dealer had done a textbook landing and was already halfway up the street when I hit the pavement.

Oh, dear ...

I gave chase but it was like a bad video game; every time I reached the end of the street, I'd just see him tearing around another corner ahead. The odds of me wearing him down were between slim and none. But I couldn't give up. It was my first job for Trident and, as one of the older blokes, I had something to prove to my team.

Seconds from a coronary, I swear, I turned another corner and pulled up, desperate to catch a breath. The man was nowhere to be seen. The only person out was an old lady who, as it happened, turned out to be a model citizen.

'Are you a police officer?' she asked.

'I – am – ma'am,' I managed to gasp out between deep breaths.

'Are you chasing someone?'

'Well – I – was – !'

'You might want to check behind those dustbins.'

Across the other side of the road was a stack of large, municipal metal dumps. But before I even got across to them, the dealer called out.

'Are you really police?'

'DI Driscoll at your service.'

'Thank God for that.'

And he marched out, wrists in front, ready to be cuffed.

'What's going on?' I had to ask. 'Why did you run?'

'I thought you were going to kill me. I thought you were from a gang.'

Well, that was a first. Slightly more comfortable was what happened next. As the collar was made half a mile from Brixton nick, that was the obvious place to take him. I whacked the geezer through the 105 – custody suite procedure – then I decided to check in with CID on the second floor. As I was running up the stairs, I found myself spinning into three blokes coming down.

'Driscoll?' one of them said.

I looked up and saw the one I had actually bumped into was the Right Honourable Jack Straw. The one speaking, however, was the chief superintendent, Simon Foy, who, if I had to describe his face, looked like he was about to have a thromby.

'What are you doing here?' he asked.

'I'm just checking some drugs in. Why?'

It soon became very clear that I should not have been there. Only once Foy and Straw had left did anyone come clean.

'What are you doing here? You were banned from Lambeth.'

'Why?'

'Because you trod on the toes of too many people.'

'Who?'

'The wrong people.'

It turned out everyone knew this – apart from me. Even Anna Tapsell had been told during her shakedown by Special Branch.

I was furious. What had I done wrong? Why was I being treated like the criminal? Someone needed to answer my questions.

I went straight round to see a colleague who I knew would be straight up with me on this occasion.

'You worried a lot of people, Clive,' he said. 'As I understand it, they even discussed you in Parliament.'

'Whatever for?'

'Who knows? But an order banning you from Lambeth had to come from somewhere on that level.'

Later this man denied saying that, but I can assure you he did. You don't forget learning your own government is out for your blood. Even if at the time I swore it was bollocks.

After that, I probably should have avoided Lambeth like the plague. In fact, what I actually did was set up camp in Brixton. There was hardly a day when I didn't have some 'business' to attend to either there or at one of the other main Lambeth stations.

No one was going to bully me out of doing my job.

But that didn't mean they wouldn't try.

One of my old SO5 jobs was helping a very young rape victim. I listened to that poor girl, I found the suspect and had enough evidence to get him to court. But it wasn't that easy. At every possible turn I met some obstruction. A lot of it was bureaucratic, much of it was people questioning my work: 'Are you sure about this, Clive?', 'Are you sure this stacks up?', 'You know she's a liar, don't you?' – but all of it was an attempt to snooker the case. And why? I couldn't say. But if I tell you the accused was Catholic, you could join the dots yourself.

As the court date drew nearer I received more and more pressure – bullying in any other language – to drop the case. Higher-ranking officers who would normally not have had any-thing to do with me flashed their credentials and expected me to roll over and have my tummy tickled like a good boy. I refused.

I certainly stopped answering my phone about a week before the court case.

On the day of the court case, once we were inside and I thought the worst was over, I was appalled to see another full turnout of luminaries in the gallery. It may or may not surprise you, but I could see those strange hand signals in every row.

To my barrister's credit, she worked the case incredibly thoroughly. As far as I was concerned, it was an open and shut case. Then the defence brief got up. I know it's her job but, bearing in mind the nature of the crime, some of the things she asked or claimed were beyond the pale. At one point she asked the victim, 'Do you know the difference between two fingers and a penis?'

She was a young child, for heaven's sake.

Afterwards I remember everyone congratulating the barrister on being so clever. But what had she done? She'd managed to win – in the jury's eyes – an argument with a vulnerable young girl who was barely out of primary school. She'd managed to convince 12 strangers that the girl didn't know the difference between fingers in her vagina and a penis. And she had got a nailed-on rape charge reduced to indecent assault so that the suspect was on the streets again before the victim had finished her school year.

I have the utmost respect for the judicial system and have worked with the most honourable of barristers but on this occasion I felt the profession had been sold a bit cheap.

In other words, the bad guys had won. Again.

A few years earlier I might have dusted myself down and got ready for the next round but this was a bout too far. The interference I'd received from outside my office just seemed like a challenge too insurmountable to make. I was but one man. Yes, I was a copper, but so were my enemies. What was I meant to do?

For once, playing the piano in the old people's homes didn't help. And so, having lost a lot of confidence and faith in the job I loved, I had a meeting with the superintendent.

'Nightingale Lane isn't for me,' I said.

'What do you want to do?'

'Anything apart from Serious Crime. I've had enough.'

I honestly had. My faith in the Met, having survived the betrayal during the Brixton riots, was now shot to pieces. My confidence in myself was just as low. I felt like I'd lost a game I didn't know I was playing against an unknown number of invisible players.

'Do you have anywhere else in mind?' he asked.

'Fulham. I want to go to Fulham.'

It was great to go to a police station where doing real police work was a priority, not an inconvenience. It was also fantastic to have a boss from the very top drawer.

If there is any justice in this world then DCI Helen Ball – as she was then – will be the first female commissioner. Her talents as an officer, a boss and a person were quite dazzling. After my previous experiences it was a breath of fresh air to turn up to Fulham Broadway and hear straight-talking from the off.

If anyone had an agenda, in fact, it was me. I'd selected Fulham only in part because I'd heard good things about Helen; the main reason for going there was because it was the area in which I had grown up and the area in which I felt most at home. And it was to be near my beloved Cottagers.

After the year I'd had, it was about time I got something out of the Job.

From the moment I started working with Helen Ball my career just took off. At the lowest point in my professional life she was incredibly supportive. Anything I have achieved since started, if I'm honest, with her. It started shortly after I arrived at Fulham, when she made me 'honorary DCI'.

But Lambeth has to take some credit, too. I learned a lot about people while I was there. Most of it not good. And that, hard as it was to learn, is a lesson they don't teach at Hendon.

But for a football fan, having Fulham, QPR and Chelsea on my doorstep was like a gift from God. What's more, as soon as Helen realised she had a CID officer who liked football, it was manna from heaven for me. There were massive problems on match days at all of those clubs.

'Sort it out, Clive, could you?'

'I'll certainly give it a go.'

I became quite the regular at Loftus Road and Stamford Bridge, as well as at Craven Cottage (I was there every fortnight watching Fulham play anyway). Touts were a big problem. Some people think it's just market forces and, if you're desperate to see a match, perhaps it's OK that you can pick up a ticket a few hours before. But touts don't care about the football. They don't care about your allegiances. And they certainly don't care where they seat you. I'd been there a week when a couple of Geordies came down to watch Newcastle play Chelsea. The touts sold them top-dollar tickets in the Shed – the most notorious part of Stamford Bridge football ground. Halfway through the match, the visitors sitting there in their black and white stripes, a Chelsea fan walked up and smacked one of them in the jaw. Over the next months I saw some very serious assaults that all kicked off in a similar way.

I'm not defending the Chelsea fan by any means, but that Geordie should never have been in the Shed. The FA have a charge called 'incitement'. The boys from Newcastle were unwittingly guilty of that, straight up.

I began by arresting the touts. A few of us dressed up as normal fans – not a hard look for me, although I drew the line at wearing a Chelsea scarf – then we identified the touts and arrested them. They generally all just said, 'It's a fair cop,' and came along quietly.

Touts, however, don't stay away for long and I realised I needed to go after the bigger fish just as I'd done with the handlers back on the Brixton burglary squad. To do that I needed the cooperation of the clubs themselves.

Eddie Ashwell was in charge of security at Chelsea, but he also happened to be an ex-copper so he wasn't entirely bad. Through him I gave lectures to the stewards at Stamford Bridge to help them spot touts and various other problem customers. More importantly, Eddie helped me trace back every ticket that we picked up as black market. Sometimes the source was a player earning a few quid on the side; more often it came from a book of tickets belonging to a season-ticket holder who didn't exist.

You needed a photograph to buy a season ticket so we were able to locate a picture of everyone who flogged theirs. When we got them all up on screen I burst out laughing.

'Well,' I said, 'either there's a lot of inbreeding among Chelsea fans, or someone's been playing in the wig box.'

Out of 25 photos there were only two different men, posing in every which way they could: hair parted down one side, parted down the middle, in a pony-tail, under a trilby, under a cap, wearing glasses, wearing sunglasses – you name it, they tried it to make themselves look like different people. When we went round to make the arrest, we didn't have a clue who would open the front door.

Buying a job lot of season tickets makes sense. Chelsea, at any one time, had about 500–600 touts buying tickets. Even if they didn't manage to sell the matches against the likes of Burnley or Bradford, knowing they could flog a £40 seat for £400 when the likes of Arsenal or United came to town made it all worthwhile. Even as a copper I could see that.

Some of the other crimes committed at the ground, however, did leave me scratching my head.

Since I'd started going to watch football matches I'd seen the gradual rise of the hooligan element. By the late 90s there were some established 'firms' of thugs who saw having a bundle after a match as a badge of honour. West Ham had a big problem with Cass Pennant's Inter City Firm, who would leave calling cards reading: 'Congratulations, you've just met the ICF.' At Stamford Bridge, what the Chelsea Head Hunters lacked in stationery, they made up for in violence. These men would travel in on match days then sit in the pub opposite – they didn't even watch the game. When the away fans came out they would attack them with sticks, glasses, fists, feet – whatever they could think of.

I was thinking of how we could combat this when I happened upon a documentary on TV one evening that contained the answer.

An undercover reporter called Donal MacIntyre had infiltrated the Head Hunters and – as an example of how bright they all are – had managed to film an awful lot of it. On his film he showed several men travelling around the country for the sake of violence. Two of them, Jason Marriner and Andy 'The Nightmare' Frain, hogged the spotlight, but it was Frain who made me sit up and take proper notice.

When you hear a hooligan boasting how he'd cut a policeman's throat, it can get your attention.

The next day I told the chief superintendent, Anthony Wills, what I'd seen. 'We can't have people on national television boasting how they've cut a police officer's throat,' I said. 'We should be doing a job on this lot.'

'I agree, Clive. Do whatever it takes.'

Wow, first Helen Ball, then him. I'd almost forgotten what a supportive boss felt like.

My first port of call was with the journalist Donal MacIntyre. I suppose, once an undercover reporter, always an undercover reporter because, even though his office had central heating, there he was wrapped in a large overcoat.

He's not recording anything, by chance, is he?

But he turned out to be a good egg and upon service of a Court Order he handed over all his recordings. All 344 hours of them.

My poor DS, the excellent Nick Elgar, won the job of scouring through every second of every tape for evidence, with a couple of helpers. I offered to help but that would have required sitting down for more than a few minutes, which has never been my style, and I don't think Nick would have let me: even when he earned a double fracture on his leg one Saturday in a rugby match, he insisted on coming in to work – wearing a great big leg clamp.

'Go home, Nick,' I said.

'I don't want to let you down, guv.'

On my life. What a team.

The second meeting I had was with the then-owner of Chelsea, the inimitable Ken Bates. He was a one-off, was Ken, and he ruled Stamford Bridge like a king prowling his castle. And a pretty obnoxious king at times too. He knew Anthony Wills hated being called 'Tony', so he peppered every conversation with the abbreviation. And as for me, the second we were introduced he said, 'Oh, you're my new DI, are you? I suppose you'll be poncing tickets off me like the rest—?'

I laughed. 'Why would I want to come and watch a bunch of clapped-out old Italians?'

That stopped him for a second.

'What's wrong with you, man? Don't you like football?'

I said, 'I love football. Would you like to borrow my pen?' And reaching into my breast pocket I produced my biro with the Fulham crest on it.

Bates grabbed it, swore at me, then flung it over his shoulder.

There was a lot of background work to be done on the Head Hunters but the bread and butter of the case was the work done by

Nick Elgar and the guys in front of the screens. The watchwords where evidence is concerned are continuity and integrity. Without those two aspects a lawyer would rip us apart. After many weeks of goggle vision, we had enough to charge Frain and Marriner.

I'm a good friend of Donal now but I was a bit put out to see TV cameras on site when we swooped in to make the arrests. He denied any involvement – still does – but, regardless, he made up for it in court.

There is no one I hold in higher regard than someone prepared to be a witness in court. Often, they are opening themselves up to public threat or potential abuse, sometimes they're opening old wounds. Always they're putting justice before their own ends and for that I, and every right-minded civilian, will be forever grateful.

Thanks to the A1 evidence, the team's diligence and Donal's contributions, we got both men sent down: Frain for seven years and Marriner for six. They were also banned from football matches for 20 years.

It's fair to say that I got a lot of my old confidence back during those early months in Fulham. So much so that I had a bit of a 'eureka' moment one morning. I went in to see Anthony Wills and said, 'Dr Valerie Sinason, the therapist I met during the Roofie investigation, has been requesting a police liaison for her clinic – I'd like to volunteer.'

Once he got his head around the idea, the chief superintendent was very supportive.

'What will it take?'

'One day a month, guv. Tops.'

'Can you afford the time to do it?'

'Can we afford not to?'

Valerie runs the Clinic for Dissociative Studies which, in old money, looks after people with 'multiple personalities'. The reason she wanted police input into her work was very simple: multiple personalities are created as a direct result of a very young child – even a baby – being sexually abused. Every single patient she saw had their own horrific past – and most of their stories had never been heard.

After the Lambeth experience there was nothing I wanted more than to help child abuse victims. But I had a problem: was 'dissociative identity disorder', DID as she called it, really a thing? Weren't people with multiple personalities, at best, just suffering from schizophrenia or, at worst, having her on?

Valerie didn't think so. The child's mind when under attack, she explained, tries to protect itself in the only way it can, which is, in effect, by creating other 'people', other personalities, to hide behind within the same body.

I did my own research and spoke with Dr Joan Coleman, Jean La Fontain, the False Memory Society and several top psychiatrists. Of two eminent professors, one said the condition was all completely true – and the other said it was a fabrication. As a subject to investigate it is wonderful as there is no middle ground: you either totally believe it or totally don't. As a police officer you just have to prove it and your own personal beliefs are irrelevant. Follow the leads and see where they take you and report the truth. Easy really.

All I can say with real certainty is that the people I met certainly seemed genuine.

And that many of those people shared a body.

One of the first people Valerie introduced me to was the woman I had been meaning to interview for a long time: Sue Castle.

'I've been looking forward to meeting you,' I said.

'Why is that?'

I explained about the work I had been doing in Lambeth. Strangely, she knew nothing about it, despite her claims that she was abused by members of that very council. That's when Dr

Sinason pointed out I was talking to the 'wrong' person. A few minutes later, her patient spoke again.

'My name's Bonny,' she said. 'Thank God you've come.'

'Bonny' was the dominant personality of Sue Castle. She was the one who had had acid thrown into her face and woken up to find her bed on fire. But she was not the one raped as a baby: that was Sue. 'No one's heard of Sue for a long while.' Even Valerie had never met her.

Among other things, Bonny said that Liverpool officers had told her they would be taking over her allegations and conducting the investigation because 'all the Metropolitan Police were bent'. Their words.

A good start.

Bonny was not, however, the one raped by a council member. But she knew all about it because of the computer files the other personality had left at home.

What I heard caused my head to spin, if I'm honest. Sue – as she was known – had been working in Lambeth Council when she was taken to a council property in Vauxhall, drugged by a male member of staff and raped by multiple strangers all dressed in robes and animal masks, chanting at every turn. It was, she said, like a church ceremony gone wrong.

It was exactly the same story I'd heard from the rohypnol victim in York. Could there really be a nationwide organisation conducting the same sick rituals on women and – as Sue also confirmed – children? It really was beginning to look like it should be investigated. Either the patients/victims have all seen the same video, all talked together and all read the same book or they have all been to similar ceremonies. The one thing I know for sure is they all believe these things happened to them and they deserve nothing less than respect and a thorough honest investigation that seeks the truth.

I wanted to do so much for Sue but, I discovered, her case was already under the Met's wing as Operation Progarda. I remembered this being discussed at a meeting with Merseyside Police officers in August, who wanted to take it on. Many weeks later I found out that the Met had refused their request.

In the meantime, Sue had lost all faith in the police. She'd been attacked, threatened and nearly murdered since reporting her assault. She'd even named certain prominent people who she claimed she had recognised behind their masks – and what had been done? In her eyes, nothing.

While my hands were tied by red tape, I could still help Sue in other ways. Through my research into dissociative identity disorder, I began to suspect that the personality within her that was the victim of the abuse was still being abused. This can come about when a child is programmed from a very young age to accept the abuse – it doesn't know any different. When that person grows up, a certain type of abuser knows how to create 'triggers' that call out the victim personality to be abused again. For some people it's a certain word spoken down the phone; for others it's a picture sent in the mail.

As I say, I have spoken to several experienced psychiatrists who say dissociative identity disorder is very real – and the same number who say it does not exist.

It's a real problem for the police. Should you get as far as court, experts will give their opinion for the prosecution and then for the defence and on occasion they are opposites. Another reason why you need a thorough investigation.

For Sue, it turned out, she thought her trigger was in emails coming in: Bonny and another personality, Patricia, recalled opening certain computer files – which would then 'disappear' as another personality took over. They both suspected what that personality was made to do.

'What can I do to help?' I asked.

'You need to get rid of our computer.'

'No problem.'

I had no idea if this would lead anywhere but I felt compelled to try. To make everything above board, I acquired a warrant, then checked again with Sue that it was still what she wanted.

'Absolutely, Clive. When can you get here?'

'Give me half an hour.'

For the sake of professionalism, I asked Nick Elgar to accompany me. To this day, he thinks it's the greatest decision I ever made.

Sue opened the door and said, 'Thank God you've come, Clive,' then, as Elgar waited by the front door, she led me into the sitting room. The computer was a proper desktop job, big and square, and still plugged in, so I went over to unhook everything – when suddenly there was this whack on the back of my shoulder.

'What are you doing? Who are you? Get out of my fucking house!'

I don't think that's Bonny.

'Sue,' I said. 'My name is DI Driscoll and I'm taking your computer away.'

'Why?'

'Because you asked me to.'

'Don't you dare touch that computer or I'll kill you.'

Before I could do anything else, she flew at me. Luckily Sue is a tiny woman, five foot nothing, but it was still a job to hold her off with one hand while I scrabbled all the cables together with the other. I called into the corridor, 'Nick, a bit of help here?' but the DS was virtually on the floor, crying with laughter. 'I'll remember this when you ask for promotion.'

Eventually I got the whole lot under my arm, which was when Sue disappeared into the kitchen.

'Oh, God, she's going for a knife.'

But when she came back out, still effing and blinding, she was carrying a pan full of water – which she let fly all over me, much to Elgar's amusement.

'Get the bloody door, Nick!' I shouted, which is when it got even more bizarre.

'It's all right, Clive, I'll let you out,' a female voice next to me said.

'Bonny?'

'Who else would it be? Thanks for coming. I really think this could make a difference.'

As I said, bizarre. But that was not the end of it.

When we got back to the station, I was told there had been a complaint made against me by a certain Sue Castle. The station had already despatched an officer round to take a statement. When he got back, I feared the worst.

'What did she say?' I asked.

'I asked if she knew Clive Driscoll and she said, and I quote, "Oh yes, Clive's a lovely man. So helpful."'

'Well, she got that right.' I laughed with relief. But another day who knows who would have answered the door – or what she would have said.

I dried the computer as best I could and Nick and I took it down to see a forensic team in Sussex. Sure enough, it was knackered as a PC but the boffins there were able to retrieve the files from the hard drive.

'Are you sure you want to see these, Inspector?' one of the lab boys said.

We went over to look and, just as I'd expected, Sue's computer was full of some of the most sickening images you can imagine with a trail of evidence proving where they had originated from. Sadly, it wasn't the first time either Nick or I had been shown such things so we managed to keep our emotions in check.

Then the technician opened a completely unrelated file and a large picture of Sir Alex Ferguson filled the screen. 'Now that *is* disgusting!' I said, and both Elgar and I, two of the only non-Man Utd supporters in London, ran out of the room, pretending to vomit.

You take your humour where you can in this job.

I handed the computer, the hard drive and all my findings over to Operation Middleton, who refused to let Merseyside have it – but did nothing with it themselves. Again the question raises its head: who did Sue Castle see during her ordeal that was powerful enough to put an entire Met operation on ice?

She and I both had our suspicions.

I began speaking to other patients at Dr Sinason's Clinic for Dissociative Studies. Because of their conditions I often heard the same story three or four times from one person – but that wasn't the only repetition. The same stories also kept being told to me by patient after patient. They were adults now but, as children or young women, they told me how they'd been abducted, taken to places and raped as part of some kind of ritual by men and women in masks and cloaks. But the masks didn't always cover entire faces. Like Sue, a number of the patients could identify some of their assailants as public figures. Some of them were exactly the same public figures Sue had seen.

The crossover was unbelievable. I spoke to people from all over the country and the same scenarios featuring the same names kept popping up.

The police were the only agency who could find out. But only if they wanted to. Again, I put it all over to SO5.

But still nothing happened. In my opinion, some of those claims could haunt the Metropolitan Police Service for years to come.

*

I could have walked away. But, I thought, *Sod it. I'm not going to roll over. You are not going to force me not to be a police officer.*

If Operation Middleton wouldn't touch these cases then I'd look into them myself. The problem was, I soon discovered, it wasn't just the Met that didn't appear to be looking as hard as it could at certain evidence. It is easier to just say these people are ill and it is all made up. I think that would be the False Memory Society's position if asked.

One young woman I knew as 'Vicky' had a slightly different take on the horror stories. She talked about a place in Kent where she had been taken, along with other children, and made to run away from dogs. They were literally dumped in the woods and given a head start before the hunting pack was released. She survived. The other kids were not so fortunate.

I'd learned my lesson about not believing people so I took Vicky's horrific story at face value and made some enquiries to the police in Kent. They had investigated her complaint but basically had shelved it because they said Vicky's description of the route didn't stack up. She'd said there was a bridge where there wasn't and a well where there wasn't. Reading between the lines, they thought she'd concocted the whole macabre episode.

I could have done a number of things with that information. The only option that called to me, however, was the one that involved getting out of the office. And so, off I drove to Kent.

I found the place where Vicky said she'd been released and I walked the entire route across fields and country walkways. It all looked exactly as the police report had said. No bridge, no well. At least, not at face value. But Vicky was about 30 when I spoke to her. The crime she reported had taken place when she was six or seven. I hailed a passing local and said, 'Has there ever been a bridge here?'

'Yes, over there, but it got washed away in the floods.'

'Thank you very much!'

Inspired, I scoured every inch of one of the fields and eventually found a bloody great hole in the ground. It wasn't a well with a bucket, but that's definitely what it had once been used for.

So, Vicky's facts weren't wrong about the route. In turn, everything else she told me needed taking seriously, including the fact that the injured children were thrown into a 'blue lake'.

Again, I went to a local and asked for help. It turned out there was a lake which, due to waste being dumped by a local cement factory, did look blue. When I checked the police records, I discovered that body parts belonging to five people had been found there.

'What did the investigation into that find?' I asked a beleaguered file clerk at the nick.

'I don't know if there was one.'

'You're telling me you find five body parts – from different people – and there's no investigation?'

'Well, there's no record of one, let me put it that way.'

I felt sweat on my back as the awful truth became clear: not being able to find papers wasn't just a London thing...

There was one other claim from Vicky that I also wanted to test. She'd said a man had used a local church for rituals involving children from local children's homes. I would have expected Kent Police to know about it.

It transpired the officer who'd taken Vicky's complaint had installed a camera in a house overlooking the church all those years ago. The camera had recorded group activity, however grainy in quality, including strange costumes, which I duly noted in my day book.

Now, this is interesting.

'Is there any chance I could see those tapes?' I asked.

'I'm afraid they went missing a while ago,' I was told.

'What about images? Computer discs?'

'Everything has gone. Files, hard copies and tapes.'

I had no evidence that the footage had been deliberately lost or even ever taken place. But, in the police, budget is rarely an obstacle to an investigation so the routine thing to do would be to start again. I spoke to two WPCs in the local vulnerable persons unit and they said they would investigate. They did, but I never saw a word of it. The week before they were due to present their findings, so I was told, the whole lot vanished from their desks again.

I told Vicky and Valerie about my findings. Rather than be as despondent as me at the outcome, Vicky could not stop thanking me. It was the same story with all the patients I tried to help at the clinic.

'They spend their whole lives looking for someone who will believe their stories,' Valerie said.

'Whether I believe them or not is irrelevant. A thorough investigation is their right.'

Over the year and a half I worked with the clinic I investigated all sorts of black magic groups and semi-religious occurrences, even tracking down the grand secretary of a cult which I thought seemed to fit the blueprint of the organisation in the allegations, although, without wishing to be boring, everyone is innocent until ... I was so certain that I informed Special Branch of my plan and they were interested enough to want two officers to come with me. On the morning of my trip, both bailed out at the last minute.

Was that suspicious? With anyone else, definitely. But Special Branch, you have to understand, is a very weird place. Cheap suits and the *Guardian*, what else do I need to say?

The grand secretary admitted his organisation did hire castles and occasionally indulge in what could be described as orgies, but that nothing untoward ever happened. The children mentioned in his ceremonies, he said, were young recruits. Again, I passed the information over, again I expected to hear back exactly what I did: nothing. Not a dickie bird. Not a peep. It was easier for them to dismiss Vicky's claims as madness rather than investigate such a taboo subject.

I don't know how much else I could have done one day a month – even with all the weekend and evening time I was throwing into it. But I do know it wasn't enough: Vicky killed herself and went to her grave knowing her alleged abusers were still at large. She starved herself to death. Killed from within. Total organ failure. Whatever Special Branch or others think of her condition, one thing is real: she is dead.

Whatever else I achieved at Fulham, Vicky's death impacted on me the most. But, after the original interference from outside forces at Lambeth, this time I handled it better. Still, when my time at Fulham came to an end after a couple of years, I took some pleasure in joining the Complaints squad – based in Lambeth. In the words of one of my earliest mentors, the legend that is Andy Cow, 'The least we can do is inconvenience these people.' And that was exactly what I intended to do. If I couldn't beat them, at least I could make them uncomfortable.

It gave me no real pleasure investigating other policemen but my interests have always lain with the victims, not covering my colleagues' backsides. The innocent ones got off, the guilty ones were sent down, just like anyone else. Best of all, I did it with very little outside interference from the government, the council or any other organisation – apart from the time I asked one of my team to work late, which meant missing his choir practice.

'Are you sure about this, sir?' he asked, grinning.

'You know we're under the cosh here. I need everyone working.'

'If you say so.'

Ten minutes later my phone rang. It was a DAC.

'Driscoll? Do you know how important this choir is?'

As he left the office the DS had the good grace to mouth 'Sorry' as he threw his tie over his shoulder... he just about shut the door before my paperweight smashed against it. The next day he brought me in a tie from the Catholic Guild. 'Put that on, guv, and you'll never get in trouble again.' He was joking – I think.

For two years I stuck to that posting and I probably could have stayed longer except that I became over-qualified. Then, in 2003, I'd applied for the post of Detective Chief Inspector – and passed, despite being the only applicant not to use a PowerPoint presentation and the newfangled whiteboards.

Even before I got back to my desk, my mobile was ringing. I could not believe who it was: Gordon Briggs. The man must have had my number on his speed dial.

'Congratulations, DCI Driscoll!'

'Thank you, sir. Can I help you with anything?'

'As a matter of fact you can. I've got just the job for a man of your qualities. Are you interested?'

'Do you remember the waves I made last time?'

'Oh, yes.' He laughed. 'And that's exactly what I'm hoping you'll do again.'

My name had been discussed in Parliament. I'd got on the watch lists of who-knew-which murky agencies. What job could Gordon Briggs possibly want me for? Chasing litter louts in the Outer Hebrides?

CHAPTER FOURTEEN

The Body's Still Warm

The job turned out to be leading one of the proactive teams of the Racial and Violent Crime Task Force, part of a wider Met unit called Athena Tower, run from an office block, not a station, in Penrhyn Road, Kingston.

Even with Briggsy in my corner, I had to actually audition for the job against several other candidates, which some might have seen as a negative but I saw as very positive. It couldn't be that bad if they were throwing it open to others, could it?

Turned out, it could. The atmosphere at Penrhyn Road was not good. I'd had a cracking team on Complaints – top-notch people at Fulham, Lambeth, Brixton; in fact, everywhere I'd ever led men and women. The faces when I walked into Racial and Violent would have curdled milk.

I've got my work cut out here.

It's funny, though, how quickly people can change. There was nothing wrong with the team at Kingston. They had no problem with me, either. They were just a bunch of really good people worn down by a series of bad decisions from on high.

I'm gonna fit right in here.

Even before I got my feet under my desk I saw an example of the sort of things that were going on. They were putting away a couple of cases before I arrived, and one of them involved a Muslim woman who had died in Southall. Her death wasn't suspicious: old age, natural causes, call it what you will. The problem – and the reason the Racial team had been called in – was because, while she was lying in the morgue, someone had draped her naked body with bacon. As the woman was a Muslim, and eating pork is forbidden in the Qur'an, this was obviously a hate crime.

I didn't have anything else to do until the DCI cleared off so I took a look at the file, just to get myself up to speed on the way the team worked. No one had been arrested so maybe I could even help.

I was pretty pleased with what I saw. Everything seemed to have been done by the book. The right questions had been asked of the right people and the evidence had been followed up in the correct way. There was only one slight, tiny thing I could fault. They hadn't arrested a bloke that the evidence clearly pointed to as a suspect.

It was there in black and white, plain as the nose on my face – and that's pretty plain, before anyone else says it. There was one person who had been interviewed – another Muslim, incidentally – who had had motive, inclination and, most importantly, time alone with the corpse, just before the discovery of the bacon. Now, I'm a student of Sherlock Holmes, yes, but anyone could have made that deduction. In the end my curiosity got the better of me and I approached one of the team – my new team.

'I've just read this file.'

'Oh, yeah.'

'It seems to me like there's a pretty stand-up suspect.'

'You're right there, guv.'

'So why haven't you arrested him?'

'He's a Muslim.'

'So?'

'We're the racial crimes squad. We're meant to stop people targeting ethnic groups.'

'But the person he desecrated was Muslim as well. Don't we have a duty to protect her faith?'

'It's not my decision.'

'Well, whose is it?'

Two guesses, but you'll only need one. The call had come from 'above'. We were not to rock the boat. To arrest a Muslim for such a heinous crime would pour oil on the flames, they said.

'Poppycock,' I said – or words to that effect.

I have not yet met the community that does not want crime solved. Just like I've not yet met a community that does not want to be protected from murder, and wants suspects of murder to be caught. You don't cover up a crime in case it causes offence or upsets people. Did I miss that class at Hendon?

The Met thought it was doing the family a service by not naming the obvious suspect. Wrong call, every day of the week. That family could have dealt with it. They weren't radicals, they wouldn't run to the press screaming 'racism' if we did our job. They were just normal people who wanted closure on a terribly disrespectful attack on a loved one.

It really made me wonder what I was getting myself into. We were the police, and we were meant to act like it – not pussyfoot around suspects in case we offended them.

I hated the decision to put over-sensitive, perceived political correctness before justice but, like a football manager uses bad press as his team talk, it gave me ammunition for my introductory speech.

'We are the police,' I said. 'We follow leads, we investigate and we nail the bad guys. Whatever colour their skin, whatever god they worship, we pursue the truth. Isn't that the whole point of us? As long as you are honest, transparent and you treat everyone with respect, you and the job you do will be respected too. You might not be liked – there will be people who despise the ground you walk on – but if you want to be loved by everybody then maybe the police service isn't the job for you.'

Respect and good intentions can get you a long way. They can also keep the noise down. When I was on Complaints, I dealt with a case that happened to be handled by Racial. A bloke had died in Brixton as a result of a road traffic accident – that's what the doctor said, that's what the original PC reported. But an autopsy revealed it wasn't the car crash that killed him. He'd been stabbed by a stiletto knife.

The reason I'd got involved was because the family were upset at a junior PC sent out to investigate the murder. To be fair, the PC thought it was a simple road traffic accident (RTA). Everyone did. But what got the complainant really upset was when one of my team on Complaints wrote back to her saying, 'I'm very sorry to hear about the death of your son.'

The victim had been her brother.

Because I immediately admitted our mistake and apologised fully, the man's sister calmed down. But fast-forward to my first week at Racial and I heard a commotion coming from another office. I knew the commander, Cressida Dick, had booked the space so I decided to stick my head round the corner to see what was going on.

'Everything all right, ma'am?' I asked.

The second I did a voice chirruped up from behind the door.

'Is that you, Clive?'

It was the sister of the stabbed victim. She'd come in and was obviously not happy with what she was being told. But because of our relationship, I got everyone talking.

Once again, I was in a job where *talking* to people was key. I've said before that I always believed that talking to people should lie at the heart of police work, and I still do. And for my first job as DCI for the Racial and Violent Crime Task Force, in October 2003, it made all the difference between solving a case and not, although I nearly caught pneumonia in the process.

It was first thing in the morning and one of the boys from Athena Tower wandered over with a note.

'You're up, Driscoll.'

Dozens of Muslim gravestones had been kicked over in a cemetery in Greenwich. It was already being run with the headline 'Racist Britain' on Al Jazeera TV right across the Middle East so the priority was obvious: clear it up, and clear it up fast.

If ever I've felt like staying indoors, that was the day. The weather was foul, the rain coming down in sheets in Kingston; by the time my DI, Danny Walsh, and I had pulled up in Greenwich, it was somehow even worse.

We slung on the waterproofs, pulled our collars up and started looking round the graveyard. Straight off I noticed that the first few stones I looked at had little etchings of a flag.

'That's the Turkish flag, isn't it, Dan?'

'I'll take your word for it, guv.'

Whatever it was, every single gravestone that had been upended carried the same ensign. Suddenly the crime seemed a bit clearer.

'This isn't an anti-Muslim attack, this is anti-Turkey.'

'But why?'

'What were you doing last night?'

'Watching the match.'

And there was the answer: racism wasn't behind the desecration, it was football. England had scraped a no-score draw in Istanbul the night before, with old Goldenballs Beckham missing a penalty. By the looks of it, a few England fans hadn't been too happy about it.

But that didn't help us find the culprits. That was only going to be done by asking questions.

'We're going to stay here and interview everyone who visits a grave and anyone who passes.'

And so we did. For a day and a half in torrential rain of biblical proportions, we stood there. We became such a feature that TV and radio crews came down and I was able to appeal for help.

And it was the standing in the rain that got us the breakthrough. Two people took pity on our drowned-rat routine and admitted they'd seen various school kids at the church on Saturday night. A few other leads took us closer and eventually we had enough to swoop and prosecute.

For a while we were heroes on Al Jazeera for solving the unsolvable. When our own media stuck cameras in my face I was able to show my gratitude: 'I am absolutely delighted with the response of the public.'

We had had three calls. I was amazed and delighted.

Our next job looked just as unlikely to be put away. Again, we surprised everyone. Awful racist cartoons and threats were being sent to indiscriminate black targets; on occasion, bullets had been posted as well. Each envelope bore a stamp from HMS something or other, which obviously led us down the path of suspecting a naval figure.

Then, while I was looking at one of the cartoons, I had a brainwave: 'How many people can draw this well?' I decided to take a punt and go back through the history books. I found a similar job from some years earlier. It had become the longest-running racial investigation ever because no prosecutions had ever been made – but that did not mean they didn't have a suspect. I compared the historic cartoons with the new ones. It didn't take my Sherlock magnifying glass to establish the similarities.

'I'm no art connoisseur,' I said, 'but this is our man.'

And it was. One of my team caught him posting a letter which turned out to be vile and abusive. Bang to rights, I think they say.

Two cases, two big challenges, two strikes. Who could have predicted that when I first joined that bunch of moping faces?

Not only had we turned the department around, but also the lucky streak continued. We tidied up a fair number of little jobs that fell under our remit. Some of them were historic or 'cold' cases that had never been cleared up, others were more current but weird.

The one thing they all had in common was they were cases nobody else wanted to touch.

Of course, it wouldn't have been me and it wouldn't have been the Met if I had been allowed to continue this successful run without obstruction: we'd been tearing through the cases for a few months when I was suddenly told the Racial and Violent Crime Task Force was being shut down. John Grieves, our division's brilliant former leader, had left, which gave others a chance to interfere.

I was called to a meeting at Scotland Yard where a commander explained what would happen to each part of the task force now it was being disbanded. As he read out the names of each department he wrote them on a whiteboard to show their new reporting structure. At the end he said, 'Any questions?'

I put up my hand. 'Excuse me, sir,' I said, 'you haven't written my Penrhyn Road team on the board.'

Deptford was also missing as well.

The commander went to the board, drew a bubble as far away from the other names as possible and wrote our divisions in it.

'We haven't got a clue what to do with you two.'

And so began the oddest six months of my career.

A few weeks later I was called back in. A decision had been made.

'We're shutting down Penrhyn Road task force.'

'Are you firing me?'

'No, we want you to head up Emerging Threats in New Communities.'

'What about my team?'

'They're coming with you.'

'Where?'

'Same office.'

All they'd done was change the name. You really couldn't make it up.

In fact, over the next half-dozen months I had to get my business cards reprinted four times but, whether we were Racial and Violent, Emerging Threats in New Communities, Southeast Asian Crime Squad or SCD2(2), my desk never moved once.

If I'm honest, it seemed like not everyone was happy with our success. When we put away the abusive artist the amount of back-slapping we got from within Scotland Yard was pretty lacklustre to be fair. I didn't want to make an issue out of nothing but I happened to mention this over lunch to my old guv'nor from Brixton, Brian Paddick.

'Am I being paranoid or are people not exactly overjoyed we're putting cases away?'

'Look at it this way, Clive,' he said. 'A lot of people worked on that case for a long time and got nowhere. You waltz in and nail the guy – their guy. You've put a lot of noses out of joint.'

'You think so?'

'I do. And long may it continue.'

Regardless of what we were called, people were beginning to notice our clear-up rate. Gordon Briggs was one of them. In January 2004, he rang me.

'I've got a murder that needs a squad. Are you up for it?'

'How old is it?' I asked.

'Put it this way, the body's still warm.'

Being given a murder was unheard of for a group like ours – proper murder squads, as the name suggests, normally took these. But around Christmas resources were tight and, Briggsy reminded me, our investigating abilities had caused people to sit up.

I got my squad together. 'This is the big time, people,' I said. 'Let's show them what we can do.'

The crime was a nasty one. Maheswaran Kaneshan was a Sri Lankan lad, 26 years old, and had somehow been tricked into working for peanuts for a gang run by Tamil Tigers in east London. There was nothing dodgy about his work: the gang basically housed a load of Sri Lankans in large houses, took their passports, and hired them out as labour or kitchen assistants to some of the top hotels and restaurants in town. The catch was in the payment: the gang was paid five or six quid for each hour the lads worked, whereas they only received a quid. Eventually, Maheswaran found a job in a BP garage earning seven times that and for a while times were good. But, if you happen to be running an organisation where the economic model is to keep your staff working for you for peanuts, the last thing you need is someone showing the others how they could earn more elsewhere. And so, on Monday 12 January 2004, as Maheswaran and two friends were leaving a restaurant at the top of Heighams Road near East Ham tube station, a gang of eight men jumped them, all armed with hammers, swords and, because it's their national sport and they all owned one, a cricket bat. The two friends survived; Maheswaran died in hospital from his injuries.

Normally when there's been a murder, a mob from the closest station will descend on the scene and keep it untampered with until the murder squad arrive. We call those first responders the 'Elastoplast' team because they're literally covering the cracks, not solving the problem. When my team arrived, however, it was so small I had to ask some of the band-aids to hang around to give us some support.

It got worse when I staged a re-enactment of the murder. Normally you have three officers on each corner of the road to control the public – I could only have one covering both sides, so he had to keep darting across the road every five minutes. But we had a functional roadblock, decent team morale and, crucially, a bit of luck. I spoke to just about everyone who passed and thanks to some very brave people ended up with three names.

We made it just in time to pick up Sivalingam Sivakuma as he was about to board a flight to Colombo, Sri Lanka. By coincidence, while he was in our custody he received a call from the other two – Sivajodi Anantharaja and Sivapragasam Rajeskanna – telling him to keep mum or suffer the consequences. We got a record of that, which was A1 evidence in anyone's book. The downside was they were phoning from Sri Lanka: we'd missed nabbing them by a matter of hours.

Sivakuma was processed in due course and found guilty of murder. He got life with a recommendation he serve 17 years.

'Well done, Clive,' Briggsy said. Others were just as impressed, in that special Met way: 'Not bad for a non-murder squad' and 'The Cockney Columbo strikes again!' was the general line!

But as good as I felt about nabbing Sivakuma, the fact I'd missed two others, each with nailed-on guilty verdicts thanks to forensics on the getaway car and weapons, plus eye-witness statements and the phone call evidence, rankled. This was where I hoped to get the support the world's greatest police force was renowned for; instead, what I got was shoulder shrugs.

'Let it go, mate – one out of three ain't bad.'

One man, whose name I won't repeat, said, 'What's the point in worrying? It's only a kid from Sri Lanka.'

I replied, 'I don't give a toss who it is! The Queen I swore an oath to at Hendon says I have to look after him, so I bloody well will.'

'Good luck with that.'

Yeah, I thought, *I'll need it. I don't have a clue what to do.*

I was hammering hell out of the old joanna keys that night when inspiration struck.

If I couldn't catch them here, I'd take the case to Sri Lanka.

*

If I'd known how hard it would be to get to Sri Lanka, I might not have bothered. First I had to present my case to the Crown Prosecution Service in Ludgate Hill. They deliberated for a while then agreed it could work and sent my application to the UK clearing authority. When their lawyers agreed, I could finally take it to court, along with my witnesses and evidence, and ask a judge for a warrant. It was a real uphill struggle and, as I ploughed from one month into the next, I could see why my colleagues had advised against it. But what's six months compared to the life of a dead man?

International law is a funny thing and even after I got my warrant it was not guaranteed that my suspects would be bundled up and posted back. Added to which, rumours of the Colombo police having been paid off were rife.

One day I said to Gordon Briggs: 'I need to go out there.'

'I agree.'

'And I need to take a credit card.'

'I was worried you'd say that.'

'And I want the Sri Lankan police on my side.'

I was authorised to wine and dine my hosts to whatever extent I deemed appropriate. The only thing I could not give them was cash. A meal and drink was being sociable; handing over hard currency was bribery. The Met doesn't do bribery.

Bearing in mind the stick I've had on an almost daily basis from Londoners who don't like the Old Bill, setting foot in Sri Lanka was a right touch. I was escorted directly from the plane to a limo, then plonked inside the opulent, wood-panelled office of the attorney general. Not bad for a Battersea boy.

Because – and I blame the dyslexia for this, of course – I don't speak a word of Tamil or Sinhalese, the two main Sri Lankan languages, I'd taken along a DC from my unit who happened to be of Tamil origin. Ramanarthan Samasunderan was to be my eyes and ears in the country. He could start off by translating my greeting to the smart geezer in the immaculate pin-striped suit. 'Constable, please inform the attorney general that Her Majesty's Metropolitan Police are honoured to be in Sri Lanka. We would like to thank him for the privilege of allowing us to travel and we're looking forward to working with the Sri Lankan police service, and government.'

Ramanarthan nodded and then repeated, in English: 'Sir, I would like to inform you that Her Majesty's Metropolitan Police are honoured to be in Sri Lanka. We would like to thank you for the privilege of allowing us to travel and we're looking forward to working with the Sri Lankan police service, and government.'

What?

In impeccable RP, he replied, 'The pleasure is all mine. Wonderful to have you here, old chap.'

If I'd bothered to look above his head, there was a picture of him and three others in a boat on the Thames. He was only a bloody Oxford blue! Obviously my smug DC had known he would speak English but hadn't seen the need to inform me.

Still, it worked and the attorney general gave us his blessing and all the help we needed.

I said, 'I'm only over here at this stage to establish good relations with your police force.'

However much it costs.

The whole force couldn't have been nicer – or more upfront. They liked the idea of our forces being friends, they liked the idea of them catching our murderers – and they weren't against being wined and dined at the Colombo Hilton on the Met's flexible friend.

'But, you know, we'd all prefer the cash.'

'I'm sorry, but the Met doesn't pay cash.'

'But you will buy us a meal?'

'Yes, and a bloody good one. But cash is not something I can swing.'

'OK ...'

I had got the feeling they were out to make a point. When we sat down at the Hilton they ordered lobsters, crabs, sushi, steaks, cocktails, champagne, more cocktails and more champagne. They then started on a local coconut spirit called arrack, which personally I wouldn't strip the paint of my house with.

In fact, although I had my share of everything, I didn't enjoy a sip. I was just worrying how I was going to explain to Commander Dick how I bankrupted Athena Tower. When the moment of truth finally arrived and the waiter slid over the bill in a cardboard wallet, I couldn't even bear to look. I just passed him the Barclaycard, signed on the dotted line and staggered out.

It was only when I got back to England that I received the statement. I still remember wincing as I tore the envelope open.

When I peered at the figures I burst out laughing. The whole evening at the Hilton had cost ... £83.80.

The next time I went out to Sri Lanka there was a lot more riding on my trip. The arrests by my friends in the police had been made and the suspects were about to be processed through the Sri Lankan courts. Again, the advice from London was to 'leave the foreigners to it'. That didn't make sense to me.

'Who knows the case better than I do? I need to be there.'

So, out I went again, accompanied by my trusted translator. We shepherded that case from the police to the courts for a warrant, and through every stage of the extradition. It was the first time a British officer had given evidence at every level of Sri Lankan courts, and it made headline news over there.

It wasn't quick, though. Days at a time in a hotel room is too long for anyone – I was so homesick I managed to find a channel showing Aylesbury versus Staines Town at three o'clock in the morning. Even though it was peeing down in the ground I remember thinking, *I wish I was there.*

Eventually the two final suspects, Sivajodi Anantharaja and Sivapragasam Rajeskanna, were shipped over and both were found guilty of murder, the former getting a minimum of 24 years for attempting to murder the other men as well, and the latter 14. I got a commendation, on behalf of the team, for chasing two bandits to the end of the earth. It proved there was nowhere villains could run without the long arm of the Met finding them.

They only had to go to Lambeth instead of Colombo and I wouldn't have been able to touch them ...

The only downside to the whole transatlantic episode was my relationship with the Sri Lankan police. Because a reward of £10,000 was put up for the men's arrests and no one had claimed it, they swore blind that me and my team had pocketed it.

I had been very clear with them and said, 'I can't take it because I'm police.'

'Give it to us then.'

'No – you can't have it either.' The reward was for members of the public only. A fact they to this day have never understood. We've never fallen out, but nor have they trusted us again, either.

Did I drink all that bloody arrack for nothing?

CHAPTER FIFTEEN

Kate at Weekends

The arrests and prosecutions of Sivajodi Anantharaja and Sivapragasam Rajeskanna took years – it was 2009, five years after Maheswaran's murder, when they were finally sentenced. Some people might have twiddled their thumbs during that time but I was desperate to get back out there straight after the first prosecution. Luckily for me there was no shortage of jobs. Not so fortunate, most of them were only available because no one else would touch them.

It was a DI over at Barnes who threw another crumb our way, in late 2004. McKellen his name was.

'Is that the Southeast Asian Crime Squad?'

'That doesn't technically exist any more,' I said. 'But go on.'

'I've got a case involving an honour killing that's been mothballed since 1998. New information has come in. Do you want it?'

'Go on then. Bung it over.' The team – despite the name changes and constant upheaval from outside – was on an upward curve. Of course I said yes.

The only hitch was, not everyone wanted us to have the case. It wasn't just my department that the top brass wanted to go away – they wanted to forget about all the unsolved or 'cold' cases on the books as well. At least that's how it seemed. Every time I opened a dusty old file I was encouraged to leave it alone. When I did press ahead, it was with very little backing. At least five times in 2003 a superintendent had said to me, 'How quickly can you close this down?'

'When the investigation is over.'

'I do not want my fingerprints on that.'

It's sad to say but I noticed there was a management style developing that actively inhibited the amazing talents the police have at their disposal – managers seemed to be more concerned with protecting themselves than encouraging officers to perform the duties they had joined to carry out. I got sick of bosses asking me, 'What's your exit strategy?'

My exit will be when I've wrapped up the case. One way or another.

I've always felt that by taking on another case there is an obligation – a moral one, perhaps for want of a better word – for me to finish it. I have to say the choruses of 'Bin it', 'Shelve it' and 'Walk away' became a regular, sometimes daily, occurrence. A lot of friends and colleagues often asked me why I was ploughing ahead – after all, what good could come of winding up my bosses like that?

Prior to Lambeth I might have caved under the pressure. But I never got into the Job for gold stars. All I cared about – all I still care about – is the victim. Do they or do they not get justice?

In the honour killing of Surjit Athwal, they most definitely had not.

Yet.

The killing in question was that of a young Sikh woman, Surjit Athwal. Surjit had married Sukhdave Athwal, before moving in with him, his mother, his brother and his brother's wife. In 1998 she had gone missing. Some people said she had been murdered; Sukhdave and the family said she had run off with a boyfriend. An investigation had got precisely nowhere after spending months working on it as a 'missing person', then switching focus

– arguably after the horse had bolted – to a murder inquiry, months later.

Now, six years after Surjit's disappearance, a new witness had come forward. What he had to say, I didn't yet know. First I needed to get up to speed on the case.

I went over to Barnes and said to the sergeant in CID, 'I've come over to pick up Operation Yewlands.'

He scratched his chin. 'Sorry, guv. I've been here years and we've never had an Operation Yewlands.'

I was about to ask to speak to McKellen when I looked up and saw 12 boxes on a high shelf with 'Operation Yewlands' written on the front.

'Humour me for a minute, will you? I'm a bit of the detective – do you think those boxes might be relevant?'

He looked up and said, 'Blimey, that shelf hasn't been touched for years.'

That was obvious from the inch of dust on each of them. By the time I got everything back to my house where I planned to read the lot that night, I was as grey and powdery as the boxes.

I sat with those 12 crates either side of me and by the time I finished, I knew less about the murder than when I started. It was so complicated. For starters, the names were so alien to me – Sukhdave, Surjit, Sarbjit – while the criss-crossing of leads and dead ends was mindboggling. For once, I don't think the dyslexia had anything to do with it …

What really didn't help, either, was that for some reason the previous senior investigating officer had logged everything on the card system. For a case as big and complex as this it needed to be computerised. So that was my first decision: to get it all typed into the mighty Met machine – then at least we'd know what we had.

The new evidence was from a gentleman called Mr Seva Singh. He was the father of Sarbjit Athwal – sister-in-law to the missing Surjit.

I visited his house in west London, and I must have been in the living room a good couple of minutes before I spotted another person there. Cowering – or, at the very least, trying not to be noticed under her traditional head covering – was an extremely shy young woman.

'Excuse me, ma'am, I didn't see you there. My name's DCI Driscoll.'

'Detective, let me introduce you to my daughter, Sarbjit,' Mr Singh said. 'It is her story that I am telling you.'

Now we're cooking.

Mr Singh told me how Sarbjit had been at a family meeting in Willow Tree Lane, where she lived with the Athwals, when the matriarch of the family, Mrs Bachan Kaur Athwal, had announced, 'She has to go.'

She'd been talking about Surjit, Sukhdave's wife. Surjit, they felt, was straying too far from the path chosen for her by her mother-in-law. She wanted to wear western clothes, she wore make-up and she had started to go to parties with colleagues at Heathrow Airport, where she worked. These parties had involved alcohol and the company of both women and men.

To you and me, she was a woman in her early twenties enjoying her life. To Bachan Kaur, she was 'bringing shame on the family' – and she had to die for it.

A plan was hatched to send her to India on the pretence of attending a family wedding. There she would be murdered and her body disposed of in the Ravi River. Her children would be informed she'd abandoned them to be with another man – and that would be the end of the matter.

As I listened to the story, I thought that Mr Singh had to be holding something back. You don't just kill your daughter-in-law because she's drinking the odd sherbet and wearing a skirt. No one in the world would think that was justifiable.

'You have to understand she was destroying the honour of the family,' Mr Singh replied to my question on this.

'You'll have to help me out here,' I said. 'That is enough to put out a contract on her?'

He nodded. 'For some people, yes.'

Throughout the entire meeting, Sarbjit didn't speak once. She didn't even look at me if she felt I might meet her eye. But I had to ask her: 'Why come to us now? Why didn't you tell the police when she first went missing? We could have done something.'

'Please don't point a finger at my daughter,' Mr Singh said very calmly. 'You see, Sarbjit did report it – *before* the murder took place.'

Oh, crap …

'Your officers had the chance to prevent the murder of Surjit Athwal and they did nothing.'

I believe implicitly in collective responsibility. I was a member of the Met and proud to be so. We're all brothers and sisters in arms and, as far as the public is concerned, we are all the same animal, so I never distance myself from somebody else's mistakes, however bad they are. When you do that, it riles everyone outside the force.

And so, as hard as it was considering the events took place six years before I joined the team, I apologised as though I'd committed the error myself. And then I asked for the details.

Having been witness to the plan to kill her sister-in-law, Sarbjit's first thought had been to get help. But who could she tell? She was living with people who would kill to protect the family name. What would they do to her if they discovered she'd spoken to the police? Or what if she dared speak to Surjit and her sister-in-law didn't believe her? That would be even worse for both of them.

And so, one morning after dropping her daughter at school, Sarbjit had made the bravest decision of her life: she had called the anonymous phone line Crimestoppers from a pay phone en route home. She told the operator everything about the plan, including the flight details, hotel plans and passport names. At the end she begged them to do something and was told it would be investigated.

From that moment on, Sarbjit lived in a haze of fear. And her paranoia was justified: her mother-in-law had commented on the unusually long time it had taken Sarbjit to do the school run that morning. She had spies everywhere – people from her temple who would tell her anything by way of gossip. What if someone had seen Sarbjit enter the phone box?

Suddenly, the enormity of what she had done hit her. If the police turned up to discuss the attempted murder, Bachan Kaur and Sukhdave would guess who had told them. And then what would happen?

She knew the answer.

But, in a perverse way, Sarbjit got lucky, as her family never found out about her betrayal – because the police did nothing about the phone call. Surjit was allowed to board the plane, attend the wedding in India, and then be murdered and her body disposed of. Just as Bachan Kaur had planned.

Sarbjit's life in the Athwal house after that was untenable, but she made one more attempt at getting justice. Too scared to physically enter a police station, she'd written a long letter, again detailing everything, and posted it to Hayes nick. Again, nothing had happened.

And then, months later, when Sarbjit had finally cracked and told her sister, Inder, everything, Inder had marched into the cop shop on the Strand in central London and relayed the entire tale. She had thought she was getting somewhere as it went to more than one meeting. But again, nothing happened. No arrests, no justice for Surjit.

And here we were, years later, when finally Sarbjit was prepared to break her anonymity and go on the record.

I knew what she must be thinking: *What's the point? They won't act – and I'll be killed for nothing.* But the pain of seeing her sister-in-law not receive justice, and Surjit's poor children believing their mum to be a bad mother, for her outweighed that risk.

I also knew it was the last roll of the dice for Sarbjit and her family. After this, if it didn't go well, they would never trust the Met again.

I listened to every word and I made a promise to get right onto the job. But then something happened to make me look a liar as well.

Is there a better time to be around children than on Christmas Day? If there is I haven't found it and 25 December 2004 – four days after I'd seen Mr Singh and Sarbjit – was another cracker for me, my wife, Harry and Thommo. I went to bed that night knowing that I had a day off the next day too, and that Boxing Day would be just as good. But then I was woken by a phone call in the middle of the night.

'Clive – you're Southeast Asia, aren't you?' a voice said.

'Why?'

'There's been a bit of a storm. You're up.'

There are times when words are never adequate but 'a bit of a storm' was the understatement of the century. By the time I threw on some clothes and got to the office it was all over the news: at just before 1 a.m. GMT, an earthquake off the coast of Sumatra, Indonesia, had caused a series of tsunamis that had wreaked destruction in 14 countries. More than 230,000 people died that day.

When there's an international crisis, the Met creates a team to coordinate UK interests: if there's a possibility of Brits being involved, we need to respond. Because of the title my team used to have, I got the gig this time. And it meant that even as similar offices began springing up all over the country to cope with the scale of the disaster, being the Met point of contact I became de facto head of intelligence for the entire country.

It was my job to piece together any clues that we had about survivors and try to get someone on site to help identify the bodies of those who hadn't survived. If a passport was found here, we logged it; if a rucksack was found there, we logged it. If we were lucky, we would find the people to go with the items. If we were really lucky we might find them alive.

Getting someone to answer a phone in what was basically a war zone was hard: begging them to travel from Phuket to Phi Phi Island to chase a clue to the identity of one guy out of 230,000 was nigh on impossible. I spent hours and hours, round the clock, trying to collate information with a meagre return. But what else could we do?

Luck was not something we saw much of that week, or the next, or the next. The horror was unspeakable. As one man on the ground over there put it: 'Imagine putting human beings in a washing machine with cars and concrete. What do you think comes out the other end?'

Identifying anyone was an almost impossible task; as time went on, it got worse. Bodies left in water for any lengthy period bloat beyond recognition, and any obvious differences between an Asian and a Caucasian are lost pretty quickly. You'd need to be a physician to tell them apart.

My phone did not stop ringing for a week and every day I conducted a video-link to Scotland Yard, briefing the top brass before they did the same to ministers and media. In fact, I was grateful for the relentlessness of the workload because it took my mind off the magnitude of the unimaginable horror.

When you let yourself think about things, you started to crumble. Any human would.

If we had it hard at our end, the men and women at ground zero must have been gods to get through it. I remember ringing a bloke who had become a makeshift mortician when the real one was lost. He picked up but quickly said, 'I can't talk to you at the moment – I'm covered in maggots.'

Once the initial clamour of the immediate aftermath had subsided, the international media began to lose interest. But the clear-up work went on throughout the year. After months of trying to work with the local teams remotely, I realised the only way to actually check up on the processes put in place on the Met's behalf was to visit.

I arrived in Thailand in November 2005 – and I honestly thought it was the previous January. The place looked like the tsunami had struck the day before with houses and cars washed halfway up a mountain. Only when I was shown a video from the start of the year did I realise how much had actually been achieved. There were bodies strewn in streets; bundles of corpses roped together and left bobbing in the sea.

Death and decay were everywhere.

For the first time I could truly appreciate why chasing passports for me hadn't been a priority. How could it have been?

I was surprised at the number of 'locals' – bodies – that appeared to be abandoned on the roadsides. Like a lot of other ills, religion appeared to be to blame. Many Thais are Hindu and, as they don't believe the body is anything more than a transport for the soul, there didn't seem to be any hurry to dispose of anyone.

Callous as you may find it, one of my reasons for being there was to ensure that British bodies were not being ignored in such a way. It gave me no pleasure to inspect pop-up mortuaries housed in gyms and schools or farmyard sheds. Everyone was doing their best in impossible circumstances but lack of electricity for refrigeration was still a massive problem.

Even as an ex-ambulance man, it was very hard to forget the images I saw. Back in my hotel on Saturday night, I watched my beloved Fulham beat Manchester City 2–1 and for the first time I felt nothing. The old Liverpool manager Bill Shankly was wrong about football being more important than life or death.

The trip to Thailand ended my run on the tsunami response team. Back in England, there was another death that I still had to deal with. It might have only been a single person and not a quarter of a million, but to the people around her she was as important as the 230,000 souls who'd lost their lives in Southeast Asia.

Yet again there was pressure from higher up for me to put the Surjit Athwal boxes back on the top shelf at Barnes and walk away. But I refused. I'd made an old man a promise and I intended to keep it. I was just a bit late, that was all.

I met Mr Seva Singh again and this time persuaded Sarbjit to talk to me. Over the next few weeks I met with her many times. During this time, I saw a transformation in her. From the shy, insecure mouse that I first nearly trod on during my first visit, to the empowered woman she became, she is a lesson for all put-upon women. Ten years later I am proud to call her a friend. But, back in 2005, she still had a treacherous journey before her.

Another remarkable person in this story is Mr Jagdeesh Singh, the brother of Surjit. Together with his father, Mr Dhillon, there was not one day when they did not campaign for action into Surjit's disappearance. Jagdeesh remains one of the most honourable people I have ever met. His relentless pursuit of the truth on his sister's behalf is commendable and was an inspiration to my team.

Unfortunately, though, honour and desire count for very little in the eyes of the law. Sarbjit was a gold-standard witness but a decent lawyer would demolish her story. For it to work I needed further evidence. I needed proof.

Thanks to Sarbjit, I knew who to go after.

Bachan Kaur Athwal denied any involvement outright while her son, Sukhdave, stuck to his story that Surjit had run off with another man. He had attended the local police station and told them about his own hunt for information about Surjit at her office at Heathrow Airport. Colleagues, he alleged, told him of Surjit's many affairs. Then one woman, called Kate, had taken him aside.

She said, 'Look, I've spoken to Surjit in India. She wants you to leave her alone. She's with her new man now, Raj, and she's not coming back.'

Sukhdave reported that to the original police investigators. He then returned with an update. Kate had found him again – this time with Surjit still on the phone.

'Look, Sukhdave, I don't love you and I don't love the kids. Fuck off and leave me alone to get on with my new life.'

When I took over the case, I asked Sukhdave about this. He trotted out the same story verbatim.

'Did you see Surjit's number on Kate's phone?'

'No, she had the screen taped up to hide it.'

'But you're sure it was Surjit?'

'I know my own wife's voice!'

A court would see his story as evidence and so I was duty-bound to investigate it. There was always the chance he was telling the truth. His legal team demanded we take up the search for Kate.

We went through Heathrow's personnel list from that time and found 156 Kates, Catherines, Katherines, Katies, Katys, some people who wished they'd been called Kate and one woman who was only Kate at weekends. If they had had a Kate Bush LP we would have spoken to it too.

It was a massive use of manpower – kudos again to the diligence of Danny Walsh and DS Alan Goodley and the rest of the team – but we got zilch.

I decided to cast the net wider. India was where the murder – if there had been one – had taken place, so that was where I needed to be. Or so I thought. Just before I was about to fly, my mother, Christine Helen Rose Driscoll née Vacher, passed away. She had been ill for some time and was eventually admitted into St Helier Hospital, Carshalton. The care and concern shown to her by everyone there will never be forgotten.

I wouldn't have forgiven myself if I'd been abroad when she'd gone. As it was, we had some wonderful conversations, right to the end. Even at her weakest, she had such concern for others. She wanted to know all about my cases and the victims and their families. Her message was simple: 'Do your best for them, son. They deserve nothing less.'

I hope she sees I tried my hardest.

Having been to Sri Lanka and Thailand, the ways of business in India should not have surprised me – but I was shocked. In Britain, for a murder case, we would have a dozen constables, five sergeants, two detectives and a DCI; over there, when I asked to speak to the person in charge of Surjit's murder, I was directed to a desk sergeant.

The bloke you would report your missing cat to also had to run a murder case.

So that answered one question. Or so I thought. But the real reason why nothing had happened came when I was speaking to some local officers, off the record.

'Why are the London Met worried about this girl? It is family business.'

'Excuse me, I think that girl was murdered.'

'For bringing shame on her family.'

I couldn't believe it. Very rarely in the pursuit of the truth do you get people handing it to you. In fact, I was told quite openly that Surjit would have been chucked in the River Ravi.

'It happens,' one bloke said. 'And the best thing about the Ravi is it runs into Pakistan – so they get our trash.'

I don't want to play the big white chief, but how had I arrived in a place where murder was OK if it was committed by a family member?

Realising I wasn't going to get much out of the local Indian police, I went to visit all the places I knew Surjit had visited, from the wedding hall to the relative's house she had shared in Pathankot. I also interviewed the two men I suspected of carrying out the actual murder. Both denied it, but there were such holes in their stories you could drive a bus through them. Still, proving it would be another matter.

Back home I had some serious thinking to do. Sarbjit was still living in a house with people capable of murder. I could not afford to let them get a sniff of her involvement.

I thought we were doing OK but then I got a call on my mobile from a terrified-sounding Sarbjit. Her mother-in-law had come to stay and, despite there being a spare bed, was demanding to share a bed with Sarbjit.

'Clive, I think she's going to kill me.'

'Right, you need to get out.'

'I can't leave the children.'

'Then I'll come to you.'

'No, not yet.'

'OK, but if anything happens you ring me at once.'

I posted two men to watch her front door and another pair to watch her back garden. The night was one of the most tense of my life but it passed without incident. Whatever plan Bachan Kaur had arrived with seemed to have been shelved – unless her whole ambition had been simply to remind Sarbjit of how powerful she was. In which case she had succeeded.

When it came time to act, I think we played a blinder. Teams were sent in to arrest Bachan, Sukhdave, his brother –

and Sarbjit. If we'd let her be, she would have stuck out as our main witness.

I have to say, to this day, Bachan Kaur remains the single most cold-blooded killer I have ever met. She showed zero remorse for Surjit because she felt none. In fact, she was positively indignant that I should interfere in her private business. Sukhdave wasn't much better. And even from inside a cell, as they awaited trial, they made sure their friends outside agreed: Sarbjit was abused by supposedly religious people in the street, and even at temple, for subjecting her family to such a wicked ordeal. It didn't matter that Surjit had lost her life.

Going to court, Sarbjit had it all to lose. If the jury voted 'Not guilty' then she would find herself back in the clutches of killers she'd betrayed. I only had my pride and moral code at stake. But I was confident, even if some of my guv'nors weren't.

'Clive,' one said, 'are you sure about this? You're going for murder against an old lady and her son when they didn't physically commit the crime, it happened on Indian soil and no body was ever found?'

'That's about right. And yes, I'm going for it. I have to. For the victim in the ground and the victims still living with them.'

Those of a conspiracy-theorist bent will raise an eyebrow at what happened next.

One Friday, two possible witnesses came to my attention, both of whom would be leaving the UK on the following Sunday. My team had been working round the clock but I couldn't afford to miss this opportunity so I asked my superintendent for permission to send a couple of lads out on overtime.

'I can't authorise that, I'm afraid, Clive.' He made noises about budget and relevance.

Both inappropriate, in my opinion. I was trying to solve a murder.

In fact, I nearly lost my rag – so much so that, outside the office, my entire team heard the ding-dong.

Unbeknownst to me, two of them, Alan Goodly and Pawalbinder Singh, agreed with me about the importance of interviewing the witnesses at the earliest opportunity – and decided to do it in their own time the following day.

Come Monday morning and I was presented with the results. I couldn't believe they'd invested their own time but I was immensely grateful – and proud. Then my phone rang.

'Clive,' said the superintendent, when I had joined him in his office, 'I regret to inform you that I am relieving you of your post.'

Talk about *déjà vu*.

'You're firing me? Why?'

'For disobeying a direct order.'

'What order?'

'I told you not to use overtime.'

'I haven't used overtime.'

'Then how do you explain two of your officers interviewing a pair of suspects in your case?'

'I only just found out about that myself. They did it in their own spare time. Nothing to do with me.'

The look on his face was priceless. He reached across the desk and ripped up an A4 form. From what I could make out, it was my official reprimand. He'd written it out in advance. Who needs corruption when red tape will do?

It was also at this time that I had to move my team to the Empress State Building in Brompton. Before I'd even had a chance to agree, I came into Penrhyn Road and discovered another chief inspector sitting at my desk!

The upshot of my run-in with the superintendent was that Cressida Dick's own boss, John Yates, personally intervened. He didn't know me from Adam but he called me in to apologise for the interference my case had suffered.

'I get that you can't work with your current superintendent,' he said, 'but you still need a senior officer to report to. What do you think about Superintendent Dickie?'

'What, Jim Dickie QPM? I love him.'

And I did. I mock him because he loves to use the 'Queen's Police Medal' tag on his signatures but, fair enough – usually that award is the domain of officers much higher in rank than him. He's a lovely bloke and really funny – so yes, in a nutshell, I could see myself working with him.

'So, what's your feeling on the Athwal case?' he asked me.

'Pretty good – if I'm allowed to do my job.'

'Point taken. Go get 'em.'

The court date soon whizzed round. I wasn't allowed to speak to Sarbjit during the trial as she was a witness but our barrister, the icon that is Michael Worsley, shepherded her through it all as best he could. He also challenged Sukhdave's story about Heathrow's mysterious 'Kate'.

Sukhdave's response? 'I made Kate up because the police were annoying me.'

Well, that's not suspicious behaviour, is it?

Wasting police time and lying do not make you a murderer – we still had to present an unimpeachable case. I like to think we did. After three and a half long weeks, during which time my testimony based on what we'd learned in Pathankot shot the defence's lies to pieces, the jury retired.

DS Goodley called to let me know they had done so, and I made my way over to the court. For me, the investigation ends when the jury retire; up to that point, I am still scrabbling around for any evidence I can possibly find. When the 12 good men and women adjourn to their room, that's the finish line for me. That's when I like to thank all the clerks and the court staff – the people who help you with photocopying, down to the ushers – for their help. The ones I couldn't find I emailed when I got back to the office, along with everyone else who had contributed to getting the case to court.

You never know for sure which way a dozen strangers are going to go but I did know that I had faith in them. I have complete respect for our jury-based justice system. If a jury sits through all our evidence and decides the accused are not guilty then justice has been served. I might not like it, but I can't blame them. I can only blame myself for not putting the right evidence in front of them to win the verdict I want.

I was in a meeting when I heard the jury had reached a decision. I flew back over to the court, but I got the news while I was still in the cab.

When I phoned Sarbjit a second later I just said one word: 'Guilty.'

Then she hung up on me. At least, that's what I thought because the line went silent. Then I realised I could just make out the faint sob of tears.

'I can't believe it,' she whispered. 'You've done it. You've saved my life.'

When I reached the court, I was told Sarbjit's life wasn't the only one in my 'plus' column. A respected member of the Sikh community said, 'You have drawn a line in the sand today, DCI Driscoll. You have shown the whole of Great Britain that murders in the name of honour, even conducted on foreign soil, will not be tolerated. I believe you have probably saved tens of thousands of lives.'

Even if the geezer was out by a nought or two, the idea that our case was a landmark stand against honour killings was an incredible honour. And, after the horror show I had witnessed in Thailand, where there had been no upside, I realised it was good news I sorely needed.

I honestly didn't return to the court for all the slaps on the back I got, but it was nice. And when a clerk came up and said, 'The judge is going to commend you for your work,' that was an honour too far.

'If anyone in this case should be commended it's the witnesses,' I said. 'It's always the witnesses. Without the bravery in coming forward of Jagdeesh and Mrs Athwal, we had nothing.'

Every award and commendation I have received should have been given to the witnesses and families who have always been exceptional to me. I honestly believe that. For Sarbjit to get up in that courtroom was a tremendously heroic act. And it was the making of her. Sarbjit today is an incredible, strong, positive woman, nothing like the person she was before tragedy entered her life.

I thought, in fact, I would never again encounter anyone as impressive as her.

But that was before I met Mrs L.

CHAPTER SIXTEEN

You Are Loved

Despite our track record, my team was universally unloved by the Job. Why? I couldn't tell you, although I suspected someone with a degree was behind it – a real policeman would have appreciated real police work. Ever since I'd become a DCI, we'd been solving crimes we had no right to. Most people would think that was a good thing. Not some of the Met. When they weren't changing our name they were trying to shut us down. And when they weren't trying to shut us down they were changing our name. By the time we were saddled with the moniker SCD2(2) it was becoming a bit of a joke. Who was going to have us as part of their group next? It wouldn't be long till we found out.

As part of the process to sweep any remains of the old Racial and Violent under the carpet, the Deptford nick was scheduled to be closed. It's flats now. Nice if you can afford them. With the old senior investigating officer, Dave Ainscough, departing for pastures new, they needed someone to clear the building and literally hand over the keys to the new tenant.

Muggins put his hand up.

It should have been a fairly straightforward, if dull, exercise. But, while I was over there, I came across rooms full of boxes marked 'Ongoing' or similar. If the station was going to be closed, what would happen to those? I thought back to Surjit Athwal's case, and those dozen boxes of files collecting dust in

Barnes. If I hadn't come along they'd still be there now, and two murderers would be walking the streets. I wanted to see if there was anything here I could have a go at.

The next four hours passed in a blur. I was like a kid in a sweetshop as I worked my way along the packed shelves. Every box I opened contained a case that had me drooling. Why hadn't people fought to work on them?

Then I entered another room and really began to get excited. The box that caught my eye had 'Operation Fishpool' printed on the front. So did the one next to it and the ones on the shelf below and on the shelves below that; in fact, when I stepped back, I realised the entire room was full of paperwork from one single case. And I knew exactly which one it was.

Stephen Lawrence.

It may as well have had 'Toxic' stamped all over it. That was the effect that investigation had on everyone who entered its orbit. This was the solvable investigation I'd heard about when I was at Brixton, just before Big Marie's boy was murdered. From what I'd heard there was evidence against several named suspects, but something had gone wrong. The family's allegation had been that the investigation team had fudged up big time. How, I didn't know. The fact the five men were still at large despite what looked like strong evidence was a bit of a steer. But the fact that Stephen's family had been forced to launch their own private prosecution because they didn't trust the Met was the harshest criticism you could get.

You know you've failed as a police force when the public cut you out of the judicial process because it doesn't think you'll do a good enough job.

This was the case that changed the police for ever. This was the case that caused an inquiry, led by Sir William Macpherson, to tear into the Met like no one else ever had. His inquiry and the subsequent report – the one that had had Ian Johnston tearing his hair out in the office at Scotland Yard – forced us to change the way we investigated all murders, insisting on full-time murder teams rather than ad hoc groups thrown together as and when. More than that, and most piercing of all for everyone who had sworn all those oaths at Hendon, he said that Stephen Lawrence's killers had not been brought to justice because we, as an entire police force, were 'institutionally racist'.

That hurt. Personally, as someone who, among many others, nearly died serving the diverse communities of Brixton, he could not have picked a more damning accusation. Yet as a group, Macpherson said, there was a culture within the Met to assume the worst of black people. He wasn't saying they were targets. But nor were they considered equal. As a group of people, he said, we were too quick to make assumptions based on race.

You have to admit he had a point. But it wasn't just us. With Stephen, the rumours about him being in a gang, about him being stabbed by his own knife, about him being the victim of a drug deal gone bad – these all came out in the media within hours of his murder.

If he'd been white, would that have been the case?

No, said Macpherson. And I have to agree.

Stereotypes, assumptions, racism – call it what you will. The upshot was a young boy's murder went unresolved. Despite a sizeable murder team, the initial investigation had failed to nail a single suspect.

In the 13 years since there had been 10 other investigations, all with the same result and increasing budgets. Operation Athena Tower was one of the biggest the Met has done outside terrorist offences. Resources were never a problem and they tried everything. It was like being given a licence to do whatever you wanted and the officers certainly did that. But still no convictions.

And so, come 2006, there it was, haunting Deptford.

It wasn't just the Met that Macpherson's report had changed. We all, as a nation, Macpherson said, needed to take a good look at ourselves in the mirror. That charge of 'institutional racism' was rolled out by politicians and cultural leaders alike, and shone like a spotlight on every major organisation within the UK. The media and the BBC, in particular, were among the many bodies given a shake-up.

Not limiting his recommendations to people and organisations, Macpherson also advocated an adjustment to a law that was nearly as old as justice itself. Since the days of the Magna Carta, it had been an intrinsic element of British law that a citizen could only be tried for a crime once – 'double jeopardy', as it was known. Macpherson trampled all over that. The police, he said, and I paraphrase the Right Honourable gentleman, had cocked up so spectacularly in failing to bring to book the killers of young Stephen – the case hadn't even come to trial – that the boy's parents had had no choice but to bring a private prosecution against some of the suspects.

Without the full backing of the Met, however, it had been doomed to failure. And it meant that, legally, under the 'double jeopardy' law, every suspect in the case found 'Not guilty' was free from further investigation.

A travesty of justice, Macpherson said. Double jeopardy had to go.

And so, with surprisingly little opposition from any political party, Jack Straw's Criminal Justice Act of 2003 had included the abrogation of 'double jeopardy' for all serious crimes on two conditions:

1. Any retrial had to be approved by the Director of Public Prosecutions.
2. The Court of Appeal would only agree to quash any prior verdicts in the light of 'new and compelling' evidence.

In other words, the spirit of double jeopardy remained, but if fresh and viable evidence came to light on a case years later, it could trigger a retrial. Pertinently, especially for my purposes, the law was retrospective. In other words, it could be applied to cases that had already been tried.

Powerful, powerful stuff – and all because the original investigating team had failed to secure successful prosecutions against the murderers of Stephen Lawrence.

How had such a balls-up been allowed to happen?

As I wandered around Deptford in 2006, preparing to switch the lights off on the whole building, that question began to niggle. We'd all been affected by Macpherson but the case that had kicked it off had seemed so straightforward. How had it become so derailed? How had it become such a nightmare for the entire Met and police in general?

The more I thought about it, the more I realised there was only one way to find out.

When I got back to Penrhyn Road, I made an appointment to see Commander Dick. The head of Trident happened to be in the building so I went straight in.

'How can I help you, Clive?'

'Ma'am, I understand Operation Fishpool is one of Deptford's?'

'Yes. Why?'

'If it's all right with you, ma'am, I'd like to take it on.'

'Seriously?'

'Yes, ma'am. I'd like to have a crack at solving the Stephen Lawrence murder.'

While Cressida Dick was delighted, not everyone shared her view. My Chief Superintendent at the time, whose name was above the door on SCD2(2), was dead against it. The department, he said, had nothing to gain and everything to lose from meddling in the case.

Plenty of others concurred. Once again, the company of Binit, Shelveit & Walkaway got involved. Friend and foe within the force said the same thing.

'Why?' I said to them all. 'A young boy died in 1993 and we failed him.'

'What makes you think you won't fail him too? There's no point letting it ruin your career like it has everyone else's.'

People were phoning me left, right and centre to commiserate with me for being landed with the Met's poisoned chalice. No one could get it into their heads that I'd asked for it. Even in an official briefing, I was told that my chances of making progress were somewhere between no hope and Bob Hope – and Bob had been dead for three years.

'You won't get anywhere, Driscoll,' I was told. 'The family are a nightmare.'

'What do you mean?'

'They won't give you the time of day. Doreen Lawrence wouldn't even let the original investigation have access to her son's school records. So much for wanting the killers caught.'

I was told to watch a PowerPoint presentation about Stephen's murder and within it again the comment about Mrs L not allowing access to Stephen's school records appeared.

That put a different complexion on things but I was too far in to back out. My ego, if nothing else, wouldn't let me. If I had to tackle the case without the family, so be it. But I didn't want to lose face, not at the first hurdle.

'With respect though,' I said, 'Mrs Lawrence hasn't even met me yet, has she?'

If there's a collective noun for a whole room of people rolling their eyes, that would have been the time to use it.

I thought of the tiny, put-upon woman who'd been crying for justice in the media for more than a decade; I thought of her husband, the giant figure of Neville Lawrence. And I thought of their marriage, another innocent casualty caught in the fallout of their son's death. Unhelpful? These people? It just went to show you couldn't judge by appearances.

In fact, a lot of people in the Met, including many of those giving me the benefit of their advice whether I wanted it or not, criticised the Lawrences – Doreen in particular – for their attitude towards the police. 'Why are they always slagging us off?' one person said. In truth, there were plenty of examples of it in print interviews, television programmes or at press conferences. After an inquest in 1997, Mrs Lawrence met assembled journalists and tore into the way the Met had handled Stephen's case. It was brutal and clinical and utterly damning. 'Why would she do that when we're trying to help?' people asked.

My answer was simple. 'She's a grieving mother. Her son's been taken and we've let her and her family down by not finding the murderers. I'd be slagging us off too if I were her.'

Forewarned was forearmed, though. If the family was going to be against me from the off, then I had to be doubly sure of any information before I stuck my head above the parapet.

Not everyone was averse to my plans, to be fair. Whereas SCD1, the murder squad, hated the case – it showed them in a bad light – and while most other departments couldn't see anything other than grief by association, I was reminded yet again how lucky I had got with my superintendent.

Jim Dickie is a wonderful police officer, as he himself will tell you – it was Jim, after all, who said in a TV interview that he was the greatest detective in Britain, and who can argue with facts like that?

I jest, of course, but Jim is about as far from one of those modern people with 'transferable skills' as I am. He's got a nose for investigating, a real instinct and, like me, he sees opportunity where others see banana skins: if we spot a light on in an empty house, we want to know who's flicked the switch; if certain colleagues see that same light, they worry who's paying the bill.

The first thing (of value) that Jim said was, 'Futureproof your investigation.'

In other words, should I ever get close to going to court I needed to be 100 per cent certain that my ducks were not only in a row but that they also had their feathers brushed, bills buffed and quacks in tune.

For example, as it was a case that had begun in 1993, it was imperative that the evidence was filed, checked and logged to 2006 standards. So much had changed – for the better, I might add – in the interim, that what was acceptable and admissible back then might not be today. It all needed looking at under a microscope.

The main way to ensure this was to have everything logged on a computer. A room full of boxes was a good starting point but in 2006 it might as well have been a room full of tea bags. Fortunately, the Met had developed a system for large cases.

As acronyms go, HOLMES is one I can appreciate. Ostensibly it stands for Home Office Large Major Enquiry System but the words are irrelevant, if I'm honest – someone in the PR department just wanted a nod to Sherlock. And why not?

HOLMES is where we key in every single piece of evidence, every single action and every single order in a large case. In a major incident room, if X needs doing, then HOLMES is the place to record that Officer A went to do it, whether or not it was done successfully and what followed. For example, if a piece of information comes to light, the 'receiver' or document reader will say to the office manager, 'Look, there's someone here who has information.' The manager will allocate an action – such as telling a DC to speak to that witness – then log what the outcome is on HOLMES. If further actions are needed, he allocates and logs those as well. Someone checks it in, another bloke processes it, a third one carries out any follow-up or action.

In theory, HOLMES was done from the off on Stephen's case. The reality was somewhat different. For a reason that I cannot fathom, one man, DS Flook, acted as receiver, office manager and action allocator. That could have been all right if he'd been the dog's wotsits at running HOLMES but, to paraphrase Lord Macpherson, he had been a lazy bastard: crucial information wasn't checked in properly or wasn't cross-checked or wasn't actioned. For example, a lot of people in Stephen's case had used the word 'juck'. If you 'juck' somebody, you've stabbed them. There were probably 40 statements recorded that used that word, but if you searched for it in HOLMES – as we did – you'd draw a blank, because someone hadn't been bothered to spell it correctly, or the same way twice or even enter it at all.

How to make a wonderful tool and an essential part of modern detective work redundant in one easy lesson.

Worse, just days into the investigation, Flook had gone away for a few days leaving everyone else, including junior members of the office, floundering in the dark.

So I was expecting it to be bad. But I had no idea how bad. A random check proved some things were on HOLMES, some weren't, and some were inputted incorrectly and were, if I'm honest, just rubbish thrown in because someone needed to look busy. After all, the computer can't read, can it? It registers that you've inputted 4,000 bits of information; it doesn't know you've just typed a comma on each page.

'It's a mess, guv,' the poor guy tasked with checking said. 'What do you want me to do?'

I'm no scientist and I didn't have any brilliant solutions. So I did what I always do and started at the beginning.

'Open box one and input everything from scratch. Do the same to box two, box three and onwards.'

'Guv, there are 540 boxes!'

'Then I suggest you hurry up.'

But he had a point. Before I'd done a stroke of investigating I had to see Cressida Dick.

'Ma'am, we've got a job on our hands here.'

'You astound me, Clive.'

'Just undoing the damage of the other investigations is going to take months.'

'How many months?'

'I need at least two years.'

She blew out her cheeks but there was only one answer she could give. The country needed young Stephen's investigation to be active and no one else was touching it. So she said, 'Whatever it takes, Clive. But do me a favour. Don't let the Met look any worse.'

'I'll try not to, ma'am.'

When I got Operation Fishpool, things had to change.

Number one, the building I was working in didn't have access to HOLMES, and young Stephen's case was screaming out for that. So, with great fanfare and not a little bit of satisfaction, I moved back into Penrhyn Road – and back into my old office.

Number two, I needed people alongside me. Luckily some of my good ones had stayed. My only DI was Shaun Keep who had been with me since the early Racial and Violent days and had been a key player in Sarbjit's case as head of intelligence. DS Alan Goodley was still around as well. You'll never find a more methodical man. Just to get the numbers up I borrowed Colin Rose and Mick Geoghan, initially on a three-month arrangement. When I retired in 2014 they were still with me.

All the various disruptions – and that's what they were – took quite a bit out of me. After just two weeks on the job I was worn out and I still hadn't done a single bit of investigating.

Finally, with my ducks as close to lined up as I could get them, it was time to put that right.

The first thing I had to do was immerse myself in the files. Being a slow reader, I'm used to taking work home to keep up. With 540 boxes to choose from, I had to be a bit choosy, and it must have been my lucky day when I chose the box I did.

The third file I opened contained a bombshell.

Right there, in black and white, was this fact: Mrs Doreen Lawrence had given permission for the Met to have access to Stephen's school records.

When you have dyslexia it's worth re-reading things. This I double-checked then treble-checked.

Mrs Lawrence had given Fishpool permission to look at Stephen's academic records.

I scratched my head. What else was there to do? It was barely a fortnight since I'd been told in an official meeting that Mrs Lawrence had refused outright to grant that permission. Not only that, but said refusal was the basis on which a whole department's opinion of her was founded.

And it was all bollocks.

The more I read, the more I despaired. There was absolutely nothing that woman would not have done, no permission she had not given, no stone she would not have agreed to overturn in the pursuit of her son's killers.

So where the hell had this other story, this other image of her, come from?

I'm not sure I ever found the answer to that. What I did discover was that no one's word was to be trusted. If I was to get anywhere at all with Stephen, I needed to start from scratch. It wasn't just HOLMES that needed fine-tuning – every single aspect of the original case needed to be checked.

To read the actual nuts and bolts of the murder I decided my comfy chair at home wasn't the thing.

There was only one place where I wanted to read about the goings on of 22 April 1993, and that was Well Hall Road in Eltham. Ground zero. The spot where Stephen breathed his last – and the Metropolitan Police Service, the law and Britain herself changed for ever.

Lord knows what people thought seeing me rock up with a satchel full of papers, a flask and a sarnie. I didn't pay it much thought as I walked along Well Hall Road; past the junction with Dickson Road where Stephen had been attacked; north towards Shooter's Hill, where he'd managed to flee; and tried to picture the events of 13 years earlier.

Outside number 320 I found the place Stephen fell. A granite stone marks the spot. On the other side of the road was a bench. I crossed over, made myself comfortable and started to read.

On that Thursday night, 22 April 1993, Stephen and his friend Duwayne Brooks had been visiting Stephen's uncle. They'd spent the night playing computer games then headed home. It was a two-bus journey, and the first one had taken them as far as the old Coronet Cinema just south of the Well Hall roundabout. For the next stint they had options: go over the roundabout and wait for a bus on Well Hall Road by the junction with Dickson Road; or go left at the roundabout and wait on Westhorne Avenue.

They decided to walk up to Dickson Road. As they set off – both lads engrossed in a conversation about Arsenal Football Club – Duwayne noticed a group of lads larking about behind them on Well Hall Road, near the railway bridge.

It was just gone 10.30 p.m. and Stephen was anxious not to be home late. When a bus didn't materialise after a few minutes, they wandered back down towards the roundabout. From there they would see a bus coming from either road, and they'd leg it to whichever stop they needed. It was worth a bit of running to make sure they caught the first bus. Duwayne went ahead.

Three witnesses at the Dickson Road stop saw them: Joseph Shepherd, who knew the Lawrences; Alexandra Marie; and Royston Westbrook. Unfortunately, the two lads also came to the attention of the gang Duwayne had spotted.

When Duwayne called out to Stephen to ask if he'd seen a bus, the gang rushed across from the other side of Well Hall Road, their leader yelling – in answer to Duwayne's question – 'What, what, nigger?' as he ran.

Duwayne sensed then saw the potential danger. Stephen did not.

Stephen was set upon by the five or six men – the witnesses were unclear – and stabbed twice. The knife or knives went five inches into his body, delivered in the sort of bowling action that would not have been out of place at Lord's cricket ground.

Duwayne instinctively fled across Well Hall Road before he could be caught. He did not see a knife, thinking the weapon was 'an iron bar'. In any case, all the reports said, it was a brief attack, over in seconds, before Stephen was able to pull away and run.

When Duwayne dared to stop and look back, he saw the gang fleeing away up Dickson Road and Stephen running towards him, alone, looking confused and scared. Stephen made it past the people at the bus stop, up the hill and across the road, heading in the direction of Shooter's Hill nick, to where Duwayne was waiting. Then, 130 yards from where he'd been attacked, Stephen fell to the ground, almost face down, outside number 320.

'What is wrong with me?' were his last words.

Duwayne had been terrified. Anyone would have been. He ran back across the road to a public telephone box – mobile phones were still in their infancy then – and dialled 999, screaming for an ambulance. It was 10.43 p.m.

By the time he got back to his wounded friend, a couple called Mr and Mrs Taaffe had found the boy. On their way home from church they had seen the boys running (at first suspecting they were up to no good but soon realising there was something elso going on), seen Stephen crash to the pavement and watched as Duwayne had tried in vain to flag down passing cars before dashing over to the phone box. As far as Mr Taaffe could tell, Stephen had been in the recovery position. His wife confirmed it: his head had looked left into the roadway and his left arm was raised. Mr Taaffe assumed Duwayne had done this. Mrs Taaffe had placed her hand on Stephen's head and whispered in his ear, 'You are loved, you are loved.'

The first police officer on the scene was off-duty PC Geddis, who happened to be passing with his wife. Their daughter, by coincidence, was in Stephen's class at school. He had turned round his car and rushed over to help. Again, he assumed Stephen had been placed in the recovery position. He made another call to 999 at 10.48 p.m.

The first on-duty responders were PCs Bethel and Gleason, arriving from nearby Plumstead nick. The first went to Duwayne, the other to Stephen. WPC Bethel found Duwayne distressed and angry. He was yelling that he'd ordered an ambulance, not 'pigs'.

The ambulance finally arrived at 10.55. The paramedics refused Duwayne permission to travel with Stephen. Another officer, WPC Smith, took him in her car.

The ambulance arrived at Brook Hospital in Shooter's Hill at 11.05. Dr Patel saw Stephen two minutes later and pronounced him dead at 11.17.

In truth, Stephen had stopped breathing before being carried into the ambulance.

Those were the facts according to the police files. When I read the Macpherson report I got them again, but this time with added comment.

Each attending officer was criticised for not having sufficient first-aid knowledge to ascertain Stephen's injuries and to stem the flow of blood. In all likelihood the blood loss had already been too great and surgery not first aid was the only solution, but the fact that none of the officers present had training adequate enough to empower them to try, however, was criticised.

Those officers, Macpherson declared, had been failed by their training; the same could not be said of an Inspector Groves, who had arrived while Stephen was still on the ground, and not taken control of the situation. Worse, according to Macpherson, Groves had wrongly jumped to the conclusion that Stephen's injuries were as a result of a fight with the obviously distressed Duwayne. The boys' race, his lordship concluded, was the reason. 'He would not have been similarly dismissive if the two young men involved had been white.'

Groves, as the senior officer, gets it in the neck from Macpherson. Without getting details from Duwayne about what happened, he went off to a nearby pub to look for witnesses. If he had asked, he would have learned that Stephen's killers had run off up Dickson Road – in the opposite direction to the pub.

Groves's failure to identify Duwayne as a victim and a witness is Macpherson's sternest criticism. Had he done so, a manhunt could have been instigated immediately, with the net closing around the estate at the top of Dickson Road. As it was, 40 men and women plus dogs were set on the area only at around midnight – nearly 90 minutes after the attack. What potential evidence could have been lost, disposed of or washed away in that time?

The Met defended Groves's initial handling of the case. Macpherson hung him out to dry. He was just as scathing about the case's first SIO.

Detective Superintendent Ian Crampton was on duty at Plumstead nick when Stephen was killed. Unfortunately, it was just one of many jobs under his gaze and, three days later, he had to leave his position as SIO to attend the Old Bailey for a contract killing case.

The timing could not have been worse. The most crucial period of any investigation, but particularly a murder, are its first hours and days. It's not an exaggeration to say that that is when most crimes are cracked, if not solved.

But between Thursday, 22 April and Monday, 26 April, when he left, Crampton still had opportunities.

Stephen died on Thursday night; by the end of Friday, there were numerous calls to police identifying suspects. The first came in at 1.50 p.m. on 23 April, naming three men. One bloke even walked into Plumstead nick to make a statement. To be fair, there were plenty of names but the same five kept cropping up: Jamie Acourt, Neil Acourt, Luke Knight, Gary Dobson and David Norris – the area's notorious 'Acourt Gang' or, as the Acourts liked to call themselves, 'The Krays'.

And so, within 24 hours, the police had received a pretty good steer as to who they should be picking up.

Crampton made the decision not to.

Sitting on Well Hall Road, I cast my mind back to my own work in the early 90s. It was a different time then. We behaved differently. In 1993, if I'm honest, we arrested almost for fun – we didn't give it a great deal of thought. We certainly didn't, as happens today, almost prepare a bloody court case before you go out and make an arrest. Back then, if you thought someone was guilty, you'd go and arrest them and work out the details afterwards. At the very least, you would search them or their property, especially within the first hours after a crime. Had so much really changed in 13 years?

Another good reason that might have been thought of for swarming out with arrest warrants was that one of the five named blokes was the son of an established local gang boss,

Clifford Norris. If his son was a chip off the old block, which you might reasonably speculate, maybe he would have been worth talking to—?

And then there was the added factor that David Norris shared the name of the man killed in the contract killing that Ian Crampton was due to oversee at the Old Bailey.

There turned out to be a connection, but in 1993 Crampton did not join the dots, Macpherson said.

Rather than give further fuel to the investigation, a lot of local people said that it was Clifford Norris's potential involvement that actually stopped the police swooping. In a case the previous year, involving the stabbing of Stacey Benefield, Norris was alleged to have prevented witnesses from coming forward, either through threats or bribes, to protect the accused.

With 'Stephen', as his case was known, all sorts of accusations flew around, the most pervasive being that Norris had officers on the payroll. One officer, in particular, had been seen with Norris at least four times in what appeared to be social situations. Locals still say to this day, it was the only reason no arrests were made.

I need to make clear that Ian Crampton himself was absolutely exonerated by Macpherson of any such collusion.

On a police level, I still don't understand why Crampton decided, on Sunday 25 April, to commence surveillance on the home of one of the suspects rather than make any arrests. If he had been worried about breaking rules, that doesn't stack up. One judge even reported back then that, in matters as serious as murder, you have to expect the police to act on slightly less evidence than they would like. Only eight months earlier, in July 1992, a young Asian lad called Rohit Duggal had been stabbed to death outside a kebab shop just down the road from where Stephen was killed, and in that instance the SIO on duty had whipped everybody in. They got their man, too.

I can tell you now that there was more than enough evidence to search the suspects named by witnesses, and almost certainly strong enough grounds to arrest most, if not all of them, by 26 April. Macpherson said there was actually enough by the evening of 24 April.

Like him, I will never understand why it did not happen.

It was specifically the not-knowing that fuelled his lord-ship's keenest attack on Crampton. Had the SIO kept adequate notes in the official policy log explaining his decision-making process, the inquiry might have had some sympathy. As it was, his note-keeping – essential for an SIO – was brief to say the least. Poor, even.

The second investigation into Stephen's death had the opposite problem. Starting as SIO on 26 April, Brian Weeden's notes were fulsome, even if his thinking was not. Presented with the same list and the same dilemma – to arrest or not? – Weeden wrote those names down in his first official log.

Just before he decided not to arrest as well.

In any murder case, there's a review after six weeks to check the investigation is up to scratch. Stephen's case was no different.

Chief Superintendent Barker came in and signed off on the investigation. Top notch, apparently. He couldn't fault it.

The Met would stand by that review for years. Whenever there was criticism, be it from the Lawrences or anyone else, they'd wave that piece of paper and say, 'No, we did everything we could have done. Look, it says so here.'

When the Macpherson inquiry kicked off, Paul Condon and Sir Ian Johnston still believed this.

Then Sir William got around to examining the Barker review.

It was not, the inquiry believed, worth the paper it was typed on. Barker himself was slaughtered by the panel. How could he have signed off on a case riddled with so many mistakes?

That was the moment Ian Johnston had turned white in my office and said it was all going 'horribly, horribly wrong'. That was the moment the Met accepted they'd cocked up.

Hindsight is easy but, looking back, it's hard to see why nobody spotted it at the time.

For the 14 months that Weeden ran Stephen's case, his methodical and comprehensive notes shed no light on why he had followed so blindly the first investigation's lead – especially as they had the added evidence of Stacey Benefield, who claimed that Stephen had been attacked as a gang initiation ritual by one of the named suspects. Weeden also had three anonymous witnesses, one of whom claimed to be very close to one of the suspects, offering varying levels of background and motive, if not proof.

It had taken outside pressures, or so Macpherson claimed, to spur Weeden into action: on 6 May 1993, Nelson Mandela visited Mr and Mrs Lawrence and then spoke to the police commissioner, while a march against racial injustice was scheduled for 8 May.

Mr Weeden had recently suffered a family tragedy that I think would unsettle most. However, on the day after Mr Mandela's intervention, on 7 May, his team arrested the suspects. Finally.

Weeden said new evidence had come to light. In truth, the only thing that had changed since 22 April was that the suspects – were they to be guilty – had had almost three weeks to dispose of any evidence and work on any alibis.

The Lawrences, meanwhile, were to learn of the arrests via television news and not via their appointed police liaison. The relationship between them and the Met, already strained, was about to snap.

What they probably didn't garner from the news was that Weeden hadn't done the arrests himself – that was left to a DS called John Davidson. Added to this, only four of the five suspects were reeled in as, according to Davidson, they didn't know what David Norris looked like.

To the outside world, at least locally, it was further fuel that Clifford Norris was exerting his strength over the investigation. David Norris was eventually picked up and, like the others, interviewed before being bailed. During those interviews he denied knowing Gary Dobson. A photograph taken during the lengthy surveillance of the suspects showed the two men together. Norris was never shown this, or made to account for it contradicting his story. This fact formed a large part of the Macpherson inquiry.

Neither Duwayne nor any of the other witnesses was able to identify Jamie Acourt, David Norris and Gary Dobson during identity parades. One witness who may have been able to help refused to cooperate after his name was said by an officer in front of the suspects during one parade. With other evidence less than concrete, further action against the three was dropped.

That left Luke Knight and Neil Acourt, both of whom had been singled out by Duwayne. But, on 3 June, the officer running Knight's identity parade, DS Crowley, reported that Duwayne had said he'd been told which bloke to choose. Weeden was adamant Crowley had misinterpreted the witness but the note had been made and, in July 1993, the Crown Prosecution Service announced that the case against Luke Knight and Neil Acourt was insufficient to proceed to trial.

It was, you have to say, a bleak time for everyone. A lot of people in the media blamed Duwayne. People are quick to forget that if he hadn't been faster than Stephen he would have gone the same way as his mate. The pressure and grief and fear, as well as the anger at the way he'd been treated by the first team, all swilled around his young head. Yes, there are minor discrepancies in some of his statements. Do they mean he is a liar? No. He was a brave but overwhelmed young man who had seen his best pal stabbed to death.

To be fair, Weeden always said good things about Duwayne. In contrast, by September 1993, it seems Weeden had lost patience with the Lawrences and particularly with their solicitor, Imran Khan. Mr Weeden said he tried endlessly to meet Neville and Doreen but was ignored by the parents and rebuffed by the solicitor. Despite the strain, Weeden stayed in the job long after he was due to retire, before finally stepping down in the summer of 1994.

Bring on the third investigation.

Detective Superintendent Bill Mellish came onto the scene after Weeden. As I recall, he did two significant things as SIO: he arrested Clifford Norris, the father of David Norris.

Mellish also had the invidious job of handing the case over to a private firm because in 1995, Mr and Mrs Lawrence announced they had lost all faith in the Met Police.

If the Met wouldn't prosecute the men believed to have killed their son, then they would do it themselves.

The trial of Luke Knight and Neil Acourt, identified by Duwayne, along with Gary Dobson, opened on 17 April 1996 at the Old Bailey's Central Criminal Court. The defendants' lawyers tried to get it thrown out before a jury could even be sworn in but Mr Justice Curtis, the judge, rejected that. However, Duwayne's testimony, given over three days (one of which was the third anniversary of Stephen's death) and around which the prosecution's case centred, was adjudged to be too weak to be relied upon and on 24 April, Judge Curtis pulled the plug on the trial.

Knight, Acourt and Dobson were free men and, in the eyes of the law as it had stood for centuries, could never be tried for the crime again.

In a lot of people's – if not everyone's – minds, that trial put the kybosh on any hope of getting a successful prosecution for the murder of Stephen Lawrence. The *Daily Mail* argued that it was summing up public opinion when, on 14 February 1997, it splashed photos of the five original suspects on the front page, naming them as Stephen's killers and issuing the challenge to sue the paper if they were wrong.

I was very uncomfortable about the role of the media in Stephen's case, as I told the Leveson inquiry in 2012. I certainly don't like to see them bypass the British justice system, however narked they might be.

Still, nothing came of it. Over the next decade there were eight more SIOs attached to the case; there was the Macpherson inquiry and its recommendations; an inquest in 1997 at which the original five attended but did not give evidence; and another review in 2004 which concluded that there still was not enough evidence to bring a trial against anyone for Stephen's murder.

David Norris and Neil Acourt were jailed for 18 months in 2002 for a racist attack on an off-duty police officer. Whether that case made it to trial because the 'institutional racism' in the Met, as highlighted by Macpherson, had been stamped out, or because the victim was Old Bill, I don't know. What I can say is that at least there was a trial, with the defendants and evidence put before a jury, which meant the investigation team had done, at the very minimum, its job.

Getting a case to trial was the least the Met should have done for Stephen. As it was, reading page after page on that bench on Well Hall Road told me that it was the Lawrence family and Duwayne Brooks who were actually made to feel on trial at times. Duwayne in particular has had to endure some wicked treatment from certain police officers and the media and, as a result, by

2006, had long since stopped speaking to anyone from either organisation. The Lawrences, too, had cited so many examples of the police betraying their trust that they were also apparently prudent in the extreme with any dealings with them.

The last thing I wanted to do was give Doreen or Neville Lawrence one single extra reason to hate the police. So how was I going to do that? Very simple. By not meeting them.

Stay away from the Lawrences until you are A1 certain, Clive.

I decided I wouldn't ask them any questions, I wouldn't send them any papers; in fact, I wouldn't even tell them I was starting a fresh investigation. Not yet.

They won't even know I exist until I've got something positive to tell them.

As I looked again at the notes of the case, I thought: *They could have a bloody long wait ...*

CHAPTER SEVENTEEN

Decision 6

I made 326 decisions on Stephen Lawrence.

I know that because every SIO has to – or should, in theory – keep a log for each case. The idea is that in a court case you can produce your log and show contemporaneous evidence of every decision and the reasoning behind it. So, if I went out and arrested Didier Drogba I'd write the reason: 'Because I don't like Chelsea.' That might be good enough for me but because it's in the log a superior officer or a court can look at it and decide whether or not that reason is logical or lawful.

As you can imagine, based on several of the other cases I've worked on, these logs can go missing and so a copy of every decision is automatically made on carbon paper and given to the computer desk to be inputted into HOLMES. It's not a bad system as it goes.

My first decision didn't set the world on fire: 'Today, 20 June 2006, I have accepted responsibility for the investigation into the murder of Stephen Lawrence.'

Having said that, there were a few dissenters even to that innocuous entry. As far as the Met was concerned, I was leading another 'review', and not an 'investigation', into young Stephen's death. If you had phoned up Scotland Yard they would have said we were 'reviewing' it. I never bought that. If you are making enquiries you're not reviewing are you? And I intended to make enquiries. To me, it was as much an investigation as the murder of Surjit Athwal. They were both cold cases and they both needed solving. I didn't ask for Stephen to check someone else's homework. I wanted to find his murderer.

Decision 2 was a bit more lively: that was the note to 'future-proof' the team's work. I also made the call to revamp security on the whole ground floor of Penrhyn Road to make it safe enough to store the papers. The way the case had gone on I didn't want someone driving by and lobbing a petrol bomb through the window. There was little enough strong evidence as there was – I didn't need the rest going up in a literal puff of smoke.

Was it likely? Even a slim chance is still a chance.

The problem with keeping records is occasionally you're just collecting evidence of your own stupidity. To get to grips with the murder, I decided to stage a re-enactment. Not a reconstruction like you see on *Crimewatch*, but just the actual murder, those moments when Stephen was set upon and stabbed. I wanted to see every angle as it happened. From that we could get clues to the height and build of the killer or killers, as well as a fuller picture.

To offer any value at all, I needed to find someone the spit of Stephen. We searched the whole of the Metropolitan Police Service to find someone who was the same height, body weight, athletic build and colour as Stephen.

What is the only thing that is irrelevant in that list?

I was so keen to make this bloke as close to Stephen as possible that I forgot his colour was irrelevant. Yes, it was the reason Stephen had been attacked but, for the purposes of this exercise, he could have been blue. I only realised it about a week later when I studied the pictures and thought, *Why did he have to be black?* Not one of my better days.

But we did find a PC who fitted the description quite eerily closely, I think. Bless his heart, it was a boiling hot day when we did it and we had him in as close to Stephen's five layers as possible. To make matters worse, we were indoors; we could hardly have done it on the street or we'd have had multiple people dialling 999 to say a bloke was being stabbed.

We put him in every conceivable pose and filmed and photographed him with a knife at his neck from behind and in front and above and underneath. It took about six hours and he never complained once. Shaun Keep, who was the assailant every time, kicked up more than him.

Three things came of that little exercise: number one, I will never make a film director, and number two, I will never live down going all out to find a particular skin colour.

And number three: this had not been a brief attack.

The more Shauny and the PC acted out the attacks, the more I realised how much had gone into it. All the original police reports, all the forensic descriptions and even Macpherson all said how Stephen had been the victim of a 'brief attack'. But it was between 30 and 60 seconds long.

If you're driving a car, that might be a 'brief' amount of time. If you're being punched and kicked and sworn and spat at – as well as stabbed – those 30 to 60 seconds are going to feel like a lifetime.

It was a massive mental breakthrough, because suddenly I realised everyone had been coming at it all wrong. If you think something was over quickly you don't anticipate finding much evidence. Whereas if you think a crime took a while to go down, you'll expect more clues so you might spend longer looking for them.

All my instincts said that the crime scene and the evidence we had already held more information than it was letting on. What information I couldn't say. But I did know one thing.

I need the best people to look for it.

Shortly after I took over the case, a reporter named Mark Daly made a programme for the BBC called *The Boys Who Killed Stephen*

Lawrence. He claimed to have new information, although what I saw wasn't necessarily new to me. But Mark did allow me to put a Crimestoppers number at the end of the programme, which lit up the phones in our Major Incident room for days after. I can't say any of it was ultimately of use but it could have been. And it showed everyone on my team that, even after 13 years, Stephen was not any old cold case. It was as vibrant in 2006 as it was in 1993 – arguably more so – as it had captured the public's imagination and it needed – deserved – to be solved.

To do that we needed evidence.

Evidence comes in all shapes and sizes. On a case like Stephen's, the Rolls-Royce stuff would be a knife with his blood and a suspect's fingerprints. Thanks, you'd have to say, to the delay in arresting anyone, any such knife was never found. Plenty of others were, but none that could be proved to have been used in the crime.

So then you have to look at other things. Everything. Any single item that could link victim to perpetrator. The original police responders, in my view, deserve some criticism for not collecting what they could and should have done at Dickson Road. For example, there was a kebab on the ground which could have been relevant because the attackers came from the direction of a nearby kebab house. No one took possession of it. According to the original reports, there was also a tissue nearby. Again, not picked up. The golden rule of any scene is you retrieve anything and chuck it away later if necessary. A kebab and a tissue next to a murdered body could be relevant. On the other hand, they could have been discarded by someone with a cold who didn't like kebabs hours before the attack. We'll never know.

So what evidence was there? All of young Stephen's clothes for a start and, because he was layered up like Scott of the Antarctic, there were plenty of them. Then, when the arrests were finally made and the suspects' houses were searched, any of their own clothes that had fitted the description of the gang members' had been taken as well.

The act of physically searching those items for evidence is where the forensic bods come in. To avoid any charges of corruption, the Met farmed such work out to the government's independent specialist forensic division, Forensic Science Service (FSS). They're the ones with the super-duper microscopes, the white coats and science kits. (They also had a torture chamber, but that's another story ...) If there's stuff to be found, they're the ones to do it.

In 1993, FSS, led by Adrian Wain, carried out hundreds of thousands of scans on the suspects' clothing and belongings in the search for Stephen's blood. Of those, 1,400 were investigated in particular detail. Nothing was found.

They also scoured Stephen's own outer clothes for transference of fibres from his attackers. Again, zilch.

You would have to say that he had done a thorough job and Macpherson commended him for this.

The only thing that struck me was that, unless you're having a blindingly lucky day, in order to find something you normally have to be looking for it. Brian Weeden, in charge of the investigation, had told Wain, 'Everything that can be done should be done.'

But I'm not sure it was.

Wain rightly looked for blood on the suspects but he didn't search for fibres from Stephen's clothes. Stephen had a coat on, the attack was 'brief' and there had been a two-week gap between the stabbing and the seizure of the clothes, so the odds of there being any chance of fibre transfer were low, he reasoned. What would be the point?

I can see two points.

The first is that FSS were told by the senior investigating officer to do everything possible.

And the second is that Wain said the odds were very low.

Low, but not zero.

A slim chance is still a chance.

Would I have thought it still worth looking for those fibres? 100 per cent. A lot of crimes are solved against very slim odds – my whole career is proof of that. That's the nature of the beast. You follow a lead until it cannot give you any more. Make assumptions and you make mistakes.

If I had a quid for every scientist over the years who has said to me, 'I can't see much point in doing that,' I could have bought Fulham a new centre forward. I always say the same thing in reply: 'You're probably right but do it anyway just to keep me happy, will you?' If you're reasonable, you normally get somewhere. Normally, not always.

I had one bloke stand in front of me and say, 'I'm a professor of this, professor of that, I've got a degree in this, a PhD in this and this, and I've got letters after my name that would fill up five envelopes and I say it's a waste of time.'

I replied, 'OK, and I nearly got a C grade in woodwork but would you please do it because I'm the police officer and this is my case.'

Whether they then did what you asked is another thing – you weren't allowed to criticise the scientists. Weeden, in my opinion, probably suffered from that.

So was he blameless in all of this?

Macpherson said not. He hammered him, in fact, for not being in control of his own investigation; for letting other people make decisions he should have been making. Was that fair?

The buck has to stop somewhere.

Fast-forward 13 years and I was in the same position as Weeden. I was the SIO. The buck had nowhere else to go, past me. Faced with the prospect of using FSS to help with my investigation, I have to admit I was nervous.

I wasn't helped by a terrible ricket made in another murder case. A 10-year-old kid, Damilola Taylor, was murdered in Peckham in 2000. The evidence was sent to FSS and they didn't cover themselves in glory. In particular, they missed spots of young Damilola's blood on one of the killer's trainers that was visible to the naked eye. If I'd shown anyone that trainer, they'd have said, 'Why is there blood on it?' FSS, with all their gear and expertise, missed it first time round. (Two brothers were eventually convicted of manslaughter at a third trial in 2006.)

And so, that brings me to Decision 6.

I wrote in my SIO's log that 'I am taking all forensic investigation away from FSS' or words to that effect.

It was a big decision. No one had ever done that before. We'd brought in outside experts to double-check our findings for court, but no one had ever moved an investigation wholesale away from the in-house unit.

The reasoning is simple. In 1993, FSS had led the forensic investigation ... I wanted to work with people who would be led by me. As the only head on the block had Driscoll's hat size, I needed to be confident my orders weren't being ignored.

I also wanted some vitality on the case. When you're looking at evidence that is 13 years old you need to keep energy levels up. It's hard to get enthusiastic about something if you've seen it a dozen times before. I thought a set of fresh eyes would come up with new ideas.

Making that decision and making it happen, however, were two very different animals. Not for the first time in my career I faced immense opposition from all quarters. Largely thanks to those other times, I was better suited to fight it.

I consulted a lot of people: Jim Dickie said he hoped I was ready for the fallout. Cressida Dick said it was unusual but she'd back whatever I decided. But the hero of the hour was Gary Pugh, the head of the Met's forensic operation. He was the one with the chequebook. He had to be persuaded to spend his money on an untested operation, and we are talking telephone numbers. Forensics is not cheap; simply doing a fingerprint is not cheap. The forensic bill in the end for Stephen would be over £3 million. It was a true leap of faith for Gary to give me my head when it would have been the easiest thing in the world for him to play safe, and for that he deserves immense credit.

Finances, it turned out, were to play a large part in the ensuing discussions. The government was preparing to sell FSS and, frankly, Decision 6 could knock some serious money off the asking price. I had phone calls from all sorts of people telling me I couldn't work that way. There was even a plea – more of an order, really – from the Home Office.

I said to them what I said to everyone: 'I think you'll find I can move the work wherever I like because I am the SIO and Macpherson says you have to listen to the SIO.'

A company who had done exceptional work on the Damilola Taylor case was LGC Forensics, based in Oxford. Their head, a wonderful jolly-hockey-sticks type of person, Angela Gallop, had actually been brought in by the Lawrences to check the work of FSS on Stephen in 1993, so she already knew the case. I had no hesitation in going with her if I could get it signed off.

Not only did I get Cressida Dick and Gary Pugh to agree, but I also got them to sit down in a meeting with me and Angela Gallop and we all signed a document that said the forensic investigation would be directed by the police. LGC might know better but if Plod – or 'Pleb' if you prefer – asked them to do something, that's what they would do. No questions, no saying, 'waste of time', no bleating that they'd already done it. This time the dog would wag the tail, not vice versa.

It's the first time in British police history that an SIO has ever got such a document signed. I thought it was a bit of a coup, if I'm honest, but no one else really batted an eyelid. When

I stuck the form in front of Commander Dick she was more exasperated than anything. Like most people, she didn't think I had an earthly of making progress and all this fuss seemed a bit of a distraction.

I think, in fact, it was the decision that made the case.

I'd like to say the handover went smoothly but for all the white coats and science talk, FSS is still full of human beings. And human beings don't like being snubbed. As soon as it was made official that we were going with LGC, I got a phone call from FSS.

'It's a shame you don't want to work with us because we've got the exhibits.'

'I was hoping you had,' I said. 'I need to arrange for them to be picked up.'

'That's not going to happen. They belong to us.'

In police science, when you apply a test to a piece of evidence, anything you use in that test becomes evidence itself. So, if the person doing the tests puts something in a pot, the pot itself becomes evidence because it's touched the original piece, so it gets bagged up and labelled. If you use tape to pull off a fibre, that tape becomes as much of an exhibit as the fibre. This means that you might send one exhibit to the lab and you'll get 800 back. You also have to keep everything that comes into contact with your evidence to prove there has been no contamination.

I knew that out of the hundreds of thousands of exhibits for the case, the majority would have been created by FSS. They still came off my original pieces, though, and I wanted them back.

Again, they said no.

'If I have to,' I wrote in an email, 'I will take out a warrant to retrieve them.'

I actually got as far as starting the ball rolling on a warrant. It was a clerk who said, 'You can't get a warrant against the police.'

'They're not police, they're government.' But I took the point.

It was actually DI Shaun Keep who sorted this out. I must have been to-ing and fro-ing with Wain's lot for a couple of months and I was about to go full bull in a china shop when I said, 'Shauny, why don't you have a go first?'

Shaun is a great DI and a natural diplomat, not someone who likes an unnecessary fight. Together we do the classic good cop/bad cop better than most. 'You've got a week,' I said and he grinned – then went off and got our exhibits. Good work from him and common sense from FSS. For a moment, anyway.

The games still continued. After all the exhibits were laboriously transported over to LGC I was told they hadn't sent any copies of their findings.

Again, back on the blower. 'Why haven't you sent your notes over?'

'Because LGC is a private company and they might steal our working methods.'

'For goodness' sake ...'

Again, though, diplomacy saved the day.

From the start of Decision 6 until the point where LGC actually got their hands on everything took a few months, but eventually I got to meet the whole team and give a bit of a pep talk.

'They said this was a "brief attack". They said there could have been no chance of transfer between Stephen and his assailants. But think of the number of times you can be hit in 30 or 40 or 50 seconds. Think of the number of times you can be kicked and spat at. And the amount of contact you might have with those who are trying to hurt you. Think of each of those seconds and think how much blood and fibres and who knows what could have jumped across in that time. Think of those fibres and, if at all possible, go and find them.'

Not exactly Churchill but I got my message across.

It was then all about the waiting. After 13 years, we weren't exactly against the clock. If I heard anything back before Christmas I'd be happy.

It took them one week.

It took precisely seven days for LGC to unearth something that had gone unreported in the earlier investigations. Angela Gallop rang one day to say that Stephen's black Raiders coat was covered in hairs. Loads of them.

'Did Stephen have a pet?' she asked, in her endearing golly-gosh way.

'Not that I know of, but I can find out. Why?'

'Because these hairs aren't human.'

On Stephen's clothing there were 45 dog hairs, 29 cat hairs, 1 from a cow and even the hair of a badger.

'Where's he come across a badger?' I asked Dr Gallop.

'Shaving perhaps. A lot of brushes use badger hair.'

After a few phone calls I discovered that the Lawrences did not have a dog – or a cat or a cow or a badger, for that matter. But one of the suspects did.

In 1993 Gary Dobson had owned a bulldog called Bullseye. The only problem was, by now, Bullseye was dead.

I explained the discovery to the head of Met forensics, Gary Pugh.

'If we can prove the hairs on Stephen come from Bullseye, we've got Dobson bang to rights.'

'How are you going to do that? The dog's been dead years.'

'I'm going to dig him up.'

I thought Gary would bust a vein in his head, he laughed so much.

'You can't go around digging up people's fucking dogs!'

'I can if I have to. And you can stop laughing because you're going to pay for it.'

I was dead serious. The ever-enthusiastic Angela Gallop sent me up to Livingston in Scotland to visit a company called Wildlife DNA Forensics, a former subsidiary of LGC. They'd recently cracked a case of bestiality, and anything animal-related was their thing. Yes, I was told, in theory, human DNA could be lifted from animal hair – so if we tested all the hairs on Stephen, we might discover Gary Dobson's DNA. As for matching the hairs to a specific creature, sadly science hadn't caught up to that idea yet. All the company could tell me that the hairs belonged to a member of the wolf family and that was it. As for which breed, that was impossible. And forget about an individual dog.

So much for digging up poor Bullseye – a fact that Gary Pugh has never let me forget.

I returned to London fairly downbeat. Still, at least there was the dog hair to comb for human DNA. And who knew what LGC might find there.

Nobody was expecting what they did find: two weeks later, the phone was ringing again.

I will never forget the name 'Avril Johnson'. She was the person who rang and asked me the simple question, 'What are all these red fibres?'

I said, 'What red fibres?'

'There are so many I thought you must have known,' she replied. 'We were going through the hair on Stephen's jacket and came across them. There are thousands of the things all over.'

'Inside or outside?'

'I've only looked on the outside so far.'

I had to scratch my head on that one. 'It must be from the ambulance blanket,' I said. 'Otherwise the last forensics would have flagged them.'

There was a pause.

'Ambulance blankets are red, aren't they?' I checked.

'Yes, but these fibres are completely different. Under magnification they're barely the same colour.'

'OK,' I said. 'Let me look into it.'

It could have been nothing; it could have been something. I always operate on the principle that it's something until proved otherwise.

On this occasion I was correct. It was something all right.

I called Avril straight back. 'I've been through the notes. Stephen was wearing five layers of clothing on his upper body, including a red polo shirt. Can you test against that?'

'Easily.'

She did and came straight back. 'The fibres are microscopically indistinguishable from Stephen's polo shirt.'

Again, it could have been something or nothing. I chose to believe the former was worth hunting for.

'Thinking out loud,' I said, 'if Stephen's polo shirt has managed to transfer fibres onto the outside of his coat, its "shedability" must be pretty high.'

Avril, to her credit, did not pick me up on my made-up word. 'I imagine so,' she said.

'So those fibres could be—?'

'—on any other item of clothing that touched Stephen's coat.'

'Blimey,' I said. 'This is exciting.'

'I agree, but let's not get our hopes up till we've checked everything else.'

She was right, of course – it could turn out to be another dead end.

But what if it wasn't?

No one likes waiting. I'm rubbish at it, so the ensuing few weeks were painful to say the least. Luckily, my night-time piano playing for the old dears was an ever-reliable distraction.

Failing that, there was always my beloved Fulham's latest terrible performance to give me something to think about.

Still, though, all I really wanted to think about was what Dr Gallop, Avril and the others were doing at LGC.

Finally, like the Vatican choosing its new pope, a puff of white smoke appeared above LGC. I was on a train to Oxford like a shot, desperate to read the boffins' faces.

I didn't have to be Sherlock to do that. They had smiles like Cheshire Cats.

'Your "Theory of Shedability" was correct,' Avril Johnson said. 'We've found red fibres from Stephen's polo shirt, via his coat, on a jacket belonging to Gary Dobson and jeans belonging to David Norris.'

As a police officer you live for moments like that.

A lot of cases fail because of loss of momentum – the original Stephen investigation is probably a prime example. In my opinion, this discovery was the spark the case had been crying out for for 13 years. It was the breakthrough to rescue the Met's reputation.

I just had to hope other people agreed. And by other people, I meant two in particular. The two I so far hadn't dared to even meet.

Imagine being Neville and Doreen Lawrence. Not only have you lost your son but the attackers are still out there – gloating, a lot of people said – and the police force entrusted with bringing you justice has fallen short more times than an overweight long-jumper. Of course you're mad at the Met. Of course you think they're, at best, incompetent, at worst, corrupt.

How many previous SIOs had called them to Scotland Yard and said, 'We're going to be doing this, we'll be doing that,' and given it the full PowerPoint presentation? They had to be sick of it. I knew I would be.

And then there were Sir Paul Condon's famous first words when he brought Mrs Lawrence to Scotland Yard: 'What do you think of the brilliant view?'

Funnily enough, Sir Paul, she was there to discuss your organisation's failure to find justice for her murdered son, not coo at the vista.

If I was going to meet the Lawrences, I decided, it wouldn't just be to shake hands and say, 'Call me Clive.' I had to have something for them. I had to be bearing gifts. And what could be better than a gift-wrapped piece of new evidence?

So why were my knees knocking before they'd even arrived?

In fact, I only met Doreen that day in early 2007. Neville, since the couple's divorce, spends half the year in Jamaica. In any case, he and his ex hadn't been in the same room for some time and liked to keep it that way. Similarly, Duwayne Brooks made it clear through his solicitor that he wanted no part of me, the investigation or the Met – yet. However, I hoped that if he saw me acting honourably he could still be persuaded.

So that left Mrs Lawrence, who did not arrive alone at the office I'd booked at New Scotland Yard. Mr Khan, her long-time solicitor, and Michael Mansfield, her barrister, were in attendance. Representing the Met there was me, Shaun Keep, Cressida Dick and the new superintendent, Neil Basu.

I still wish we hadn't come out in such numbers, because it made it look like the red corner against the blue. It just goes to show how much of a tinderbox the whole case was for the police. No one else would have got the royal treatment.

Commander Dick did some preliminary introductions and, looking at our guests, I have to say that 'frosty' was a word that sprang to mind.

To be fair to Mrs Lawrence, Mr Mansfield and Mr Khan, they all thought they were arriving to be told we were officially shutting the book on young Stephen's investigation. They already had an opinion of the Met lower than a snake's belly, so it was no surprise their attitude, certainly at the start, was reflective of this.

Right from the off, then, I regretted meeting the family for the first time in that environment. There was being professional and showing you were doing a good job, and there was making decent people feel awkward. Even I felt uncomfortable sitting around that table in an over-lit meeting room. Allowances always had to be made for visitors. And for these visitors more so than usual.

When I was called up to bat I introduced myself and cut straight to the chase.

'I believe we have found new evidence linking Stephen to several suspects.' I then slid across the table printouts of a robotic figure marked where fibres had been found. For some reason it seemed of the utmost importance to me then that I pointed out that the figures in the diagram weren't real people. I can only put it down to nerves. As soon as the words came out of my mouth I thought, *Well, everyone's going to believe you're a detective, aren't they?*

Fortunately I don't think anyone noticed. Mr Khan, the lawyer for Mrs Lawrence, actually smiled.

'This is really exciting news,' he said. 'Well done.'

Mr Mansfield agreed.

Mrs L, on the other hand, refused to let her guard down.

'I think we've been down this path before, haven't we?' she said.

'No, ma'am,' I said. 'I honestly think this is something new.'

'Well, I'll believe it when you show me a conviction.'

Slightly deflated, I moved on to a second line of enquiry.

Since the FSS had looked at Stephen's case, there had been massive scientific progress, particularly in the area of DNA testing. For the benefit of new tests LGC were planning, I asked

Mrs Lawrence if she and her family would agree to supply a sample of their saliva to get a record of their DNA, in case we found samples on Stephen's clothes.

That's what I said. What she heard was: 'Please can we get a sample of your family's DNA to check them against outstanding crimes on the police computer.'

'Why would I agree to this?' she demanded. 'Haven't you demonised my family enough?'

I was shocked. The request couldn't have been more innocent. We wanted to discount family members from spit found on Stephen's clothes. How had it turned into us wanting to pin various crimes on her family?

It was a rude awakening, whichever way you looked at it.

What hell has this poor woman gone through at the hands of the Met that this is what she thinks?

Obviously I hadn't explained myself particularly well – she was actually furious.

'I'm sorry if I've given the wrong impression, ma'am,' I said. 'I can assure you our intentions are 100 per cent honourable. This is not some backdoor attempt to entrap you or anyone in your family. I'm not going to test your aunts and uncles against some burglary in Greenwich.'

'Really?'

'Really. I can offer you no more than my word but I swear the only reason I want your DNA is to progress the case against your son's killers.'

'If you say so.'

'I do. So will you trust me?'

'For now.'

'That's good enough for me.'

I thought the meeting went OK in the circumstances. The commander and superintendent both warned me not to read too much into it. I wouldn't be the first SIO Mrs Lawrence had chewed up, they said.

She's not the enemy, I reminded myself. *She's a victim. Whatever she has said about the Met was probably justified.* As long as I didn't let her down, I figured I'd be OK. This was my investigation. I was in complete control.

When I saw a record of our meeting splashed all over the *Daily Mail* the following day, I realised I was in control of nothing.

It took about 15 minutes from that newspaper arriving on front door steps all over the country before we got a call from one of the lawyers acting for the family.

'Same old Met, leaking everything to make yourselves look good.'

I was horrified that Mrs Lawrence thought I'd have done something like that. I'd already rattled her with the saliva request. Now this had happened, she had to think I was as full of hot air as the rest. How was I going to prove otherwise? I was also shocked because the *Mail* had printed secret information. On reflection, we could have been victims of the phone hacking scandal but I had no idea how such information could have leaked at that time. Solving a crime or building a case against someone is like a game of chess; the longer you prevent your opponent knowing what you're up to, the greater your chance of knocking their pieces over. So, yes, it was a good news story and, for once, it showed the police in a half-decent light where Stephen was concerned, but I was worried it now had my suspects on red alert.

Still, newspapers I could deal with – or, ideally, not deal with. Even tipping the suspects the wink could be salvaged. But a leak within my own organisation? That could prove fatal in the investigation and I knew I just had to do everything I could to make everything as failproof as possible.

Decision 6

As the weeks went by and no further good news came in to tip the scales back in our favour, Cressida Dick could see it was vexing me.

'What are you going to do?' she asked.

'I'm going to have to turn on the old Driscoll charm.'

'And if that doesn't work?'

'I'm going to buy Mrs Lawrence a bun.'

CHAPTER EIGHTEEN

Dig Him Up

The Stephen Lawrence Centre was officially opened in Deptford High Street on 7 February 2008 but it had been open for business since early 2007. When I arrived in March that year, armed with doughnuts I had bought at the local bakers, I noticed the impressive building had already been vandalised more than once.

I went up to the smiling lady on reception and said, 'Hello, my name is DCI Driscoll—'

'Have you come about the window? It was only smashed this morning. That was quick.'

'Actually, no. I'm looking after young Stephen's case. I wonder if I might have a word with Mrs Lawrence?'

By coincidence, the woman in question happened to walk past at that moment. 'Hello again, officer. What can I do for you?'

Well, at least she remembers me ...

'Hello, Mrs L,' I said. 'If you wouldn't mind sticking the kettle on, I've brought us some doughnuts.'

Her face didn't crack. So much for the Driscoll charm. But, as we walked away, I swear I saw her share a smile with the receptionist.

Get in ...

I take people as I find them. With Doreen Lawrence I saw a fragile, fifty-something woman who had lost a son, who had been a victim of police incompetence and probably corruption, and who had run out of patience with the police. But she hadn't run out of patience with me. Not yet. She also took people at face value. If I said I wanted to help, she would believe me. If I could prove it.

First of all, I apologised – between slurps of coffee and bites of doughnut – for the leak.

'I swear it didn't come from me.'

She accepted that. We even discussed where it might have originated and both rolled our eyes. Then we went back over some of the facts from my presentation, only this time without the audience or the idiotic explanation of the robot diagrams. This time she was more upbeat and, by the end of the meeting – despite not touching any of the doughnuts – she was actually very supportive of what I hoped to do. Despite her obvious and fair mistrust of the Met, she even seemed to warm to me.

But then, when you're talking to someone with sugar all over his face, you know it's not exactly Hitler's Third Reich, is it?

I can honestly say that, from that meeting, I have never experienced anything other than the fullest support and friendship from Mrs L.

But, despite being the most vocal and arguably the most important, she was still just one of the three people I needed to win over. The next two would prove a real challenge, even for me.

If I failed, the case could fall apart.

Previous SIOs on Stephen's case have met Neville Lawrence in Florida; they've met him in Jamaica; they've met him in Scotland.

I met him in a noodle bar in Plumstead. And I bought the noodles.

The person who says Neville Lawrence isn't lovely is a liar. Despite going through everything he has – including the break-up of his marriage – he remains the most upbeat, kindly gent you could hope to meet. It's been a pleasure, from day one, and that first encounter was no different.

As I brought him up to speed on where we were, where we were aiming and where we hoped to get to, he just said, 'Do your best, officer. That's all we've ever asked. Do your best for Stephen.'

The third cog in the wheel, historically, wasn't a family member: it was Duwayne Brooks, the boy who could have died with Stephen. *Instead* of Stephen. People seem in a hurry to forget that. The 'What, what, nigger?' shout wasn't directed at Stephen. It was aimed at Duwayne. He was the one calling out to Stephen. He was the one being answered by the murderers.

He was the one who could be dead instead of his friend.

By the time I started putting serious feelers out to him it was 15 years since the murder. He'd been invited to the meeting at Scotland Yard and declined, but after getting somewhere with Stephen's parents I was hopeful of being able to convince him to come on board.

I soon got told where I stood – by his solicitor.

Jane Deighton is very good at her job. Her client, Duwayne, had clearly instructed her not to let the Old Bill through the net. So she didn't. My original approach by phone was rebuffed so I reverted to email. For a dyslexic that's not as straightforward as it sounds. Still, I hope I gave Jane Deighton a game, because that's what it felt like. I would send an email with a request and she would knock it back. I would return it and she would send a reply, which I would pounce on. Just when I'd think I was getting somewhere she'd slam the door and I'd have to go again. It was classic tennis, in its way.

Nice serve from Driscoll, Driscoll comes into the net ... passing shot from Deighton – Driscoll dives, but it's too little too late ...

But even a Brit's luck has to turn at tennis – look at Andy Murray – and eventually I served down one or two unreturnables and she let me have a message from Duwayne.

'If you pay Jane Deighton's fees I will speak to you.'

How I would have loved to have done that, but there was a problem.

'Please tell Duwayne he is a witness and not a suspect, however other officers have made him feel. I can't pay the solicitor of witnesses. How would that look to the defence team? Cash is changing hands for a performance in court I want? I'm sorry, I can't do it.'

There are all sorts of rules and regulations around the correct way you treat witnesses. In the right defence lawyer's hands, should it get that far, what was being proposed could have been seen as tainting the evidence if we paid over a penny.

The sound of a door slamming is never nice, even by email. I wondered if I'd ever be able to prise it open.

But, when I thought about it, I knew a man who could.

I had not worked with Brian Paddick since leaving Brixton in 1995 but we'd stayed in touch as old colleagues do. After leaving the force in 2007 he had entered the political arena, throwing his hat into the ring to stand for the position of Mayor of London for the Liberal Democratic Party in May 2008. (He would also appear on *I'm A Celebrity Get Me Out Of Here* in the same year, but nobody's perfect.) The reason I mention it is because, come 2008, Duwayne Brooks was considerably active in the political arena himself. And his party? The Lib Dems.

I don't know how he did it, considering the feelings involved, but in 2007 Brian turned up at a hotel opposite my office at Tintagel House on Albert Embankment accompanied by Duwayne Brooks himself. After six months, minimum, of email ping-pong, this was manna from heaven.

In the years that have followed, I've called Duwayne Brooks an absolute pain in the arse. To his face, as well. Because he was. On the one hand, he was charming, erudite, really, really supportive and desperate to help; but on the other, as soon as I stepped over a line that he could see and I couldn't, he'd just shut up shop and the shutters would tumble down.

More than a decade of being on the rough end of the Old Bill will do that for you.

It happened the first time when I asked if he, like the Lawrence relatives, would give us a DNA sample.

'Why do you want that?'

'We're asking for samples from everyone, including Mr and Mrs Lawrence, to eliminate them from our enquiries. We don't want to get excited about something on Stephen's jacket if it turns out it came from you.'

'I don't buy it.'

'What do you mean?'

'You're trying to frame me for something else.'

Mrs Lawrence had said the same thing. What must these people have gone through at the hands of the police to have come up with that as my reason for wanting their DNA?

Duwayne believed passionately that we would fabricate evidence against him. You name it, he believed it. When he took me on a walk around Lewisham, we always took the back streets where there was no CCTV. He was that aware of unseen forces trying to trip him up.

'You're my best witness,' I said. 'Why would I do anything to damage you?'

'It's never stopped your lot before.'

Days after Stephen's death, Duwayne took part in an anti-racism rally outside the local offices of the BNP. For no obvious reason, he believes, other than his skin colour and recent history with the police, he was arrested and charged with violent disorder. Those charges were dropped. In 1999 a charge of indecent assault – reduced from an initial rape charge – was thrown out of court by the judge as an abuse of process amid allegations of errors and inconsistencies in the police and prosecution's case.

With history like that, you can see where the lad was coming from. Whatever I said, why should he have believed I was any different to the coppers who'd been after him for a decade and a half?

Eventually he said, 'I don't see why I should give you anything – you've got my DNA from that trumped-up case against me.'

'It's quite simple, really,' I replied. 'DNA degrades over time.'

'I don't believe you.'

'OK,' I said. 'Would you take the word of our chief scientific officer?'

He nodded.

I've done a few things I'm not proud of in my life but getting Alan Tribe to explain the lifespan of DNA to Duwayne was perhaps the most cruel. Alan is an absolute hero for his outstanding work in young Stephen's case and I love him to death. But asking him to tell someone about a scientific process is like handing down a sentence to the listener. There is not a detail he does not relish going into. It must be a thing about scientists because another crucial player in the case was Ed Jarman at LGC, who is as meticulous and brilliant and excited by detail as Alan. An hour in a room with them can feel like a day for a normal person.

Alan alone was enough to break Duwayne. After about 15 minutes, just as he got around to elaborating on the construction process of test tubes, Duwayne cracked.

'I believe you,' he said. 'You can take my DNA.'

By February 2008 I really felt we were getting somewhere on Stephen's case ... and we were moved, yet again.

Is someone actively trying to derail this investigation? I wondered. *Because they're going about it the right way.*

The real reason was far more benign. It was all Jim Dickie's fault, really. The old boy had decided to move and, as I needed a new superintendent, someone without Jim's experience of solving crimes thought it would be a whizz to use the opportunity to shift us again.

The good news was I didn't have to move desk; the even better news was we were going to Trident – run by Chief Superintendent Helen Ball.

I have so much time for Helen but it's fair to say that her team was less blown away by the arrival of the old Racial and Violent mob.

I was called into a meeting with Trident's head honchos. The fact that I'd been part of their squad very recently counted for nada. One police officer addressed the entire room as though we weren't there. Bearing in mind his audience included several faces, like Helen, who I knew, I was surprised when he said, 'I'm very unhappy about this union. I'm not sure the skill sets of our two groups are compatible.'

Time for me to interject.

'It's not ideal for us, I admit, but if you're prepared to at least try to meet our standards, then I suppose we could give you a chance.'

The Trident DCI was furious; Helen and anyone else who knew me was in fits.

Afterwards, she introduced our new superintendent, Jill Bailey, who immediately asked for a briefing. We had an hour and I barely skimmed the surface. Even then I'd have required a fortnight to get anywhere near the full story.

To her credit, like Jim Dickie, Jill was happy for me to continue the investigation as I saw fit. If that was what being part of Trident meant then I was happy.

All I could do was prove people wrong. In order to do that, I needed to prove other people guilty. And in February 2008, that wasn't looking too likely.

'Gary Dobson is innocent of the murder of Stephen Lawrence.'

That, in 2008, was the legal state of affairs in a nutshell. He, along with the two others who had made it to trial in 1996, had been acquitted. In the eyes of the law, therefore, he was untouchable.

Or so he definitely would have thought at the time.

Macpherson's report had changed that with the recommend-ation of ending 'double jeopardy', which Jack Straw brought into statute in 2003 and active law in 2005.

In 2006 we saw the first example of it at work. William Dunlop had stood trial twice for the murder of Julie Hogg in 1991 and both times the jury had failed to reach a verdict, leading to him being officially cleared. After tireless campaigning by Julie's mother, Ann Ming, who had actually demanded a repeal of 'double jeopardy' herself, new evidence was brought against Dunlop and he was jailed for life after admitting the murder.

Evidence, I thought. *It's all about the evidence.*

There was no room for error – even the new Criminal Justice Act would only allow a retrial once – so I put Shaun Keep on the job of researching every aspect of the new law. When he returned with his report he had a face like a smacked bottom.

'I hope you're not bringing me bad news about Dobson,' I said.

'I'll be honest, guv, it doesn't look good.'

The evidence we had on David Norris and Gary Dobson was very nearly top drawer. Although the red fibres on the suspects' clothes were microscopically indistinguishable from those forming Stephen's polo shirt, at the end of the day fibre evidence is not as good as DNA evidence. With fibre you have a 1 in 500,000 chance of error; with DNA, it's 1 in a billion.

Norris, because he had never previously been charged, was looking at a straight 'guilty' in my eyes – and hopefully those of a jury – on the fibres alone. To nail Dobson with the same evidence we needed it to be 'new and compelling'.

Anyone would agree it was compelling all right: fibres linking victim and suspect? I will take that all day. But was it 'new'?

To us it was. To the entire Met it was brand spanking new. But this was where Shaun's research rained on the parade.

It was 'new' because it had not previously been found. At the same time, it could be argued it was 'not new' because it really, really should have been found the first time around – the original forensic team had had the equipment and the know-how to have discovered the fibres. The Criminal Justice Act 2003 was designed to avoid miscarriages of justice – not to let police cock up and then have another go.

Even though we hadn't used them this time around, the bloody FSS was still casting a very long shadow on my investigation. It's fair to say my office was not the place to be that afternoon.

'We've still got Norris,' one of the team said, trying to be cheerful.

'But I want both. So do you all know how we're going to get Dobson?'

'No, guv.'

'We're going to find more evidence.'

I hope ...

It was a blow, I admit, but keeping enthusiasm levels up was key to the investigation. I didn't want one setback derailing us. Nor did I want one achievement in the evidence department to mean we could stop searching. I wanted to go for as many targets as possible – in fact, we had fibre evidence linking one other person to Stephen's red shirt. For legal reasons I cannot divulge a name.

The next few weeks were topsy-turvy. Every time I rang Angela Gallop she seemed to have a new snippet of evidence for me. I let myself believe the suspects list could grow to as many as four.

It wasn't all good news, however. A lot of material seemed to have vanished in the transfer from FSS to LGC. In particular, items pertaining to 1995–2000. It would be months before that mystery was solved.

It was very simple, really. According to the notes from FSS, there should have been some tapings – fibres collected on sticky tape – from clothes belonging to David Norris and Gary Dobson. After months of searching, it was discovered the original files had been mislabelled: instead of David Norris's blue cardigan being tagged with 'Stephen Lawrence' or 'Operation Fishpool', it had been filed as part of a Brixton burglary.

Regardless, by March 2008 there were enough extra little bits of information to make it worth another family update.

It should have been straightforward but, like the scientist who didn't file the exhibits correctly, I must have been daydreaming when I made arrangements. I was at the Buckingham Gate Hotel early enough to welcome Mrs Lawrence who, I'm glad to report, couldn't have seemed happier to see me.

How things can change when you win someone's confidence, and they don't think you're out to get them.

However, her smile vanished when the door opened again and Jocelyn Cockburn, Neville Lawrence's solicitor, walked in.

'What's she doing here?' Mrs L asked.

She knew, as well as I did, that if Ms Cockburn was there, her client probably wouldn't be far behind. The Lawrences hadn't been in the same room for years – and here I was playing matchmaker by accident.

We got over the awkwardness – and my momentous cock-up – pretty early, I have to say, but it still wasn't right that Jocelyn was there and Mrs L didn't have any representation, so we put a call through to Mr Khan and he turned up a short while later. I think he was as shocked as anyone.

Afterwards, we all went to the bar to mark the occasion. I bought Neville a pint, Jocelyn a gin, water for Mr Khan and a huge glass of wine for Mrs L.

When she saw it arrive she said, 'Clive, if I get drunk will you arrest me?'

'Well, I think we can safely say you'd have tomorrow's front pages sewn up if I did.'

The next time I would meet them all would be on 22 April. We couldn't forget it. It would be the fifteenth anniversary of young Stephen's death.

It's not every day you feel sorry for Gordon Brown.

It was Tuesday, 22 April, 2008 at St Martin-in-the-Fields, just off Trafalgar Square and, like the rest of the congregation, I was belting out 'All Things Bright And Beautiful'. I was next to Cressida Dick, Assistant Commissioner John Grieve (retired) and Deputy Commissioner Paul Stephenson.

But it was the prime minister who was unlucky enough to be in front of me.

Alongside him, and slightly safer, were the leaders of the opposition, David Cameron and Nick Clegg, as well as the Home Secretary, Jacqui Smith, her predecessor Jack Straw, and other household names. It was a right *Who's Who* of public life.

None of those politicians had met Stephen – some of them never came within a postcode of him – but in death he'd changed our country for ever. They knew that, and so did the banks of dignitaries lined up behind us, faces craning to be seen, voices straining to be heard. And overseeing it all was the giant poster at the front of the boy himself: young, beautiful, innocent and full of hope.

His face loomed over the room but I swear he only had eyes for four people standing stoically on the other side of the aisle, the only ones who counted: Doreen, the miniature powerhouse; Neville, the nicest man on the planet – two of the loveliest, bravest and most incredible human beings I've ever had the pleasure to meet. And of course, sitting next to them, Stuart and Georgina, Stephen's brother and sister.

If I had been in any doubt before how much of an impact Stephen's death meant to the country – and I wasn't – this nailed it. People cared. Important people. People who had the power to effect change. Jack Straw, sitting just along from me, had got rid of the 'double jeopardy' law. No one had imagined that 10 years ago. I just hoped I could mount a case worthy of using it.

If ever there was a scenario to bring out a reflective mood, it was there, in that church, during a service led by Dr Rowan Williams, the Archbishop of Canterbury, and surrounded by love for young Stephen. Without the personal invite from the Lawrences maybe I wouldn't have come. Unlike Jack Straw, what had I achieved for them? I had launched yet another as yet unsuccessful investigation. I felt a bit of a fraud for being there, if I'm honest, hollering into the PM's ear like I was on the terraces at Craven Cottage. I could tell that proud couple that I was in pursuit of the truth until I was blue in the face but nothing, I realised, would make me feel better until I was able to look them in the eye and say, 'I've got the evidence to nail your son's killers.'

The service ended and with it any further chance of reflection as the flashbulbs of the media popped at every exiting dignitary. Doreen Lawrence generally can't go anywhere without being mobbed by the press and, with this congregation all desperate to have their photo taken with her, it was like a free-kick wall of cameras outside the door.

I'd come with John Grieve who, by then, was in a wheelchair. As I popped up the back to collect it, my phone vibrated in my pocket. It's never good form to answer in a church but with the noise the great and the good were making, I thought I could get away with it. Especially when I saw the number.

It was DS Peter Birdsall, one of my team. He knew exactly where I was and he would not have called unless it was important. I rang back immediately.

'Guv, you need to call Ed Jarman at LGC.'

I've been told the press can read your lips and so, as there were hundreds outside all facing my way, I turned my back on the door to make the next call. After all the leaks I wasn't taking any chances.

I found Ed's number and while it was ringing looked up. There was Stephen, about eight foot by ten, in that famous black-and-white striped shirt of his. It always reminded me of the West Brom strip, which I'm sure would have offended him as an Arsenal fan.

Suddenly the familiar voice of Ed Jarman answered.

'It's Clive Driscoll,' I said. 'Is everything all right?'

'It's more than all right, Clive. We've found Stephen's blood.'

'Where?'

'On Gary Dobson's jacket.'

I looked up at Stephen's picture and couldn't help talking to him.

'Not long now, son. Not long, I promise.'

CHAPTER NINETEEN

Sir Woy

Picture the scene. I'm pushing John Grieve, one of the most respected Met officers of my acquaintance, up the aisle behind the prime minister, leaders of the opposition and the Archbishop of Canterbury ... and I'm going too fast, weaving through the masses to get alongside Cressida Dick. I lean over to her. She's tiny – they call her (behind her back) the 'pocket Spitfire' – and it must look like I'm trying to nibble her ear.

'Ma'am, there's something I must tell you.'

She just stops short of swatting me away. Then she sees my face. I'm serious.

'What is it?'

It's hard to whisper something you want to shout from the rooftops.

'We've just found Stephen's blood on Gary Dobson's jacket.'

'Oh ... *wow*!'

'Oh, wow, indeed, ma'am.'

'What next?' she asked.

'For now we keep it between you and me. I'm not even telling my team.'

'Agreed.'

John Grieve couldn't have heard the conversation but he must have sensed my good mood because when we got to the door and the church contributions plate was there, he looked up and said, 'Have you got any money on you, Clive? Because I haven't got anything to put in the tray.'

'Don't worry, guv, I'll cover you,' I said, weighing in with a couple of twenties from me and him.

I wouldn't normally mention it but has he, with his massive ex-assistant commissioner pension, ever paid me back? Has he heck. But I'd pay £20 for him any day because he's a good copper.

As agreed, I did not tell my team, not immediately. Instead, the very next day I went up to see Ed Jarman with Alan Tribe, because if anyone could verify the findings it was him.

I sat with them in Oxford, mouth open as they showed me what they had found.

It was a fibre of Dobson's jacket, with Stephen's blood around it.

'Do you realise what this means?' Alan asked.

'Tell me.'

'It means the blood was wet when it went on. It couldn't have been transferred in any way other than during the attack.'

'Oh, this is *quality*.'

And that, believe it or not, was actually a problem.

Ten investigations, plus an inquest and an inquiry, have looked into the murder of Stephen Lawrence, and got nowhere. Fifteen years later, Driscoll comes along and he finds blood.

A1, Rolls-Royce, cherry-on-top evidence.

Hello? Does anyone else find that a bit suspicious?

It's true: the evidence that LGC had found was so good that there were genuine fears from my team (when I told them), and myself, that it would be considered staged. Too good to be true.

In our defence – and, for once, in FSS's defence – the evidence was the 'newest' there was. The technology to find it had not existed back in the early 90s to have found it. Adrian Wain and his team were clear on that charge.

As for 'compelling' – it was blood. You don't get much more compelling than that.

Still, before we did anything else, I took the decision to test our case. If we were even thinking of going for a 'double jeopardy' conviction, we needed the most robust case imaginable.

I put a whole team of people together whose specific task was to attack our evidence. I wanted it pulled this way and that, stretched to the limits and beyond.

'Think like a defence barrister – what would they say? And how would we prove them wrong?'

I have to say, my team went at it with gusto. Particular mention goes to Richard Dixon, a lovely bloke – but you could have knocked his lights out some days with some of the defence theories he came up with.

'Guv, what if a Martian came down, melted the blood with his laser and teleported it onto Dobson's jacket while it was in the bag?'

We never dismissed any argument, however crackpot, so just for the hell of it I said, 'OK, well, this Martian – how tall is he ...?' And on we went, coming up with every possible permutation of defence and using everything we had at our disposal to knock it down.

While one part of the team worked on the 'what if' scenarios, another group worked on making sure that what we did know was in perfect working order. Any defence brief worth his salt would try to attack the 'integrity' of our evidence. In other words, they'd say, 'Those fibres found on our client's coat were transferred when the coat was put in the same evidence bag as Stephen's shirt.' They would be bluffing, of course – there was no way they could have known that happened (and, in fact, it never had) – but if it caused one member of the jury to question the evidence, they'd have done their job: the role of the prosecution is to prove 'beyond reasonable doubt' that a crime has been committed – if the defence can get a few doubts going, they've won.

It's a system I fully support, but when you're the one mounting the prosecution it's tough. So, how do you beat a defence that is allowed, in law, to challenge every part of your evidence without coming up with any of their own?

You work bloody hard.

I have seen so many nailed-on cases fall apart because the prosecution believed their evidence was enough. Look at my first case: that geezer who jumped the lights. We had proof that he'd done it. He'd admitted he'd done it. We probably rested on our laurels a bit and thought, *Job's a good'un*. What we didn't do was think like a defence counsellor. We didn't run through the possibilities of what he could say in mitigation. And it cost us that day.

I'd sworn then I'd never be caught out again. On Stephen I had the chance to prove that in front of the whole Met and the country's media. So no pressure, then.

I wanted to anticipate and make sure we had a comeback for every possible claim or accusation, however far-fetched or fanciful it sounded to us. The way we would achieve that was with facts. Hard, irrefutable facts.

And I knew the man to do just that job.

When I first took over Stephen's case, nobody wanted to touch us with a bargepole; after 22 April 2008, everyone wanted to be in our gang. Few of them, though, were better than the people who had been with me for years.

Alan Taylor, I knew, was built for a job like this. I stuck him in charge of continuity and integrity and marvelled as he tracked down the life story and history post-1993 of every single exhibit in the police's possession. And remember, there were thousands of them.

They'd been collected by one officer; bagged, then examined by FSS; shipped to Kent for review into the case; brought back to FSS; then handed over to us. Each exhibit could tell its own story – and Alan Taylor knew each one by heart. You could ask Alan about any individual fibre and he'd be able to say, 'It spent this long at this nick in this cupboard, this long under this microscope ...' and so on. We even went down to Kent to examine the cupboard the evidence had been kept in there, in case that was thrown at us.

It was an outstanding job.

By midway through 2009 I felt we'd crossed as many t's as we could so I went to Jill Bailey.

To her credit she wasn't convinced.

'We can't afford one single error,' she said. 'My advice is to keep checking.'

So we did. I always listen to people and reflect on what they say. If she was nervous, Cressida Dick would be. So it was back to testing – for six more months.

Finally, in 2010, I was confident we had it. Angela Gallop and her team in Oxford had been over every millimetre of our evidence and applied it to every known test. Alan Taylor had the full biography of every item. We'd even managed to exhaust Richard Dixon on plausible and implausible permutations.

It was time to go.

The case against David Norris was simpler but the evidence against Gary Dobson was stronger. As he was protected under 'double jeopardy' we couldn't just go straight to trial. There were three steps – or hurdles, depending on your outlook – in between.

1. We needed to persuade the Director of Public Prosecutions that we had a case against Dobson.
2. If we passed that, we would have three weeks to arrest Dobson and Norris and whomever else we felt we could nab. At that stage I had plausible cases against four names.

3. Then we would have to go to the Royal Courts of Justice with our 'new and compelling' evidence to get Dobson's acquittal overturned. Without that, Dobson stayed a free man.

You have to start somewhere and so in 2010 I went to Commander Dick to get the ball rolling. Someone of my rank couldn't just write to the Director of Public Prosecutions so she was the one to jot down all the evidence, stating why the evidence was new and compelling, then we posted it off to Keir Starmer, the DPP at the time, along with every piece of our case.

After that there was nothing we could do but wait.

And wait. And wait.

For nine days we waited, with no word. In a way, that was good news. It meant the press hadn't got wind of our case. If they had, I was worried they'd print one wrong thing and ruin everything we'd worked for. Journalists always tell me they're helping by publicising stories but if you're Gary Dobson and you have no idea Driscoll's about to arrest you until you read it in the the *Sun*, you've got a tip-off right there. How is that helpful? The media interest in Stephen – thanks to stories like that printed by the *Daily Mail* in 1997 and various documentaries – was huge, and the money offered by the tabloids for any titbit of information was, I imagine, very tempting to some people at the Met. As I already knew to my cost. Which is why I was planning to ask the DPP for a total press blackout on the case. It had never been done before. I didn't know if it could be done, even. But if I couldn't stop the Met from leaking like a sieve – and nobody has ever been able to do that – then if I ensured the press couldn't report on received information, it was the next best thing.

In any case, I hadn't even told the Lawrences about Stephen's blood, or the plans to arrest, and the last thing I wanted was them reading about it in the press before I'd had the conversation with them. The 1993 investigation had made that mistake and never recovered from it.

Finally, after the 10 most nerve-wracking days of my life, we got the call: Keir Starmer would see us that afternoon.

Accompanying me to the DPP's office opposite Sea Container House on the Thames was the Met's solicitor. Three things about him stood out: he was numero uno when it came to getting press restrictions; he was the spitting image of the king from *Shrek*; and he had no sense of humour. All three of those would be proved by the time the afternoon was over.

We were shown into an office, and all thoughts of the case left my mind for a fleeting moment. Palatial doesn't do the place justice. I looked at the DPP's uninterrupted views across the river and thought, *You're being paid too much.*

Or was he worth every penny? I would decide when I heard his verdict.

The sight of my bundle of files – four years' hard graft – stacked on the top of his desk shook me back to the present. Instinctively, I scanned the room to check for unwanted eyes. We were safe.

And so, finally, the DPP began to talk us through his decision. After a few minutes he paused, looked me in the eye and said, 'Do you know? I think you have enough to move forward to the next stage.'

I said, 'Excuse me, Mr Starmer, you couldn't just say that one more time for me, could you, please?'

My own solicitor snapped at that. 'You heard the man. He said it once, didn't he?' I said he had no sense of humour.

Starmer smiled, then obliged.

'I think you have enough to move forward to the next stage, DCI Driscoll. Congratulations.'

'Thank you, sir. That is such monumental news I just needed to hear it twice.'

The case would only be against Dobson and Norris, however, and not the four names I'd submitted. But I could live with that. For now.

For all his faults, the solicitor was blinding at his job and we won a total press blackout. Unfortunately, it would not kick in until the point of arrest.

I looked at the files on Starmer's desk and considered all the eyes between my office and his who must have seen them over the last 10 days. Would we seriously be able to contain any leaks until arrests? I would do everything in my power to ensure it. But when it's not just people on the outside you have to worry about, that difficult job becomes a bit harder.

I don't think I'm speaking out of turn when I say that prior to that decision by the DPP, our investigation had flown under the radar at Scotland Yard. If I had the impression that people didn't think we stood a chance then that was because that was what I was constantly being told. I thought that being told by the DPP that we had done enough work to invoke the double jeopardy law would gee the Job up. It had the opposite effect. Not for the first time in my life I had calls from people questioning whether I knew what I was doing.

'You haven't done enough.'

'You're going to fail.'

Of course, what they all actually meant was, 'The Met is going to be shown up again.'

There really was a definite feeling of 'let sleeping dogs lie' where young Stephen was concerned. The whole case was a hornets' nest which had been kicked too many times by the Met. For certain people, their most fervent wish was to get through the rest of their lives without being stung by Stephen's case again.

Even if it meant not going for a prosecution.

I never understood that. I trusted my team. I trusted my case. And I trusted the jury system to get to the truth. That was what we had all signed up for at Hendon, wasn't it? To get to the truth? To any doubters I said, 'We have a case,' and left it at that. There was no way I was backing down, either by choice or coercion. I'd made that mistake once in Lambeth. I'd never make it again.

If they'd happened in isolation I could have dismissed the Chinese whispers and vaguely veiled threats as sour grapes, or nerves, from people that should have known better. But they didn't: at the same time that my investigation was being shot at verbally, it was also being attacked physically. With the investigation in full swing I was told we were being moved – again – this time to Tintagel House near the MI5 building on the Thames.

'Why?'

'We're shutting down Kingston.'

Moving is always a pain but when you've spent months acquiring and logging thousands of files, the last thing you want is for them to be shifted. It was a massive disruption and it cost us weeks of double-checking that everything had arrived safely. Our entire case could disintegrate if one piece of paper went missing.

Surely the people who had made this decision knew that? Or was that the point?

To minimise the threat of leaks you have to limit sensitive information to a controllable number of people. When it came to making arrests, some people think I went too far. The people of East Ham, on the other hand, were grateful I did.

The planning was intricate. Working backwards, I needed a police station that had capacity to hold two suspects far enough apart that they could not communicate or collude. What with the various closures, the list was shorter than you'd think. In the end there was only one choice: Sutton – where I'd had so many great nights on my bike and where life for me as Old Bill began.

There was no point trying for secrecy and then booking the cells under the names 'David Norris' and 'Gary Dobson' because there wasn't a copper alive who didn't have those names etched in his memory. So – and this is where it got elaborate – I went on a Tamil baby names website and gave them both Sri Lankan names with their own initials. Thus, Gary Dobson became Gurutither Dobaranga and David Norris Daaresh Nattar. I got pictures of two Sri Lankan lads from a dating agency and added those to the file.

The duplicity didn't end there. I had to give Sutton nick a story so I told them we were working on 'Operation Sir Woy' – named after the Fulham manager, Roy Hodgson, who had just taken us to the Europa League Final. (As far as I'm concerned, anyone who could do that with our team deserved a country named after them, not a fake operation, but that was as far as my powers extended.) Although I gave myself sleepless nights about taking the mickey out of Roy's inability to pronounce his Rs. The crowds singing 'Woy, Woy, Woy' was one thing, but since when had police officers made fun of speech impediments ...? I honestly thought I'd get a complaint, or worse, for that.

(Speaking of Woy's finest moment taking on Atletico Madrid in Germany, I thought I might share this little insight. Ten minutes before kick-off, I was standing on the terraces in Hamburg with three out of my four sons. Being abroad with my club, let alone in a European cup final, was a dream. I thought I would wake up at any minute and find it was Fulham v Leyton Orient and we were two nil down. My phone rang and a familiar voice said, 'Is that you, Clive?'

'Mrs L! What can I do for you?'

Before she could answer we were cut off so I ran to find a better signal then went to ring back. Before I did, I noticed she'd left a voice message.

'Clive,' it said, 'I think that team you support is playing tonight. I called to wish you luck.'

If only she'd played, we might not have lost 2-1.)

Whatever its faults, Operation Sir Woy was basically an operation over in east London, in particular a raid on the Tamil Tigers. And, just in case anyone on the inside put two and two together and thought, *Hang about, this must be a wind-up – Driscoll was on Fishpool, wasn't he? Let me call my friend on the* Daily Mirror ... I despatched the fantastic DC Ramanarthan Samasunderan – who had accompanied me to Sri Lanka for the Kaneshan case – to East Ham nick to work our 'investigation' from the ground.

Bless Ramanarthan. I'm not sure he ever got that East Ham was a spoof operation designed to mask my real intent, because he was there three weeks and he solved eight crimes – from blackmail to GBH.

I'd phone him up and he'd say, 'Oh, guv, bad things are happening in East Ham – but I'm dealing with them.'

'Ramanarthan, you do remember that Sir Woy is not a real operation—?'

But enthusiasm and talent for police work like that you can only applaud. I wasn't just keeping the Old Bill and the media in the dark. In the years since the discovery of Stephen's blood on Gary Dobson's jacket, I must have spoken or met with Mrs L ninety or a hundred times. Not once did I reveal the secret to her. But nor did I want to lie. Right from the off I said, 'Look, this is awkward but I know something that I cannot tell you for operational reasons. It would mean a lot if you would trust me to do the right thing.'

And do you know what? She said, 'Whatever you think is best, Clive. I trust you.'

She could not have been more supportive, then or any time since. Neville is exactly the same. When I read about other officers blaming them for the failure of earlier investigations, it is so much cobblers as to make you wonder what the true agenda is.

But, come September 2010, as we prepared to arrest Norris and Dobson, it was time to show my hand. I called a meeting at Scotland Yard where Cressida Dick, Alan Tribe, Shauny Keep and a representative from the Crown Prosecution Service all greeted Imran Khan, Doreen, Neville and – wearing an awful Arsenal shirt – Stevie's brother, Stuart.

Despite our closeness, the fact we were at the Yard meant there was business to be discussed. I kicked things off by saying, 'I really don't want to offend anyone, but we are going to talk about Stephen today.' I looked at Stuart and pictured his older brother sitting there as well. 'The thing is, we have found Stephen's blood on Gary Dobson's jacket. As a result, we are preparing to arrest and charge Gary Dobson and David Norris within the week.'

There was an audible gasp around the room. Quickly, though, it turned to anger from Mrs L. As happy as she was that we had made such astounding progress, she couldn't hold back her hurt that the two men would have been behind bars in 1994 if the Met had only supported her private prosecution properly. Even allowing for the fact the blood could not have been discovered forensically back then, I had to admit she probably had a point.

Still, my ducks, as Jim Dickie liked to say, were in a row. Time to move. First stop: Belmarsh Prison.

When you're going to arrest someone, the first step is knowing where they are. Since 7 July 2010 I'd known exactly where Gary Dobson was: that was the day he was sentenced at Kingston Crown Court for five years for trafficking cannabis worth

£350,000, and had been driven straight to his new home at Belmarsh Prison in Thamesmead.

David Norris, on the other hand, following excellent work from our Department of Professional Standards Team, was found living in a hostel above a real problem pub in Greenwich.

I wanted both arrests to happen at once so that neither man got the chance to warn the other. 'Divide and conquer' is an old army tenet for a reason. If the suspects got a whisper of our plans they could put their heads together and come up with I didn't know what.

Obviously I couldn't be in two places at once. Of the two arrests, Norris threatened the most possible cock-ups, so that's where I went. But I really wanted to go to Belmarsh just to see the look on Dobson's face.

We'd had a word with the governor of the prison via our police liaison officer who also deserves real credit. He agreed to ship Dobson out on the pretence of something to do with his drug bust.

On the morning of the arrest, Dobson was taken from his cell, through security and out into the courtyard where a police van was waiting for him. The guards handed him over to us and the second he got into the van our man DC McGuinness – who'd obviously drawn the lucky straw – got to say the immortal words: 'Gary Dobson, I am arresting you on suspicion of the murder of Stephen Lawrence.'

To be fair, Dobson didn't respond how we'd all have liked, so it's just as well I didn't go. By all accounts he rolled his eyes as if to say, 'This again?'

There was not an inch of his body that thought we could get him on anything.

As the crow flies, David Norris was only about 2½ miles away. And so was I. The pub he was living over was a real no-no for anyone who wasn't after trouble – the police only went in there in twos and threes during opening hours. Which was why I chose the crack of dawn. Even then I noticed there were a few prying eyes coming from the office block opposite.

I was only on hand in case anything went wrong. Technically, I could have stayed at home but we'd had so much criticism about SIOs not taking the lead in the past that I had to be there. Peter 'Birdie' Birdsall and Derek Reid, the DCs doing the arrest, probably thought, *Soppy old sod, what is he doing here?* but, if Norris got away because of our decisions, I didn't want one of my officers in the cack.

As it turned out, it couldn't have gone more smoothly: it was a textbook arrest. We covered all exits then a team entered the pub, swooped upstairs, knocked on Mr Norris's door and read him his charge.

I watched it all from the end of the corridor and I couldn't believe how much he took it in his stride. He actually started talking to me like I was his mate.

I thought, *I'm not your mate, actually. I'm your worst nightmare. You just don't know it yet.*

When we got back outside the blinds of the office block opposite were still twitching. Then my phone rang. It was the borough commander of Greenwich.

'Is that you outside the nick, Clive?' he said.

'What nick?'

It turned out that Greenwich station had been shut for decorating so they'd all shifted to the office block behind me. The nosey parkers I'd seen were all Old Bill. So much for keeping it secret. But I could try.

'What are you up to out there?'

'Nothing, guv. Nothing at all.'

Apart from the Greenwich nick, you would never have known we'd been there. In fact, that afternoon I received a call from the pub landlord. 'Have you been in my pub today?'

'Yeah.'

'But nothing was broken.'

Apparently we were the first of Her Majesty's finest to leave without a bundle. We had not even damaged the door and no other occupants of the flats had known (1) a police raid had taken place and (2) that someone had been arrested. I think George Dixon would have approved and even Sherlock may have thought the police had done OK.

There were more surprises when we all pulled up at Sutton nick. Norris was in one blacked-out van and Dobson another. Neither knew the other was there and they were taken in separately.

The second the desk sergeant saw the first he obviously recognised him because he just stared at me.

'Really, Clive?'

I shrugged.

'Well,' he said. 'I suppose we won't be needing that Tamil translator, then.'

In movies, the arrests are the big scene where the police get to show their toys. It's the bit where you get to play cops and robbers for real. I admit, there was a rush of exhilaration picking up two suspects, but the real buzz for me was knowing everything had gone like clockwork. We'd planned every detail so carefully and it had paid off. I hoped the rest of the operation would go as well, because the arrest was just the beginning.

In a well-timed pincer movement, while I was en route to Sutton, Superintendent Jill Bailey was at court with our top barrister arguing for the press ban to kick in. They got it just in time. Seconds later we made the two arrests.

Sutton nick had changed out of all recognition since my day, and it wasn't just the accommodation that sold it to me. Anyone arrested has to go before a magistrate within 24 hours but, after the effort of bringing Dobson and Norris in, I didn't want them leaving again for a long, long time, so I'd arranged in advance for a videolink room to be set up.

Norris and Dobson were both marched in front of a camera and they chatted to the beaks at Camberwell Magistrates' Court like they were in the same room. Incredible, really.

I had also gone to the trouble – and vast expense – of training officers to level three of interview techniques. If there was information to be drained from Norris and Dobson, I wanted it. We trained enough pairs to work on all the suspects I wanted, but only needed four in the end. In charge of the operation was DS John Smee. He did a fantastic job coordinating interviews and deserved a lot better than me yelling 'Smee!' in the style of Captain Hook every time I saw him.

Whatever we did, as polished as we tried to be, at no time did either Norris or Dobson look worried. At best they were put out. Dobson, after all, probably had a nice little routine in Belmarsh. We were just an inconvenience to him.

Not for long, sunshine. Not for long …

Despite the DPP saying we had a case with which to go forward, in order for that to be worth anything we still had to get Dobson's acquittal overturned. On 23 October 2010 we applied to the Royal Courts of Justice and a three-week hearing was set for the following April.

Now the gloves were off.

From the moment we'd arrested the suspects, their solicitors had been entitled to see our evidence. With the court date set, they threw everything at it. They sent scientist after scientist to go over the fibres, looking for some inconsistency with our findings. I was particularly worried when an American expert was flown in. If anyone could shoot down our theory it was him.

I do love our justice system but it has given me sleepless nights. You spend years working hard on a case and they get to pull it apart without providing any proof themselves. As long as justice is served – that's all that matters.

But keeping morale up on the team while this was going on for six months would be no picnic. In fact, just prior to this I had to remove an officer from the case following complaints from the rest of the team. It's a part of being a DCI I don't relish but I acted for the greater good, I made a note of it in my Decision log and we moved on. At least we tried. To my disappointment and confusion, the officer was posted back onto the team two days later, causing huge problems. He lasted about two weeks before the full extent of what he had originally done came out and he was then moved again. Disruption or mistake, I still do not know.

Finally, 11 April 2011 arrived and so did we, at the Royal Courts of Justice. The man in charge of our case was none other than the head Fred, the top judge, Lord Justice Judge himself.

There would be nowhere to go after this. What he said went. And the press would finally be allowed to report it.

Without doubt, this was the most nerve-wracking period of the entire investigation. If we'd found no evidence and I'd just wasted Gary Pugh's money digging up dead dogs, that would have been a shame but we'd all move on. If we'd fudged up the arrests, it wouldn't have been the first time. Even if there had been leaks we would have recovered. But having done all the hard work, having got all our ducks in a row, it was now up to one man to decide whether all our hard work had been in vain. Or not. Did we have enough 'new and compelling' evidence to overturn Gary Dobson's original acquittal?

We opened in the morning and started presenting our evidence. I tried to read the judge's face as the prosecution went through each piece of significant evidence. His lordship was a closed book.

The defence team, on the other hand, was not.

When the prosecution had finished, Lord Judge threw open the witness to the defence.

'No questions, your honour,' came the response.

In other words, all the international scientists had not been able to prove our physical evidence wrong.

At lunchtime, Lord Judge adjourned proceedings until the following afternoon. When we returned, it was my 15 minutes of fame in the box, then Alan Taylor.

After each of us, the defence registered the same comment: 'No questions.' While it meant nothing in real terms because the decision was not theirs to make yet, it did mean that our three-week trial was over in a couple of days.

Small mercies.

Despite wrapping up early, Lord Judge said it would require further time to reach a verdict. I knew that probably meant weeks. Despite having 100% faith in our case, you'd have to have artificial knees for them not to knock in that situation. 'What if this ...?' and 'What if that ...?' The questions and doubts would not stop buzzing around my brain.

I've said it before, and I'll say it again: the Stephen Lawrence case was different. The Met didn't appear to know how to deal with it. That didn't change, even after I appeared to be getting somewhere.

No sooner had Lord Judge retired than the whispering campaign started. Bearing in mind the press ban, it could only have come from within the Job. People from Scotland Yard were ringing with worries that I hadn't done a thorough enough presentation. One senior person claimed that he'd heard Lord Judge's assistant say we'd wasted everyone's time taking the case to him. I never believed a word of it. I was in the minority.

'What were you playing at, Driscoll? We're not going down for your cock-ups.'

But would they be my cock-ups? Yet again, external forces seemed to be hellbent on disrupting the smooth running of

Fishpool, or certainly misinterpreting it at the very least. When I was told we had to vacate our offices at Tintagel House, I nearly laughed.

'Oh, yeah? What's the reason this time?'

'It's being sold.'

'Fair enough.'

Did I believe it? Well, the fact they moved another squad in as soon as we left and spent thousands of pounds renovating it to accommodate Firearms soon answered that question.

Our new home was Jubilee House, on Putney Bridge Road. Perfectly adequate but open plan – therefore, no office for a senior investigating officer on the most high-profile and contentious case in recent British history to close the door and have confidential discussions or phone calls.

Honestly, it wasn't just the timing that concerned me. It was either the worst form of stupidity ever or someone, somewhere was trying to cause problems. I'm sad to say that with each passing month on young Stephen's case, I was getting more and more hardened to the unsavoury truth.

Not every cock-up can be blamed on someone out to disrupt the investigation. That doesn't mean they don't hurt.

We got the message from the High Court that Lord Justice Judge would be delivering his verdict on the hearing at 9 a.m. on 18 May. Unfortunately, from my point of view, he'd decided to tell everyone at the same time: us, our suspects – and the media. His lordship saw no gain in denying some basic information, whichever way the decision went.

With a date finally set, the real nerves kicked in. Jill Bailey, for example, suddenly started asking, 'Did we do this? Did we do that?'

I had to say, 'Jill, relax. I ain't worried. We did everything we could.'

We arranged a room in the Royal Courts of Justice so that the family could wait in some privacy. The judge would tell the Crown Prosecution Service and the press the verdict and the CPS would come and tell us.

Should have been simple. Except we arrived at the room and the usher leading us, a sweet old dear, shook the locked door handle and said, 'Damn, I should have brought keys for this.'

She was only gone five minutes. In the meantime, Neville took a call. Then he said to me, 'Well, this is a bit embarrassing, Clive.'

I said, 'What is?'

'I've just had a call from Jamaica. We did it. It's a thumbs up from the judge.'

And that's why I had wanted a media blackout. Within 30 seconds of Lord Judge reading his verdict, it was front page news on websites in Australia and all points in between.

The little old lady came tottering back and, pointlessly, we went into the room. Moments later an official from the CPS came to tell us that there was, Lord Judge said, 'new and substantial' evidence against Gary Dobson, and on those grounds he had quashed the previous verdict. Just as I always believed he would. *Honest...*

You have got to love Doreen and Neville. Even though they'd both been texted congratulations a dozen times by then, they both pretended to be surprised!

'What did you do that for, Mrs L?'

'I didn't want to hurt the CPS's feelings.'

Then, I have to admit, we all allowed ourselves a smile. We were going to trial – this time, the Lawrences and the Met shoulder to shoulder, together.

CHAPTER TWENTY

I've Had Worse Days

The trial of Gary Dobson and David Norris for the murder of Stephen Lawrence was slated to begin on 12 November 2011.

For my money, we had nothing to worry about. Our evidence had been raked over forensically and they'd found nothing. The DPP said we had a good case and the leading judge in the land had declared it substantial. The High Court was a higher test of proof than a trial would be.

But, as some of my team pointed out, that was decided by a professional. The jury would have to listen carefully.

My reply to that? 'There is no such thing as a crap jury. If we don't win, it's because we haven't done enough. There'll be no one to blame but us.'

A lot of cases have crashed over the years because SIOs put their feet up as soon as they got the court date: 'I have nicked the bloke, I've handed over the evidence, let the CPS take over now.'

Wrong attitude. You have to work equally hard, if not harder, during the lead-up to the trial or what was the point in all that work? The servicing of the trial takes a monumental amount of work and you need to be up to it. Making sure the CPS have everything they need, making sure your lead barrister is supported, dealing with the other side's lawyers – they're equally important in the process – by answering their questions, giving full disclosure so there's no technicalities you can be had on, making sure your witnesses are looked after and ready to go, checking the coffee machine for sugar ... it all needs doing and doing with a thoroughness that is beyond most people. Again, Alan Taylor and his team need to take a lot of credit for this.

To be fair, though, it wasn't as though I had many people to choose from. Once again, an unseen hand above me had intervened and printed in police notices was news that my team would be disbanded after the trial.

I couldn't believe it. I wrote straight back to Chief Superintendent Stuart Cundy and said, 'If I didn't know better I'd think you were trying to disrupt this case.' At the very least, it wasn't exactly a morale-boosting cheerleading dance, was it? Mr Cundy apologised, which I accepted, but for a while it caused waves.

Luckily – and I mean that sarcastically – there weren't many of us left to cheer. Not content with moving my team around again and again, the top brass had also been plucking out my men and women for other posts over the previous 18 months. Others had just seen the writing on the wall and decided that, in the face of continued opposition within the force, staying with me could jeopardise their careers. I couldn't blame anyone for leaving, but it did mean that we had a period where two or three of us were trying to finish bits and pieces started by others. Again, it was disruption. Again, it was avoidable, and again, it could really have cost our investigation and trial dear.

If I thought I was imagining the whispers against the team and myself, pretty much any doubt was removed three days before the trial was due to start. At a meeting at Scotland Yard, in the presence of numerous people assembled to help us, I received the mother of all bollockings from one of my superiors.

Great preparation that was.

I couldn't see any particular need for what he said but I know that some people within the police were uncomfortable that we were on the verge of finally solving the most unsolvable murder since Jack the Ripper... and for some people it just didn't look good.

We'd never be on each other's Christmas cards list, let's put it that way.

The sad thing is, I wasn't surprised. At numerous stages in the investigation we'd been interfered with through one means or another.

Still, come show time, I'd put it behind me. I had never taken on the case to please the murder squad – or the Met, for that matter. I took it on to give justice to a young boy and his family.

I also wanted to honour the memory of my mother. One of the last things she said to me days before she died was, 'You have got to help that poor family.' And that, over the next few weeks, was what I intended to do.

If there are two better barristers than Mark Ellison and Alison Morgan out there, then bring them on. Since working with Michael Worsley on Surjit's case, he had been my legal icon, but the way these two handled Stephen's case blew me away. Ms Morgan's attention to detail during the disclosure was unbelievable, and Mr Ellison was just a really honourable man from the start. Along with Alison Saunders, the head of the CPS, we were in their hands from the moment Judge Treacy called Court 16 to order for the first time.

Again, that didn't mean our jobs were over. Because of the massive media interest in the case, just the simple matter of getting Mr and Mrs Lawrence and their families safely to and from the Old Bailey was a nightmare. I'd send drivers every day to Catford for Mrs L and east London for Neville, then meet them at the back door. We had a private room put aside for the police team so I shielded them there until the court was in session. I remember one of Neville's family friends, however, being terrified by the crowds and the shouting as they arrived. It was not for the faint-hearted.

None of it was, if I'm honest. Because the suspects' families would be seated in the public gallery, I didn't want Mr and Mrs L anywhere near them, so we got seats underneath the gallery at the back of the court reserved in their names. In breaks and adjournments, it became a game of cat and mouse in ensuring the Lawrences didn't bump into anyone connected with the accused in the corridors. A DC was given the job of looking after them. I wanted to minimise what I knew was going to be an extremely painful few weeks.

There were a lot of lows. The worst moment came when our physician, Dr Richard Shepherd – a man I admire greatly – was listing Stephen's wounds. It was graphic – it had to be – and I couldn't help looking at Doreen and Neville. My heart went out to them. Hearing in forensic detail how your young boy was beaten and stabbed, blow by blow, is something no one should have to endure.

There was also a horrible quiet in the courtroom when the jury were played video and audio recordings of David Norris and Gary Dobson, captured via secret surveillance in 1994. In them, Norris and Dobson are heard using racist and violent terminology. For example, Norris: 'If I was going to kill myself do you know what I'd do? I'd go and kill every black cunt, every Paki, every copper, every mug that I know ... I'd go down to Catford and places like that, I'm telling you now, with two sub-machine guns and I'm telling you I'd take one of them, skin the black cunt alive, mate, torture him, set him alight ... I'd blow their two legs and arms off and say, "Go on, you can swim home now."'

Dobson: '... He said, "The fucking black bastard, I am going to kill him." I cracked up laughing. I went, "What black geezer?"

He went, "The Wimpy one. The fucking black nigger cunt, fucking black bastard." I went, "What, the Paki?" ...' And so on.

The recordings were disgusting and they confirmed, in my opinion, the fact that Stephen's death was random. He was the wrong colour in the wrong place at the wrong time. Any other black person would most likely have gone the same way that night.

One in particular nearly did.

Duwayne Brooks had sworn years ago never to give evidence for the Metropolitan Police Service. He'd also fallen out, irrevocably it appeared, with Mrs L. So persuading him to appear at the trial was a coup for me and a humbling decision from him. It was, as I've said, Brian Paddick I had to thank for his full support in helping Duwayne through the process.

I thought everything was ready for him. Then, on the day he was due to give evidence, Duwayne rang me at 5 a.m.

'Clive,' he said, 'my dad died this morning.'

'Duwayne, I am so sorry. Is there anything I can do?'

'Will you still meet me at the court?'

'Seriously? You don't have to do this today. The judge will understand.'

'No,' he said, but obviously still shaken, 'I want to.'

I've never had more respect for anyone than at that moment.

I'd agreed to meet Duwayne by St Paul's. Not the best decision. At the time of the trial a massive camp of New Age Travellers and anti-debt campaigners had taken over the area around the cathedral. There were hundreds of tents in every direction.

Politicians always travel in twos so I shouldn't have been surprised to see Duwayne arrive with Brian. We picked our way through the maze of canvas, and went for a coffee.

There's a thin line between interfering with a witness and ensuring his evidence gets heard. In my opinion, Duwayne had never before had the chance to give his whole story to a court. He gave clear and concise evidence in the witness box. His father would have been proud of him.

I sometimes wonder if some of the ill-feeling between Duwayne and Stephen's family was orchestrated by people passing poor information between them. It saddens me that both sides are hurt by this conflict when they have all suffered enough.

Of my team, only Alan Taylor was called upon to give evidence. He did a sterling job, as did Alan Tribe and the marvellous Dr Angela Gallop. No one could have heard their evidence, in my opinion, and not been persuaded.

So, why was I reading a different version in the papers? I couldn't understand it. Every day I went home satisfied that we'd scored a goal – or drawn, at worst. Then I'd pick up the papers and see the same facts with a negative twist.

One morning I bumped into a crime writer from one of the daily newspapers.

I said, 'Hello. Are you in Court 15 today?'

'No,' he said, 'I'm in Court 16, covering your case.'

'Are you sure about that? Because from what you're writing, I swear you're seeing a different case to me. I don't know where you get half your information.'

He looked surprised. 'We get it from your press office.'

He wasn't the only journo I spoke to about negative coverage and they all said a similar thing: 'The Met press office told us this, that, the other ...'

Was it intentional? Was someone still trying to knock us off track, hoping the jury would read a negative story and change their minds? Or was it just another error? The problem with the Met is you're never far from either.

Our trial began in mid-November, which meant we were always going to get close to the festive season. Judge Treacy gave us Christmas and Boxing Day off, plus the 27th December in lieu of the weekend, then said we'd be sitting the rest of the time. I had every faith that the eight men and four women across the room were honourable people, but it wasn't the best decision. Just a little thing like missing family holidays could turn an opinion if someone was undecided. It's human nature. The fact none of them reacted like that showed why the jury system is as good as it gets. As a team we felt humbled to have served them all.

And, eventually, we got there. Mr Ellison's team concluded their prosecution and the defence theirs. And on Wednesday, 28 December 2011 the judge began his summing up.

This, for me, is where you get a sense of how it's gone. A judge might interject and question and badger during a trial but his opinion is normally hidden. What he says in summing up can give away a few clues.

I have to say, inscrutable just about covers it. But there was one clue. After instructing the jury to ignore any sympathy for Doreen and Neville, or hatred at Norris and Dobson for what they'd seen on the video, he then said that the jury had to be 'sure the new evidence is reliable and free from contamination'. Well, I knew our experts. I knew the diamond job they'd done in the dock. This was a good sign.

Then he took the unusual step of handing out an 11-point plan in the form of a flow chart. He called it a 'route to verdict'. I saw it as a pathway to conviction. In it he laid out the various steps the jury should go through.

Numbers 1–8 dealt with the integrity and validity of the fibres, blood and forensic evidence. If they had any problem with those items, then that was it – game over. The case was to be thrown out.

However, should they accept the evidence was accurate and uncontaminated, then they were allowed to proceed to weighing up numbers 9-11, the rest of the evidence. In particular, should they wish to see the video or any other exhibit again, they could do so.

It was a lot to take in. My favourite line was this: 'It's not necessary for every question raised in a case to be answered or for every loose end to be tied up. This is real life. It's not a detective novel.'

If it had been a novel I'd never have finished it, because it was all so implausible.

By the time the jury was sent out to consider their verdict, the new year was nearly upon us. To me the evidence was straightforward. Even the naysayers at the Met, the ones briefing the press saying the case would fail on points 1–8, couldn't dent that resolution.

Even so, I made sure that I was out that night playing my piano, surrounded by a cheering and happy audience. For two hours – arguably the only two hours since summer – any thought of Stephen left my head. The case had been presented, the evidence heard, the police's job done. All that was left for me to do was an encore of 'Knees Up, Mother Brown' and then bed; and then do it all again.

Until, that is, we got the call that the jury had a request for the judge.

In front of a packed courtroom the jury foreman stood up and said, 'We would like to see the video again.'

I nearly punched the air. This was point number 9 on the pathway to conviction. It meant they'd accepted our evidence, points 1–8. It was the home straight from there.

Even the defence barrister, Mr Batten, as he walked past my seat, had to concede, 'I expect it will all be over soon.' And, as much as I liked and admired him, I couldn't hold back a rather satisfied nod.

The jury returned their verdict on 3 January 2012. We knew it was coming and the judge warned the whole court that he didn't want any hollering or shouting. That didn't quite work out.

When the foreman declared 'Guilty' for both David Norris and Gary Dobson, Dobson yelled out, 'You have condemned an innocent man.' His sobbing mum had a few things to say as well, but I wasn't interested in them. All my attention was focused on Mrs L, suddenly looking so frail as she cried her heart out, and lovely old Neville a few seats behind, blowing his nose to hide the tears.

It was a moment of pure happiness, pure relief. People I didn't know came up and hugged me, and one woman kissed me, squeezed me and just kept repeating, 'Thank you.'

Rightly, the judge adjourned for the day and said he'd sentence tomorrow. Everyone wandered out in a daze, of joy or despair, depending on your connection to the case. The first person I bumped into outside was John Aza, the head of the Independent Advisory Committee.

'Well done, Clive,' he said. 'How are you feeling?'

I was still speechless. Then, in the words of the Bard of Peckham, Del Boy Trotter, I said, 'I've had worse days.'

Before we left the court house, Mrs L called me over. 'Thank you, Clive,' she said, 'for never losing faith. I owe you so much. You're a credit to the police.'

Then she went outside and gave a speech on the steps where she laid into the Met, big time. I do not blame her. Our victory that day could not make up for the years where we'd let her down.

Neville was also very generous in his thanks, and Duwayne rang to congratulate me as well. The whole world seemed to be buzzing with the news.

I celebrated that night with a quiet curry, with Alan and Shaun. Nothing rowdy, just a dignified meal to mark our respect for the work of each other, our colleagues, and the suffering of one family. We raised our glasses to Stephen in silent respect.

As I entered Court 16 I realised I was too late for my usual seat. In fact, there were already more people standing than sitting. Ushers were flying left, right and centre emptying other courts of chairs, but we were still a few short. Then one of the clerks said, 'Judge Treacy says you can take the chairs from his office.'

Entering a judge's chambers during a trial is a real no-no for Old Bill but the judge was as good as gold. 'Just hurry up, will you?' he said. As Shaun, Richard Dixon and I lugged the last few out, his Lordship Treacy said to us, 'I bet you didn't expect to be humping furniture today, did you?'

There were two reasons for the extra demand. First was the media – you have never seen so many journalists in your life. And second, there was the phalanx from Scotland Yard. I only really noticed it as I walked out from the judge's chambers but there they were, the great and the good and the highly decorated, all clamouring to get near the case they all – or mostly – told me I had had no chance of winning.

It was pathetic really, if I'm honest. One minute I was practically on my own; the next everyone wanted to be my friend. Or so I thought. When we had given the press interviews the previous Thursday, I had found myself competing for airtime with Jill Bailey, who was being introduced as the SIO on Stephen's case. Since 2006 I had been honoured with that title and never lost it until the press wanted interviews, and then on briefing notes and in front of the press I was the IO. How to undermine everything that is good in the Met Police in one easy step.

But that's people for you.

I was feeling quite low when Judge Treacy entered the court. He gave his opinion of Dobson and Norris – scum, basically –

and said they had committed 'a murder which had scarred the conscience of a nation'.

As they had been juveniles when the crime was committed, their life sentences were only 15 years and two months in Dobson's case and 14 years and three months for Norris.

Then, when he had finished his summing up, he said, 'Is DCI Driscoll in the court?'

I was half asleep when I realised all eyes had turned to yours truly. I raised my hand and was led by an usher over to the witness box for the judge to talk to me.

He's going to bollock me for going in his chambers ...

'DCI Driscoll, have you been working on this case since 2006?'

'Yes, I have, your honour.'

'Then I congratulate you. This case has been dreadful for the police and a stain on the United Kingdom. However, you and your team have done an excellent job and through you I commend them all. At least a measure of justice has been achieved at last.'

Well, this is unexpected.

Thinking of the high and mighty watching, I couldn't help smiling.

But there was a sting in the tail: 'Now, DCI Driscoll, I expect you to bring their associates to justice as well.'

Well, I'd better cancel that holiday then ...

As I left the box I thought back to my childhood hero, Sergeant George Dixon and how he loved to wrap up a case every Saturday night, and I realised I'd never been happier. Yes, it had taken me six years when he used to do it in 30 or 40 minutes. Yes, we only got two suspects out of a possible five. And yes, I'd done it with some of the Met seemingly out to stop me. But, do you know what? I'd done it all the same. I'd gone looking for the truth about the night Stephen died and, in the eyes of the law, I'd found it. Maybe not all, but enough to make a whole country sit up and take notice. Even Sherlock would have said well done, or at least have sent Dr Watson to say it.

And if that wasn't what George Dixon was all about, then I don't know what was.

How was it he ended his show? It's elementary.

'Goodnight, all.'

You're Rushing This

In 2013 I found myself standing outside a little terraced house in south London. A man answered when I knocked on the door.

'Hello,' I said. 'My name is DCI Driscoll from the Metropolitan Police Service. I understand you have information on Stephen Lawrence.'

The man laughed. 'You're rushing this job, aren't you?'

Some 20 years earlier, shortly after Stephen's murder, the man had made a phone call to the police saying he had information. Thanks to the brilliant record keeping of Sgt Flook and his colleagues, all trace of that call had been buried. We had only come across it after the court case of Gary Dobson and David Norris, and even then only by chance.

But what a result. Judge Treacy had told me directly not to close the case on Stephen and I had taken him at his word. With this 'new' witness – who had waited two decades to speak to anyone – there was a real chance that a third person could be prosecuted. And while his word alone might not be strong enough to persuade the CPS to go forward, along with other evidence we already had in our locker, I was sure there was a case.

And, if we'd missed one crucial witness, how many more were out there? I couldn't wait to get looking.

Unfortunately, the Job had different ideas.

Dobson and Norris were sentenced on 4 January 2012. On 6 January I attended a meeting at Scotland Yard, where I thought we were going to talk about how best to pursue the case.

It turned out to be the opposite. For 45 minutes I listened to how the powers that be had written this marvellous report saying we had exhausted every opportunity of further convictions in Stephen Lawrence.

I said, 'I don't believe that we have.'

To which I was told, 'But it's in the report.'

'But I haven't seen this report. How can I argue against something I haven't seen?'

I was left in no doubt that certain people around that table wanted the investigation shut down. If I'm honest, they'd wanted it buried years ago. How else do you explain my team being disrupted the way it was: moved five times, including once to a building without HOLMES computers, and briefed against in the press? Report or no report, I could not stand by and let that happen without a fight.

'Didn't Judge Treacy just tell us to keep looking?' I said. 'Since when do police start disagreeing with judges?'

A compromise was agreed. A murder review panel would investigate all further options. If I could show promising leads or potential roads to go down, maybe it wasn't the end.

Except, looking around that table, I knew they'd already decided.

The murder review group came in and I told them everything I had: all the little leads and avenues I wanted to explore. Bearing in mind I felt I had a case against four suspects until the CPS, in their wisdom, had said it would be safer to concentrate on the strongest two, there was definitely potential to be exploited.

However, in the spirit of openness, I said, 'I have to tell you that other people disagree with me. Apparently there's a report, which I recommend you see.'

It seemed only fair.

'Have you got a copy of this report?' they asked.

'No, I've never seen it.'

A month later I got a call from Cressida Dick. 'What's this report the murder review group is chasing me for?' she asked.

'The report we were told about after the trial.'

'What report?' It was obvious she had no idea what I was talking about.

So what had I spent 45 minutes arguing about in that meeting? More terrifyingly, if I hadn't dug my heels in, the investigation would have been closed *based on a report that didn't exist!*

If I didn't know it for certain before, I knew it then: the Job wants Stephen to just go away.

Unfortunately, events in 2012 meant that was never going to happen.

Once our trial was out of the way and therefore unable to be affected, certain files were released to the public for the first time. One of the contributors to the BBC programme *The Boys Who Killed Stephen Lawrence*, a 'supergrass' and ex-copper called Neil Putnam, had named several policemen as corrupt, allegedly taking backhanders or dealing in drugs they had confiscated from criminals. One of them, the former DS John Davidson, had played a major part in the initial Stephen Lawrence investigation.

According to Putnam, Davidson cherry picked his work so that he was the one to interview key witnesses and suspects. It was Davidson who hadn't pushed the fact that Dobson denied knowing Norris, despite photographic evidence. Why is that relevant? Because Davidson later told Putnam that coppers like him 'looked after old man Norris'.

If that was true, then a lot of the historic questions surrounding Stephen Lawrence, like 'Why did they wait so long to arrest?' or 'Why was David Norris arrested days after the others?' suddenly made more sense. If a bent DS was steering the investigation away from the truth, of course it would have taken longer.

An investigation into police corruption, led by Detective Superintendent John Yates, had begun in January 1998. The Criminal Investigation Bureau, as they were known, targeted a dozen or so officers of interest. One of them was Davidson. In a note to his superiors, Yates wrote that Davidson 'developed a corrupt informant/handler relationship' dealing in predominantly Class A drugs plus 'all aspects of criminality when the opportunities presented themselves'. This note has been shown to many journalists and several authors must have received briefings from CIB due to the information contained within some books.

Clifford Norris was a notorious dealer of Class A drugs.

Despite the operation work and Putnam's testimony, Davidson has repeatedly denied the accusations and was never tried. He retired from the force to run a bar in Spain. He was prepared to come to England and give evidence at the Stephen Lawrence trial but he was never called as a witness, although he did travel.

There are two lightning bolts in this story. The first is that a police officer allegedly scuppered, for his own financial gain, the original investigation into Stephen Lawrence. As Mrs L said, 'It's what we suspected all along.'

But do you know what is worse? That we – the Met – tried to cover it up. Macpherson found us out. I understand several investigations are currently looking into allegations that cover the period of Stephen's investigation. I hope it is a search for the truth.

I've always been an advocate of telling the truth. It might get a bit sticky, especially if you've made a ricket, but at the end of the day if you can prove you acted in good faith people tend to go, 'All right, Clive, don't be such a wally next time,' and everyone moves on. If you try to cover things up, they get magnified when they finally come out. And, trust me, things always come out eventually.

Yates had his suspicions and his evidence in early 1998 – when the Macpherson inquiry was in full swing. John Davidson was actually called as a witness.

A decision was taken – many decisions probably – that the findings of some of the corrupt investigations would not be shared with Sir William. It has been alleged on many occasions that this was to prevent him from finding out that corrruption had played any part into the failed investigation into Stephen's death. Whenever asked, the Met Police have always said Stephen's was a bodged or unfortunate operation – not a bent one.

If it is true that the police decided not to mention these operations to Sir William then, at the very least, he was denied relevant information. Hopefully future investigations will get to the bottom of all of this and everybody can be sure they know the truth.

By 2012, what was already contentious had become explosive. Mr and Mrs Lawrence reacted as you'd expect. Both of them had always said corruption had to have played a hand, right from the start.

The thing about Mrs L, though, is that she doesn't just speak about these things to her friends and family – she calls the Home Office. Bang, just like that, she'd got a meeting with Theresa May for the following Monday.

Even at this point, the Job had choices: come clean with Mrs L and do everything they could to uproot all traces of previous corruption – while promising to re-open the investigation into her son's murder; or say it's all in hand, nothing to see here, there's no need to go bothering that busy Mrs May ...

Based on previous form you can imagine which way they went. I was sitting at home one Friday – it's allowed on days off – when I got a call from Commander Peter Spindler, head of the Directorate of Professional Standards (DPS) – basically the Met's complaints desk.

'Can I help you, guv?'

'I need to speak to Doreen Lawrence. Can you get her to come in today?'

'I'll see what I can do.'

It tells you everything about the Job's relationship with her that he felt he needed to go through me. Everyone has Mrs L's number. They're all just afraid to use it.

I went to New Scotland Yard and rang Mrs L from Mr Spindler's desk.

'What's this about, Clive?'

'Ma'am, is there any chance you could come to New Scotland Yard today? Mr Spindler, head of DPS, would like to see you.'

She agreed to shift a few things around to make the meeting. The commander was delighted and, to be fair to him, he sent a car to pick her up. His police chauffeur-driven car.

It didn't require my magnifying glass to deduce that Mr Spindler has a dog or two. The back seats looked like a mohair coat, covered in enough hairs to keep LGC Forensics busy for a decade. I started manically scrubbing away at the back seat and in the end I said, 'You sit in the front, ma'am. I'll sit here.'

'Don't be silly, Clive, it's fine.'

Mrs L is not the sort of person to worry about things like that. She's seen me pitch up on my bike in all sorts of outfits without complaining. Laughing, yes, complaining, no. If she had a problem she'd tell me. We both knew that.

The commander never got that.

I opened Peter Spindler's office door for Mrs L and his first words to her were, 'I noticed earlier that Clive called you "ma'am".'

'Yes, he did.'

'I just want to check you're OK being called "ma'am"?'

Oh, Peter, Peter, Peter.

Admittedly it wasn't as bad as Sir Paul Condon dragging her up to the eleventh floor and showing off his beautiful view when she's a grieving mum. But anyone would think it was just a little bit patronising.

Mrs L certainly did.

'Sometimes he calls me ma'am, sometimes he calls me Mrs L, sometimes he calls me Your Majesty,' she said. 'If I weren't OK with it, I would tell him – I wouldn't need anyone to do it for me.'

Afterwards she said to me, 'I do not believe a word he said. Why did he say them? Is he foolish?'

I said, 'Far from it, actually. He's a very clever man.' (He would go on to do good things on Operation Yewtree.)

'So why is he acting like an old slave trader, thinking they have to do things for me because I'm too weak or stupid to do it myself? They're all the same here, these officers.' Mrs L, over the years, would say that many police officers assumed the role of slave master when talking to her.

'It's not his finest hour, I'll give you that.'

It got worse. Peter Spindler then tried to talk Mrs L out of going to see the Home Secretary the following Monday, which was probably a little dodgy in itself. His reason? He had documentation showing the Met hadn't done the things the papers and everyone was saying we had.

'Who wrote that report?' she asked.

He told her.

'OK.'

He then mentioned the name of a retired senior officer.

'Hmm,' she said. 'There were some concerns about him, if I remember correctly.'

At which point Peter said, 'If I may challenge that—?' and he put his hand up like a stop sign in front of Mrs L's face.

If there is one person you don't want to be doing that to, it's Mrs L. From that moment on, he might as well have been talking Japanese. She wasn't listening. The only reason she didn't tell him what she thought of him and storm out was because she was raised better. But, as far as she was concerned, Monday's meeting with Theresa May could not come soon enough.

It troubled me that I didn't even question whose side I should have been on in the argument between Mr Spindler and Mrs L. Yes, I was a proud member of the Metropolitan Police Service, honoured every day to get up and serve my Queen and country. But for me, the serving part was the priority. Helping, policing and protecting citizens was why we were there. I got the distinct impression that some people were only interested in serving themselves.

My relationship with Mrs L has been one of the highlights of my police career. Through her, I've met some wonderful people I would never have been allowed within 50 yards of on my own: politicians, prime ministers, world leaders, celebrities – you name it.

I believe the benefit goes two ways. I knew I'd cracked it with her when she rang one day to ask, 'Clive, do you know how to prune roses?'

The bottom line is she knows she'll get an honest answer from me. Everyone does.

When she managed to persuade the Home Secretary to instigate a review into police corruption on Stephen's investigation, she asked me who I thought should run it.

'Mark Ellison QC, no question.'

Mr Ellison was never intending to speak to me. I had no specific knowledge of Stephen's case prior to 2006 and the alleged corruption took place in the 90s.

Circumstances brought us together. When the DPS struggled to find one or two essential files requested by the inquiry, he got in touch and I stepped in to help. Given that one of the questions Mr Ellison was considering was 'Was the Macpherson inquiry provided with all relevant material connected to the issue of possible corrupt activity by any officer associated with the initial investigation of the murder of Stephen Lawrence?' it was outlandish to assume they'd withhold anything from him.

And, what do you know? I located everything that was needed within half an hour.

The Job absolutely came down on me for this. Everything, I was told in no uncertain terms, had to go through the DPS.

'But you can't find anything!'

What the Met wanted or didn't want Ellison to know became irrelevant in 2013, when another explosion rocked proceedings. A one-time undercover officer, Peter Francis, went public with accusations of surveillance on the Lawrence family carried out in 1993.

Just when you thought it couldn't get any worse.

Not only, according to Francis, was there a concerted effort to discredit the Lawrences because of their attacks on the police investigation, but he had also been one of the men responsible for going through video evidence of the 'violence' Duwayne Brooks had been charged with in 1993.

His arrest and subsequent court appearance were both, he said, 'arranged' by the Met.

To Duwayne, this was nothing he hadn't suspected all along. To Mrs L, however, it was a bombshell. She already knew her son's death had been poorly investigated because of racist attitudes. She knew a corrupt officer had prevented anyone from being brought to justice for years. She had even learned that the Met knew about this corruption and had hidden it from Macpherson. But now she was being told that she and her family had been investigated, in secret, because they were considered dangerous to the police.

You couldn't make it up.

Mr and Mrs L had a right to criticise the Met, of course they did. We'd let them down. And, in 2013, it looked like we were still doing it.

In September 2013 I got a phone call from my old friend, Brian Paddick. A month earlier he'd been appointed into the House of Lords, and deservedly so. When you accept the honour, tradition says you choose a place to represent in your title, for example: Lord Clive of Battersea.

'Where do you think I've chosen?' he asked.

Brian's a Balham boy, so obviously it wouldn't be that. 'Not Brixton!' I said.

'Spot on. You are now talking to Baron Paddick of Brixton. Fancy coming to lunch?'

Lord Paddick wasn't the only one recognised for his work for the community that year. A month later, Mrs L was made a life peer in recognition of all her tireless campaigning and local work – arguably the closest the Establishment would come to admitting how much she'd been wronged. It's a tremendous honour and, as with Brian, one well deserved. But take it from me: the OBE and the seat in the House of Lords would count for nothing with the new Baroness Lawrence of Clarendon if Mark Ellison's report even hinted at covering up the truth.

She needn't have worried. The report was published in January 2014, and firmly pointed the finger at the Met for the outrageous way they had treated Mr and Baroness Lawrence and Duwayne in life, and Stephen in death.

As members of the Met we all had to take it on the chin, as we had had to do when Macpherson had tarred us all as 'institutionally racist'. Some needed to look at themselves more than others, however. I'm not sure they did.

To me, the way to appease a family so publicly wronged by the police force created to serve them would be to say, 'We apologise for what has gone on in the past and we want to rectify that by throwing everything we have at continuing the investigation into Stephen's murder.'

What they actually did was wind it all down.

The way they did it was very simple: they got rid of me.

That's what the Baroness will tell you, anyway.

In law, they did nothing wrong. The way the police service works is you do 30 years then you retire on a decent pension. If you happen to be quite young, your contract can be extended on a rolling agreement. In 2013 I had done 32 years and I was 62 years old. Not only was I over the limit on age but on service as well.

However, it was within the Met's power to say, 'Stay on for a few more years, Clive, and be our Stephen Lawrence guru.' To which I would have said, 'It would be a pleasure.'

In March 2013 I met with a chap called Dean Haydon, a nice bloke, who was my chief superintendent. I said, 'You have three choices with Stephen Lawrence. Number one, you shut it down now and I wish you well on that.' With Mark Ellison's report ongoing and Mrs L banging on Scotland Yard's door it didn't seem an option. 'Secondly you could extend the whole team for a year and we will pursue the leads that I consider to still be out there.' My team – Shaun Keep and two superb detectives, Mick Geoghan and Colin Rose – was due to be disbanded on 31 December 2013. Mick and Colin, like me, were already over the 30-year point. 'Or there is a third option: you bring in another SIO now to work alongside us and then on 31 December, when we will go, at least there will be some continuity.'

Mr Haydon said he'd get back to me but I left the meeting with the distinct impression I'd be extended until at least December 2014. Subsequently, I was told this by other people.

In May 2013 and again in June, July, August and September, I kept asking, 'What is your decision?' and they kept saying, 'We haven't made a decision yet, we're not too sure.' But it still seemed that they were going to extend the team, including me.

Only they will know if my working with Mr Ellison directly influenced the decision but, in October 2013, I was told that a new SIO had been recruited for Stephen's case, and I would be let go in June the following year. Some of my team would go a few months earlier. I honestly didn't expect it.

For her part, the Baroness went for the jugular in the press, calling the decision to let me go a backdoor way of shutting down her son's case. For once, despite her supporters in the media offering dozens of column inches and TV minutes, this was one fight too many.

I was honoured to be a police officer and work with the teams I did through the years. I will always admire every PC, PS, DC and DS. I know how talented they are, how hard they work and what bravery and kindness they show every day.

The ACPO – the Association of Chief Police Officers – I do not hold in such high esteem. In my opinion, they have let down the police force, the public and the spirit of George Dixon. For more than a century Britain had a policing model that was the envy of the world. It placed policing at its heart, starting with the honest constable, and was proudly independent of politics and other influences. In my career I've seen decisions made that challenge that. For democracy to work, we need that model to be strong once again. The ACPO could do this. They should do this.

But will they?

I officially stopped working on Stephen's case on 28 February 2014. I wished the new DCI and his team all the luck in the world. Unofficially, I will never refuse to help the Baroness and her family get justice. That is why I told the Job I would be on permanent standby in case my replacement needed any help.

If they want to pursue the truth about Stephen, I am at their disposal.

I'm still waiting for that phone to ring.

ACKNOWLEDGEMENTS

When I was asked by my publishers Random House to write acknowledgements for all those who have helped me through my life, my first thought was that there is not enough paper in the world for me to say thank you to all the people who have both touched and inspired me. All the victims' families I have worked with have left me feeling very humble and the same can be said for all the witnesses that have stood up and done their duty. My career has been one of the most enjoyable studies of human beings' ability to cope and thrive when faced with conflict and adversity. To all who I have met and who it has been my privilege to serve, thank you.

During one's life one person will always stand out as being a great role model at different times and I would like to thank the following with all my heart.

Firstly, to my mother, Christine Helen Rose Driscoll, née Vacher. Without you, your dedication and your love, I would never have achieved the happiness I have achieved. It would be impossible for me to repay you for your support and, most of all, for the sacrifices you made to ensure Barry and me had a happy – even though on occasions hard – childhood. I cannot respect you more than I do at this moment.

To Robert Driscoll, my grandad and Nell, my nan who aided and abetted my mother at every stage. I hope I have passed the lessons you taught me on to your great grandchildren, and that they in turn will pass those on to their own children.

To my father, who for many years I felt anger towards for the way he treated my mother. However, as time has moved on and I have found out more about this man and the very difficult life he faced – and the almost inhuman way he was treated as a child – I now both understand and respect the efforts he made with Barry and me.

To Barry, my brother who I lost many years ago to pancreatitis. Baz, you were and will always be my big brother and the cherished meetings I have with your son Jonathan just remind me how much I miss you and how much you helped me through my early life.

To Margaret and Linda, thank you for the times we spent together as a family.

To my children Robert, Bonita, David, Thomas and Harry. There are no words I can find to thank you as much as I want to say thank you. Watching you all make your way through your lives is an honour and a joy, and something I thank every god for. I am so proud of all of you.

To Carly and Sarah, thank you for being such wonderful mothers to my grandchildren and for making Robert and David so happy. To Darren, the support you have shown Bonita has allowed her to grow from strength to strength and for that I will always be eternally grateful.

To my wife Anne – without you I would have failed these last thirty years and if I have had any success in that period it all belongs to you. You would be perfect but for the fact you support Chelsea. Everybody has a cross to bear.

To Alf and Doreen Laurence, my in-laws – I miss so much the times we spent together. And to Jill, Anne's sister, sorry, I know she deserves better.

To Paul, my brother in Wales – we should be ashamed of ourselves that we allowed 10 years to go by without keeping in touch but now I am very proud we meet regularly, and it has been a pleasure to get to know your wonderful daughter.

To my extended family, some of whom I lost contact with, thank you for the times we have spent together. As children we had some fantastic moments. Uncle Bob, Uncle Ron and Uncle Cyril, Auntie Phyllis and Auntie Pat and Auntie Ivy – I will never forget you. Bob, you started my love of the piano and many a residential home I play in has suffered as a result but I will always be very grateful to you.

To all the teams and police officers I have worked with, thank you. Thanks also to all the service personnel I worked with during my time as an ambulance man – great times and great memories.

I need to make a special mention to the teams I worked with whilst employed as a Detective Inspector and Detective Chief Inspector. My admiration for you all will never diminish. To the team that worked on Stephen's case, you are and always will be the top team. Of all the stupid things the Metropolitan Police have ever done, not recognising that and treating you the way they did is the most upsetting.

To Mr Andy Cow, thank you for your kindness and support whilst I was a clumsy dyslexic Police Constable. To PC Bert Stephens and PS Nick Prouse who we lost this year, you will remain in my heart forever.

Thanks also to Donal MacIntyre, Nick Elgar and the Chelsea Head Hunters team for the most enjoyable operation. Football and police work – it does not get any better. Thank you.

To my publishers Ebury Press, Kelly Ellis, my editor Ciara Foley and Mr Robert Smith, my literary agent, I hope I have not let any of you down. The encouragement you have shown me has again left me feeling unworthy. And Jeff Hudson – thank you for all your hard work. I have enjoyed working with you, even if I have lost money on the biscuits you consumed.

To Graham Le Petit and Les Gale, thank you for putting up with my Les Dawson style of playing the piano. And to all the other musicians who have come and gone during Twin Tubbs' 34-year life span, I have really enjoyed our time together. To Stephen Henniker, who we lost many years ago to a motorcycle accident, I can still hear your guitar playing every time we perform. To all of you, as the great Eric Morecambe said, 'I play all the right notes but not necessarily in the right order'.

To Jeff, Geoff and Brendon who I met in a male sauna years ago, thank you for all your support during the last seven years. Our trips away are very special to me; they prove you cannot export culture. Stephen Frankham, John Hayes, Ted Morris, Stephen Jones and all your families, you are all legends. To anyone else I should have thanked, thank you.

To all at Fulham FC since 1957 until now, please try harder.

And last but by no means least...

Thank you to Baroness Lawrence for showing me what courage and determination can do if they are used in the right manner. You are a British treasure – please do not stop trying to make us all better. Thank you for your support and encouragement during Stephen's investigation; meeting you has been one of the highlights and I hope my mother knows that I tried my hardest for your family.

To Neville Lawrence, thank you. You have always acted with such dignity to me and helped in every way you can.

Stuart Lawrence – why Arsenal?! Thank you for always being supportive and for bringing your beautiful young son to Craven Cottage... even if Arsenal did beat God's favourite team. And to Georgina Lawrence, thank you for all the kindness you have shown me. Yours and Stuart's bravery and resilience is an inspiration to me.

To Duwayne Brooks, thank you for being such a brave witness during the trial and placing your faith in the team. I apologise again for the scientific explanations!

To Alison Saunders and the CPS team, Mr Mark Ellison QC and Alison Morgan, the junior barrister during Stephen's case and all the scientists from LGC – from an unworthy and humble police officer, you were simply the best. The word 'magnificent' does not do you justice, thank you.

And a special thank you to the Metropolitan Police and all the police forces and 999 services across this wonderful country, and the armed forces who protect my family. You will always be my heroes – never stop being proud of what you achieve. To the Criminal Justice system and all who work within it, and to juries past, present and in the future – thank you. The one good thing about retiring and becoming a member of the public is I can now say with all my heart, thank you for what you all do. It was a privilege and an honour for me to work alongside you all.

Thank you
Good Night All

Clive D